T0301120

MARK

The Hodder Bible Commentary

Edited by Lee Gatiss

MARK

CHRISTOPHER K. W. MOORE

HODDER &
STOUGHTON

The Hodder Bible Commentary
Series Editor: Lee Gatiss

First published in Great Britain in 2024 by Hodder & Stoughton
An Hachette UK company

I

Hardback ISBN 9781473695023
eBook ISBN 9781473695207

Typeset in Bembo Std and Utopia by Palimpsest Book Production Ltd, Falkirk, Stirlingshire

Printed and bound in Great Britain by Clays Ltd, Elcograf S.p.A.

Hodder & Stoughton policy is to use papers that are natural, renewable and recyclable products and made from wood grown in sustainable forests. The logging and manufacturing processes are expected to conform to the environmental regulations of the country of origin.

Hodder & Stoughton Ltd
Carmelite House
50 Victoria Embankment
London EC4Y 0DZ

www.hodderfaith.com
www.hodderbiblecommentary.com

Contents

Dedication

To Mary, my wife, whose patient lovingkindness
has created a happy home and marriage.

To Joshua, Jonathan, Joel, Judah and Jadon, our sons, who
have given us so much life (and to Alison and Olivia
who have taken two of them on as husbands).

To Alan and Mary, my parents, whose long
support has made so much possible.

Series Preface

The unfolding of your words gives light
(Psalm 119:130)

The Hodder Bible Commentary aims to proclaim afresh in our generation the unchanging and unerring word of God, for the glory of God and the good of his people. This fifty-volume commentary on the whole Bible seeks to provide the contemporary church with fresh and readable expositions of Scripture which are doctrinally sensitive and globally aware, accessible for all adult readers but particularly useful to those who preach, teach and lead Bible studies in churches and small groups.

Building on the success of Hodder's NIV Proclamation Bible, we have assembled as contributors a remarkable team of men and women from around the world. Alongside a diverse panel of trusted Consultant Editors, they have a tremendous variety of denominational backgrounds and ministries. Each has great experience in unfolding the gospel of Jesus Christ and all are united in our aim of faithfully expounding the Bible in a way that takes account of the original text, biblical theology, the history of interpretation and the needs of the contemporary global church.

These volumes are serious expositions – not overly technical, scholarly works of reference but not simply sermons either. As well as carefully unpacking what the Bible says, they are sensitive to how it has been used in doctrinal discussions over the centuries and in our own day, though not dominated by such concerns at the expense of the text's own agenda. They also try to speak not only into a white, middle-class, Western context (for example), as some might, but to be aware of ways in which other cultures hear and need to hear what the Spirit is saying to the churches.

As you tuck into his word, with the help of this book, may the glorious Father 'give you the Spirit of wisdom and revelation, so that you may know him better' (Ephesians 1:17).

Lee Gatiss, Series Editor

Consultant Editors

The Series Editor would like to thank the following Consultant Editors for their contributions to the Hodder Bible Commentary:

Shady Anis (*Egypt*)
Kirsten Birkett (*UK*)
Felipe Chamy (*Chile*)
Ben Cooper (*UK*)
Mervyn Eloff (*South Africa*)
Keri Folmar (*Dubai*)
Kerry Gatiss (*UK*)
Kara Hartley (*Australia*)
Julian Hardyman (*Madagascar*)
Stephen Fagbemi (*Nigeria*)
Rosanne Jones (*Japan*)
Henry Jansma (*USA*)
Samuel Lago (*USA*)
Andis Miezitis (*Latvia*)
Adrian Reynolds (*UK*)
Peter Ryan (*Australia*)
Sookgoo Shin (*South Korea*)
Myrto Theocharous (*Greece*)

Acknowledgements

My interest in Mark was first sparked as I spent three years preaching through the Gospel at Salem Baptist Church in Cheltenham. My steadfast guide was James R. Edwards's commentary on Mark in the Pillar Series, and my interest in Mark's use of the Old Testament took root. A few years later I undertook doctoral studies on this theme, dipping also into John, and am grateful for the wise supervision of the Revd Dr Ernest Lucas and the Revd Professor Frances Young. The research helped me to finally answer a question written at the end of an essay which had been marked by Dr Robert Forrest a few years before.

It was Professor Young who introduced me to the Fellowship of St Alban and St Sergius, whose conference that year was on Scripture and Tradition. From that and future conferences sprang enduring friendships with many in Eastern and Oriental Orthodoxy from across the globe, and the beginnings of an interest in patristic biblical interpretation. I began to understand Old and New Testaments as a single book, a product of the inspiration of the one God, and to expect deep connections between both Testaments.

By the time I had finished my doctoral studies I had returned to the Church of England (that's another story), and was working in twelve churches scattered up the south slope of Clee Hill in Herefordshire, Shropshire and Worcestershire. Every three years the lectionary would bring me back to Mark, and every three years I would find more depth in his Gospel. No naïve Gospel this, but rather a deep work with solid Old Testament foundations. I soon moved down to my current post, and for the past dozen years the good people of Fownhope, Mordiford, Brockhampton, Woolhope and Checkley – a Narnia-like corner of Herefordshire – have heard me attempt to distil Mark's wisdom as I mount the steps of their pulpits. The land itself speaks of the high handiwork of creation and has forth-told the glory of God. Well did the poet John Masefield put it: 'I know of no land more full of the beauty and bounty of God than these red ploughlands and these deep woodlands so full of yew trees, those apple orchards and lovely rivers and running brooks.'[1]

Over this time my interest in Reformed theology deepened, as did my understanding of its place within the flow of patristic and medieval theology. I was but a few months into part-time studies at Edinburgh Theological Seminary when the Revd Dr Lee Gatiss suggested I work on this commentary. What a patient editor he is. As I tapped away, I was helped by the comments of those who read all or parts of the manuscript – Kerry Gatiss, Joie Davies, Alison Moore, the Revd Drs Steve Langford and Owen Pembery, the Revds Rob Oram and Mark Melluish, and my wife Mary. I am grateful for their time, but any errors you find in these pages are mine alone. All the while Mary was wondering where on earth her husband had gone.

As I write this, the church in England – this little corner of the globe – weakens. Census returns and statistics speak of a decline, and churches struggle to stay open. Yet Mark's Gospel reminds us that God works in centuries, and the gospel we proclaim is founded upon the unchanging nature of God. The land of Bede, Anselm, Wycliffe, Tyndale, Bunyan, Owen, Whitefield, the Wesleys and Spurgeon is not forgotten by God. We may lie fallow as the church in other parts of the world flourishes, but we do so awaiting the fresh dew of God's blessing once more. And as we wait, we look to God and cry out:

> Oh, that you would rend the heavens and come down,
> that the mountains would tremble before you!
> (Isaiah 64:1)

---

[1] From a speech given when the poet was made an Honorary Freeman of the city of Hereford in 1930. George Herbert Clarke, 'John Masefield: Poet-Laureate', *The Dalhousie Review* 12, no. 1 (1932): 25–46.

Introduction

Mark: the Gospel and the author

The Gospel according to Mark

The titles of the Gospels are strangely formed. In the ancient world, the custom for naming books was to first name the author and then give the title: Mark's Gospel. In the Gospels, we have a construction that is virtually unique: the Gospel *according* to Mark.

This may sound obscure, but it makes an important point. This is not *Mark's* Gospel, but rather Mark's telling of *the* gospel. There may be four Gospels, but they are simply four tellings of the same gospel. The core is the same, but the authors have different aims and so may look at the same incident from a different angle. Each Gospel complements the others. The oddness of the phrasing of the title makes this clear: this is *the* gospel, according to Mark.[1] As Irenaeus of Lyon (*c.* 130–200) comments, 'the Word . . . gave us the fourfold Gospel, which is held together by the one Spirit'.[2] This 'holding together' should encourage us to confidently look for harmony between the Gospels, and not simply assume that apparent contradictions have no solution.

In the mid-second century, Justin Martyr (*c.* 100–*c.* 165) captured this nuance by referring to the Gospels as memoirs: 'The Apostles

---

[1] For an interesting discussion of this, see Martin Hengel, *Studies in the Gospel of Mark*, trans. J. Bowden (London: SCM Press Ltd, 1985), chapter 3.

[2] Irenaeus, *Against Heresies*, 3.11.8. Translation from Irenaeus of Lyon, *Against the Heresies: Book 3*, trans. Matthew C. Steenberg (New York: The Newman Press, 2012), 56.

in their memoirs, which are called Gospels. . .'[3] This implies that the core of Mark's writing, as well as the writings of the other Gospel authors, is their experience of Jesus himself: his life, teaching, death and resurrection. This is *the* gospel, and this is why Christianity can have multiple Gospels from different authors that speak of a single message, rather than a single holy book from a single author. Their authority does not come from the authors themselves, but from both the subject of the work and the fact that the authors are, to use a phrase from 2 Peter, 'carried along by the Holy Spirit' (2 Peter 1:21).

Much has been written about the inspiration of Scripture, and the extent of that inspiration, but for now it must be acknowledged that any doctrine of inspiration derives directly from the doctrine of God. If God is all-holy, all-loving, all-powerful and all-true, would he rely upon an unreliable method to reveal himself to us? Certainly the earliest church was in no doubt, and at the end of the first century Clement of Rome wrote, 'You have studied the Holy Scriptures, which are true and inspired by the Holy Spirit. You know that nothing contrary to justice or truth has been written in them.'[4]

This is not to suggest some sort of automatic writing, or that the authors themselves did not have a hand in composing the works that bear their names, but it is to suggest that they did so under the influence of God. The phrase from 2 Peter is a happy one: 'carried along'. The traveller on a boat makes all sorts of decisions and carries out all sorts of actions, but in the end the destination is set by the captain.

The 'gospel'

'Good news' (in Greek, *euangelion*) is a term that was used in the wider Greek culture to announce some happening to be celebrated or

---

[3] Justin Martyr, *First Apology*, 66. Translation taken from Justin Martyr, *The First Apology, the Second Apology, Dialogue With Trypho, Exhortation to the Greeks, Discourse to the Greeks, the Monarchy; or the Rule of God*, trans. Thomas B. Falls (Washington: The Catholic University of America Press, 1948), 106. He also uses the term frequently in the *Dialogue*.

[4] Clement of Rome (*d. c.* 100), *First Letter*, 45. Translation from *The Apostolic Fathers*, trans. Gerald G. Walsh, Francis Grimm and Joseph Marique (Washington: The Catholic University of America Press, 1947), 44.

some historical event that was to be acclaimed. However, that should not mislead us into thinking that in the Jewish world *euangelion* was simply a joyful proclamation. There was something deeper in mind.

In Isaiah 40:9–11 (LXX)[5] the word describes the coming of the LORD in power and speaks of him tending 'his flock like a shepherd'. In Isaiah 52:7–10 the word is used in the context of the LORD returning to Mount Zion, and the watchmen 'will see it with their own eyes' (reminiscent of Palm Sunday). There is more than just a Jewish response in mind: 'all the ends of the earth will see the salvation of our God'. Further on, in Isaiah 61:1–2, we discover that this good news is to be delivered by one on whom the Spirit rests, an event we encounter at Jesus's baptism. The good news is, though, double-edged: it is both the 'year of the LORD's favour' and the 'day of vengeance of our God' (Isaiah 61:2). God is both merciful and judge.

In all of this it is important to note that the good news is not simply the message Jesus preached, but the entirety of his life, death, resurrection and ascension. The very name of Jesus speaks of this good news, being translated as 'the LORD saves' or 'the LORD is salvation',[6] and our entire hope is founded solely upon that life. Our salvation rests not upon what *we* might do but on what Jesus *has done*. His actions within the historical context of ancient Israel are as much the gospel as his teaching, and the gospel is not fully preached if we simply draw moral lessons from Jesus's words. The full gospel encompasses our reconciliation to God by means of the sacrifice of Christ. All of the Old Testament sacrificial system led up to that one moment: the once-and-for-all sacrifice of the cross whereby sins are eternally forgiven.

Mark the author

From very early days there has been a tradition that Mark was closely connected to Peter, working as his interpreter, and that his Gospel

---

[5] The Septuagint (LXX) is a translation of the Old Testament into Greek made some two hundred years before Christ.

[6] See also Matthew 1:21, 'you are to give him the name Jesus, because he will save his people from their sins'. The name is the Greek form of the Hebrew 'Joshua', and so brings to mind the leader who finally brought the wandering Hebrews into the Promised Land.

was drawn from Peter's teaching. Irenaeus (*c.* 130–*c.* 200) stated that Peter and Paul evangelised Rome, founding the church in that great city. After their departure (a word which more plausibly should be translated as death) 'Mark, Peter's disciple and translator, handed down to us in writing what was preached by Peter'.[7]

In his historical writings, Eusebius of Caesarea (*c.* 260–*c.* 340) quoted Papias, who himself was a hearer of the apostle John. Papias was recorded as saying that 'the elder' used to say:

> When Mark became Peter's interpreter, he wrote down accurately, although not in order, all that he remembered of what was said or done by the Lord. For he had not heard the Lord nor followed Him, but later, as I have said, he did [hear] Peter, who made his teaching fit his needs without, as it were, making any arrangement of the Lord's oracles, so that Mark made no mistake in thus writing some things down as he remembered them. For to one thing he gave careful attention, to omit nothing of what he heard and to falsify nothing in this.[8]

The New Testament itself gives us some evidence of this relationship between Mark and Peter. Peter made mention of 'my son Mark' (1 Peter 5:13), and after his escape from prison, he made his way to the house of Mary the mother of Mark (Acts 12:12).[9] He was clearly close to the family and it is most likely that, as tradition asserts, this Mark is the author of our Gospel.

Given all this, we might accept that the material in Mark's Gospel finds its origin in the preaching of Peter, such that we have Peter's account of Jesus's words, ordered for the purposes of teaching. In fact, the Gospel itself has the flavour of a storyteller or preacher. It is urgent, driven on by the repeated use of 'and', 'immediately' and 'at that time'. It makes much use of the historical present tense, putting

---

[7] Irenaeus of Lyon, *Against Heresies*, 3.1. Translation from Steenberg (ed.), *Against the Heresies Book 3*, 30.

[8] Eusebius of Caesarea, *Ecclesiastical History*, 3.39. Translation from Eusebius of Caesarea, *Ecclesiastical History, Books 1–5*, trans. Roy J. Deferrari (Washington: The Catholic University of America Press, 1953), 206.

[9] From this passage we discover, too, that Mark was also known as John.

the past into the present. Since it was designed as an oral text, which would have been read aloud, it would have conveyed the urgency of an eyewitness to the hearer. Even today, there is much benefit in finding a quiet corner and reading the whole Gospel aloud.

The oral flavour of the Gospel can also be seen in the techniques Mark used to hold the attention of the hearer. Alongside the urgency of the language, he made frequent use of a 'sandwich' technique, whereby one story is placed between the two halves of another story. One example of this is the cursing of the fig tree (Mark 11:12–26): the tree is cursed, the Temple is cleared and the fig tree is withered. The two accounts help interpret each other: the fig tree is a symbol of the Temple. The sandwich might also contain a flashback, such as the retelling of John the Baptist's execution being placed between the Twelve being sent out and their return (Mark 6:7–30).

We also find paradoxes throughout the Gospel which help grab the attention of the hearer: for example, the demons recognise Jesus, but the religious authorities do not. The good teacher (Mark 10:17) is sent to the cross where the Gentile centurion recognises the one condemned by the authorities as none other than the Son of God (Mark 15:39).

This Gospel is a good listen.

Who was Mark?

The Mark of Acts 12:12 is identified as 'John, also called Mark', and this same Mark a little later set off with his cousin Barnabas and Paul for the first of his missionary journeys (see Colossians 4:10). For some reason he left them in Pamphylia, which caused some friction between Paul and Barnabas, who was keen that Mark rejoin them (Acts 15:36–40). In the end Paul took Silas with him to Syria and Cilicia, and Barnabas took Mark to Cyprus. There was a reconciliation. Paul later asked for Mark to be sent to him in Rome 'because he is helpful to me in my ministry' (2 Timothy 4:11), and he was with Paul in Rome by the time the apostle wrote to the Colossians (Colossians 4:10) and Philemon (Philemon 24).

There is an early and widespread tradition that it was in Rome that Mark composed his Gospel, alongside Peter, probably before the apostle died.[10] After that, Mark went on to the North African city of Alexandria and served as the first bishop of that metropolis, a tradition proudly held by the Coptic Church to this day.[11] Rather less celebrated is the fact that he was nicknamed 'stump-fingered'.[12]

This leaves us with the question of when the Gospel was compiled. Given the link with Peter (whose death is normally dated to AD 64 or 65), and the probable age of Mark himself, a date in the 60s seems most probable, with a likelihood that it was composed in the early part of that decade.[13]

Matthew, Mark and Luke

This leads us to consider the precise relationship between the first three Gospels, a question much debated over the past century or more. Any reader of these three Gospels will notice a strong similarity, but also some distinct differences. How do we explain this?

The issue is the order in which the Gospels were written. Was Mark written first, and then expanded by Matthew and Luke for their own contexts? Or is Mark a distillation of Matthew and Luke? If that is the case, then why would Mark omit the birth of Jesus and the resurrection appearances?[14] The issues are complex, but the most likely solution is that Mark was written first in the early 60s, with Matthew being an expansion for a Jewish audience and Luke for a Gentile one. Too much can be made of the significance of this question, and it is vital to let the Gospel of Mark stand on its own. Let Mark be Mark, and not simply part of the synoptic puzzle.

---

[10] See the discussions in R. T. France, *The Gospel of Mark: A Commentary on the Greek Text* (Grand Rapids: Eerdmans, 2002), 36–41; Hengel, *Studies*, chapter 1. They draw on the writings of early writers such as Papias, Irenaeus, Clement of Alexandria, Tertullian, Origin, Eusebius and other early sources.

[11] Eusebius, *Ecclesiastical History*, 2.16.1 and 2.24.1.

[12] Hippolytus (c. 170–c. 236), *The Refutation of All Heresies*, 7.30.

[13] It is notable that the apocalyptic material of chapter 13 makes no reference to either the First Jewish Revolt which began in AD 66 or the fall of the Temple in AD 70.

[14] W. D. Davies and D. C. Allison Jr, *A Critical and Exegetical Commentary on the Gospel According to Saint Matthew, Volume 1* (London; New York: T&T Clark International, 1998), 109.

Mark and the Old Testament

When Jesus spoke to the two on the road to Emmaus, 'he explained to them what was said in all the Scriptures concerning himself' (Luke 24:27). Those Scriptures, of course, are known to us as the Old Testament. This was no isolated incident. Earlier, when addressing the Jewish leaders, he had said, 'You study the Scriptures diligently because you think that in them you have eternal life. These are the very Scriptures that testify about me . . . If you believed Moses, you would believe me, for he wrote about me' (John 5:39, 46).

The New Testament fulfils, not replaces, the Old, and the two sit firmly together as a single revelation of the grand narrative of God reconciling the world to himself. They should never be separated. Augustine (354–430) put it well: 'In the Old Testament the New is concealed, in the New the Old is revealed.'[15] The Old Testament is the unfolding of God's revelation, a process that finds its pinnacle and goal in the person of Christ. As Jesus said, the 'Scriptures . . . testify about me'.

This is why, for example, the early apologist Justin Martyr, when he was defending Christianity to the Roman Emperor Antonius Pius, was keen to point out that Jesus's coming was anticipated from antiquity. He wrote that Jesus 'was foretold, in truth, before He actually appeared, first five thousand years before, then three thousand, then two thousand, then one thousand, and, finally, eight hundred. For, in succeeding generations new Prophets rose time and again.'[16] The Old and New Testaments operate as one. This is key to fully understanding Mark's Gospel, and Mark makes particular use of Isaiah as he shows us Christ. In fact, a prophecy from Isaiah sits at the beginning of the Gospel: 'Prepare the way for the Lord, make straight paths for him' (Mark 1:3).

This quotation about 'the way' provides a significant background to Mark's Gospel. Many of the later prophets dealt with the shock of the Exile and the deportation of the Jews to Babylon, but it is Isaiah who is the prophet most associated with this idea. Imagery of the Exodus abounds in his prophecies, especially after chapter 40, and a new 'way' is envisaged that will bring the exiles back home

---

[15] Augustine of Hippo, *Questions on the Heptateuch*, 2,73.
[16] Justin, *First Apology*, 31, Falls (tr.) *Apologies and Dialogue*, 68.

to Israel (compare Exodus 13:21 and Isaiah 43:16–19).[17] Of particular importance in these passages is the understanding that it is the LORD himself who will lead the people in this second Exodus as he did in the first from Egypt. The exiles are told that the LORD 'will be with you' (Isaiah 43:1–3) and will lead them as a shepherd leads the sheep (Isaiah 40:11).[18] The LORD will 'lead the blind . . . I will guide them' (Isaiah 42:16, compare 49:10), and the pinnacle of this new Exodus is the return of the LORD to Jerusalem/Zion.

When the exiles did return from Babylon, however, they were faced with disappointment. Zerubbabel may have been a descendant of David (see 1 Chronicles 3:19), but he was now a governor and not a king (Haggai 1:1). As the Second Temple was built to replace the first, which had been destroyed by the Babylonians, those who had seen Solomon's magnificent structure wept at the sight of the new Temple (Ezra 3:12). The word of the LORD through Haggai was scathing: 'Who of you is left who saw this house in its former glory? How does it look to you now? Does it not seem to you like nothing?' (Haggai 2:3). Things weren't quite right. The promises of Isaiah were only fulfilled in part.

The prophets writing after the return from the Exile took up this theme and looked forward to a time when the LORD would once more return to the Temple (Zechariah 2:10–12; 8:3; Malachi 3:1–2). However, it is evident from the writings of the centuries leading up to the time of Christ that this hope had yet to be fulfilled (e.g., 1 Enoch 25:3; Jubilees 1:26–28). The community that produced the Dead Sea Scrolls looked forward to a future dwelling of God in his Temple, and they thought ritual purity was the key to this.[19] To varying degrees, so did the Sadducees and Pharisees.[20]

---

[17] See, for example, the monographs of David Wei Chun Pao, *Acts and the Isaianic New Exodus* (Tübingen: Mohr Siebeck, 2000) and Rikki E. Watts, *Isaiah's New Exodus and Mark* (Tübingen: Mohr Siebeck, 1997). See also Bernhard W. Anderson, 'Exodus Typology in Second Isaiah', in *Israel's Prophetic Heritage: Essays in Honor of James Muilenburg* (New York: Harper & Brothers, 1962), which has proved influential.

[18] See Exodus 15:13: 'In your unfailing love you will lead the people you have redeemed. In your strength you will guide them to your holy dwelling,' and Psalm 78:52: 'But he brought his people out like a flock; he led them like sheep through the wilderness.'

[19] *Temple Scroll* 29. See also 45:12–14; 46:4–12; 47:3–18; 51:7–10.

[20] Jonathan Klawans, *Purity, Sacrifice, and the Temple: Symbolism and Supersessionism in*

This, then, is the background to Mark: the hope for a return of God to his Temple and a full realisation of the prophesied return from the Exile. As we have seen, Mark picked up this hope in the very opening verses of his Gospel and this theme continues throughout the remainder of the work. Rather than chronicling the start of some new work of God, Mark presents us with the fulfilment of a long-awaited act. As we read this Gospel, Mark reveals to us the Christ who is also the returning presence of God – who, in fact, *is* God.

Mark's Christology and the Messianic Secret

As Mark presents us with Jesus, he sets out a narrative Christology. That is, he does not boldly state that Jesus is God, such as we find in Thomas's confession 'My Lord and my God!' (John 20:28), but rather Mark demonstrates Jesus's divinity by showing us Christ doing the things that only God can do. Jesus is acting like God because he *is* God.

The question of Jesus's identity runs through the Gospel. People were amazed at his authority (Mark 1:22),[21] and the authorities were outraged that he dared to forgive sins, a divine act (Mark 2:7). The disciples were terrified as they witnessed Jesus stilling the storm and asked, 'Who is this?' (Mark 4:41). A synagogue congregation wondered at his wisdom and miracles (Mark 6:2). Throughout the first half of the Gospel, we are faced with the question: who is this who does these things?

Of course, we the readers know. At the outset of the Gospel, Mark describes Jesus as the 'Messiah, the Son of God' (Mark 1:1) and, ironically, the demons knew precisely who he was (Mark 1:24, 34; 3:11; 5:7). The disciples, too, had some sort of idea of Jesus's true identity (see Peter's confession in Mark 8:29), but it is clear that their understanding was limited at best. When granted a glimpse of Jesus's glory at the transfiguration, Peter, who had just recognised Jesus as the Messiah, simply 'did not know what to say' (Mark 9:6).

---

the *Study of Ancient Judaism* (Oxford: Oxford University Press, 2006), 161.
[21] See also the amazement expressed in Mark 1:27; 2:12; 6:2, 51; 7:37; 10:24, 26; 11:18; 12:17.

It is this persistent misunderstanding of Jesus's messiahship and deeper identity that lies behind the theme of secrecy in the Gospel, which has puzzled so many.[22] John stated that at the feeding of the five thousand, the crowds wanted to make him 'king by force' (John 6:15). There was a longing for Israel to be free from its Roman occupation and for a truly Jewish monarchy to be restored. The Messiah was understood in those terms, as a religious/political leader, but this was not the understanding of messiahship that Jesus held. His was a deeper work, and there is a deep irony that not only was his work revealed to all at the crucifixion, but the person who truly understood his messiahship was a soldier from the occupying forces (Mark 15:39).

Jesus's secrecy surrounding his messianic identity was to prevent misunderstanding, and to guard against him being made into a figure-head for a Jewish revolt against the Romans. He was more than a mere pretender to the throne. However, now that Jesus's true identity has been revealed in his death, resurrection and ascension, there is no longer a need for any such secrecy. He is to be proclaimed to all the world.

Where does Mark end?

There are questions surrounding the ending of Mark. The NIV text notes that 'the earliest manuscripts and some other ancient witnesses do not have verses 9–20', and so a decision needs to be made as to what to do with those extra verses.

This is not a new question. In the early fourth century, Eusebius commented on the debates about Mark's ending. He noted that the text of Mark 16:8 'is where the text does end, in almost all copies of the gospel according to Mark', but also mentioned those who were 'diffident about athetizing [marking as spurious] anything at all in the texts of the gospels'.[23]

The earliest manuscripts we have stop at verse 8, and many of the

---

[22] See Mark 1:25, 34, 43–4; 3:12; 5:43; 7:36; 8:26.
[23] Eusebius, *Questions to Marinus*, 1. Translation from Eusebius of Caesarea, *Eusebius of Caesarea: Gospel Problems and Solutions*, trans. Roger Pearse et al. (Ipswich: Chieftain Publishing Ltd, 2010), 97f.

later manuscripts that do include the longer ending have marked it to show it is of doubtful provenance. The fact that there are also alternative shorter endings would suggest that the rather abrupt ending to Mark left some scribes with the desire to tidy it up. Most early church fathers make no mention of the long ending, with Irenaeus being the most notable exception,[24] but the longer ending grew in popularity from the fourth century.[25]

The longer ending is stylistically different from the rest of Mark and sits rather uncomfortably with the rest of the chapter. For instance, while the NIV has added the word 'Jesus' to verse 9, it is missing in the Greek text and it is not clear to whom it is referring. Mary Magdalene is introduced as if she were not referred to in the earlier verses. Most scholars conclude that the longer ending is not in the original manuscript of Mark's Gospel, known as the original 'autograph'.

If this is the case, and it is my view that it is, then that would affect its status as Scripture. J. Gresham Machen (1881–1937) neatly sets out the traditional, Reformed view of inspiration:

> Now we believers in the inspiration of the Bible do not believe that the scribe who made any one of these manuscripts that we have was inspired. Every one of the manuscripts contains errors, no one of them is perfect. What we do believe is that the writers of the Biblical books, as distinguished from scribes who later copied the books, were inspired. Only the autographs of the Biblical books, in other words – the books as they came from the pen of the sacred writers, and not any one of the copies of those autographs which we now possess – were produced with that supernatural impulse and guidance of the Holy Spirit which we call inspiration.[26]

---

[24] Even there, the longer ending only survives in the Latin translation of his text.
[25] For a full discussion of this see Philip W. Comfort, *New Testament Text and Translation Commentary: Commentary on the Variant Readings of the Ancient New Testament Manuscripts and How They Relate to the Major English Translations* (Carol Stream: Tyndale House Publishers, Inc., 2008), 156–63.
[26] J. Gresham Machen, *The Christian Faith in the Modern World* (Grand Rapids: Eerdmans, 1947), 39.

If the longer ending of Mark did not come from the pen of Mark himself, as seems likely, it would not fall within the category of 'inspired'.[27] That said, the longer ending has been widely accepted throughout the history of the church, and is still accepted by many, so I will offer some brief comments on it in an appendix for those whose churches hold it to be original. Since it contains no doctrine that is not found elsewhere in the Gospels or Acts, there is no danger in preaching on it.

The subject: Son of God and Messiah

The Messiah

At the outset of the Gospel, Jesus is identified as 'the Messiah', and we would do well to consider how that term would have been understood. In the first century AD, the Messiah had come to be understood as a king from the line of that greatest of Jewish kings: David. Having endured centuries of occupation under first the Greek and then the Roman Empire, the Jewish people longed for a king from that Davidic line which had been established by an eternal covenant (2 Samuel 7:11–16; see also Psalms 2, 89 and 110). A king who could save them from the Romans.

Isaiah had spoken of a person who 'will reign on David's throne and over his kingdom, establishing and upholding it with justice and righteousness from that time on and for ever' (Isaiah 9:7; see also Jeremiah 33:17). Intriguingly, the opening verse of Isaiah 9 introduced the prophecy with the words: 'in the future he [God] will honour Galilee of the nations'. Two chapters on, Isaiah returned to the Davidic theme, looking for one who would come from the 'stump of Jesse' (David's father) on whom 'the Spirit of the LORD will rest' (Isaiah 11:2).

Jeremiah, too, looked forward to this future king, a 'righteous Branch' for David, who was given the name 'The LORD Our

---

[27] For a recent argument taking the contrary view, see Jeffrey T. Riddle, 'The Ending of Mark as a Canonical Crisis,' *Puritan Reformed Journal* 10, no. 1 (2018).

Righteous Saviour' (Jeremiah 23:5–6), a designation that echoes the name 'Jesus'.[28] Ezekiel foresaw that a future king would shepherd the people (Ezekiel 34:22–4; 37:24–5) which, when taken with Isaiah 40:9–11, suggests the involvement of the LORD himself.

This hope was widespread and can also be found in Hosea 3:5 and Amos 9:11. In Zechariah 9:9–10 we read of a returning king, and later that same prophet wrote that: 'the house of David will be like God, like the angel of the LORD going before them' (Zechariah 12:8).[29]

This is not to say that all Jews at the time of Christ held the same view, or even hoped for a Messiah at all. The evidence from other Dead Sea Scrolls shows a variety of views, and other writings of the time interpret the Old Testament hopes in a variety of ways. That said, the messianic hopes of the Old Testament prophets were widely distributed and clearly converge on the person of Jesus.

The Son of God

The second of the titles by which Mark introduces Jesus gives a further focus to the nature of the Messiah: he is the Son of God.[30] In the Old Testament we find heavenly beings referred to as sons of God (e.g., Genesis 6:2–4; Job 1:6 NIV footnote; Daniel 3:25), as well as the Israelites as a whole (e.g., Exodus 4:22–3; Jeremiah

---

[28] 'Jesus' is the Greek form of 'Joshua', which means 'the LORD is salvation' or 'the LORD saves'.

[29] This thought developed in the years between the Old and New Testaments and can be seen in the Dead Sea Scrolls. One scroll, known as the *Florilegium*, is often dated to within a century of Christ's birth and contains this passage: '"Moreover the Lord decl[ares] to you that He will make you a house," and that "I will raise up your offspring after you, and establish the throne of his kingdom [fore]ver. I will be a father to him, and he will be My son" (2 Sam. 7:11c, 12b, 13b–14a). This passage refers to the Shoot of David, who is to arise with the Interpreter of the Law, and who will [arise] in Zi[on in the La]st Days, as it is written, "And I shall raise up the booth of David that is fallen" (Amos 9:11). This passage describes the fallen Branch of David, "[w]hom He shall raise up to deliver Israel".' Michael O. Wise, Martin G. Abegg and Edward M. Cook, *The Dead Sea Scrolls, Revised Edition* (New York: Harper Collins, 2005), 257.

[30] The NIV notes that some manuscripts do not include the phrase 'the Son of God'. Its presence in a wide variety of early manuscripts from different sources suggests that this might have been an accidental omission. After all, the 'Son of God' is, as we will see, an important theme in this Gospel.

31:9, 20; Hosea 11:1), but the most telling Old Testament use for our purposes is the idea of the king as a son of God. This is not to say that the Old Testament kings were understood as divine, but rather that their kingship was given by God and that kings were agents of God.

This idea of royal sonship was introduced by the covenant made with David in 2 Samuel 7 and was further developed in the Psalms (e.g., Psalms 2 and 89). If the Messiah was the long-hoped-for kingly descendant of David, then it followed that he would exemplify the royal status as God's son.

However, as the Gospel develops, we discover that there is more in mind than simply royal lineage. At Jesus's baptism, a voice from heaven proclaimed: 'You are my Son, whom I love' (Mark 1:11), and the demons recognised him as such (Mark 3:11; 5:7). At the transfiguration a voice was once more heard, declaring, 'This is my Son, whom I love' (Mark 9:7), and Jesus can call the Father '*Abba*' (Mark 14:36). When asked by the high priest whether he is 'the Messiah, the Son of the Blessed One', Jesus responded, 'I am' (Mark 14:61–2). Finally, when the Gentile centurion witnessed how Jesus died, he concluded, 'Surely this man was the Son of God' (Mark 15:39). The irony in all of these passages is that Jesus's *divine* Sonship was recognised by the Gentiles and the demons, but not by the religious authorities. In fact, as we will see, the nature of this Sonship would become a point of debate between Jesus and the teachers of the law in Mark 12:35–7 as the 'large crowd listened to him with delight'.

The Son of Man

Within Mark's Gospel, Jesus referred to himself as the 'Son of Man' on fourteen occasions.[31] The Greek phrase translated as 'Son of Man' might literally be translated as '*the* Son of *the* Man', and in the New Testament is rarely found outside the Gospels.[32] It was

---

[31] Mark 2:10, 28; 8:31, 38; 9:9, 12, 31; 10:33, 45; 13:26; 14:21 (twice), 41, 62.

[32] Moule notes of the Greek phrase (*ho huios tou anthropou*), 'Neither is it linguistically odd, as has been asserted. It is an exact and idiomatic rendering of the sense "*the* Son of Man". The definite article with the second noun represents a

clearly intended to catch the ear and operate as a title, rather than simply carry the meaning 'a man', as some suggest.[33] Moreover, Jesus taught that the 'Son of Man' had a particular role and particular powers. He had 'authority on earth to forgive sins' (Mark 2:10) and was lord 'even of the Sabbath' (Mark 2:28). He was to come 'in his Father's glory with the holy angels' (Mark 8:38; see also Mark 13:26; 14:62) and rise from the dead (Mark 9:9, 31). Here was a figure of some significance.

In the book of Daniel, we find coming together a number of themes connected to Jesus. We have seen how the Messiah was thought to come from David's line and to be the inheritor of his throne. In Daniel 2:44 this hope is restated: 'In the time of those kings, the God of heaven will set up a kingdom that will never be destroyed, nor will it be left to another people. It will crush all those kingdoms and bring them to an end, but it will itself endure for ever.' A few chapters later, in Daniel 7:13–14, we find the prophetic fulfilment of the establishment of this 'kingdom . . . that will never be destroyed':

> In my vision at night I looked, and there before me was one like a son of man, coming with the clouds of heaven. He approached the Ancient of Days and was led into his presence. He was given authority, glory and sovereign power; all nations and peoples of every language worshipped him. His dominion is an everlasting dominion that will not pass away, and his kingdom is one that will never be destroyed.

At the time of Jesus, some had already identified this figure with the Messiah,[34] and Moule is surely correct in suggesting that the emphatic phrase *the* Son of *the* Man is intended to point to a particular figure: *that* Son of Man. Within Judaism there is no better

---

well-known Greek idiom.' C. F. D. Moule, '"The Son of Man": Some of the Facts', *New Testament Studies* 41, no. 2 (1995), 277.

[33] Juan B. Cortés and Florence M. Gatti, 'The Son of Man or the Son of Adam', *Biblica* 49, no. 4 (1968), 466–7.

[34] See, for example, 1 Enoch 37–71, 2 Esdras/4 Ezra 13.

target than Daniel 7,[35] and given that Jesus quoted from this passage at his trial before the Sanhedrin (Mark 14:61–4), this vision should provide the background not only for the term 'Son of Man', but also for his rule in the kingdom of heaven. Christ, the Son of Man, has been given an everlasting kingdom. Here we have the reign of God and the Davidic monarchy coming together.

It should be noted that Daniel 7 is set in the context of suffering and persecution at the hands of the four beasts. This is made all the clearer by the interpretation of the vision given to Daniel (Daniel 7:15–27). The Son of Man was a figure who would suffer, a recurrent theme in Mark,[36] and would then be vindicated. In fact, Mark portrays a Son of Man who 'had authority on earth during his human life (Mark 2:10, 28); was destined to suffer, die and rise again (Mark 8:31; 9:31; 10:33–34; and related sayings); and would come again in glory (Mark 8:38; 13:26; 14:62)'.[37]

We have, therefore, in '*the* Son of *the* Man', a rich description of Jesus. Here is a figure who is human, yet one who may approach the Ancient of Days and who will also be worshipped (Daniel 7:13–14). He will have a kingdom, and thus will be a king. He will suffer yet will be vindicated and, in his vindication, will share his kingdom with his 'holy people' (a phrase that may be translated as 'saints'). He will be given glory and sovereign power. In other words, *the* one like a Son of Man is much more than merely a man's son.

The kingdom of God

Mark uses the phrase 'kingdom of God' fourteen times in his Gospel, and in all but one of those instances the words come from the lips of Jesus.[38] As we have seen, in Isaiah the 'good news' was closely identified

---

[35] C. F. D. Moule, *The Origin of Christology* (Cambridge: Cambridge University Press, 1978), 12–13.

[36] Francis J. Moloney, '"Constructing Jesus" and the Son of Man', *The Catholic Biblical Quarterly* 75, no. 4 (2013), 733 note 69.

[37] Adela Yarbro Collins and John Joseph Collins, 'The Influence of Daniel on the New Testament', in *Daniel: A Commentary on the Book of Daniel* (Minneapolis: Fortress Press, 1993), 98.

[38] Mark 1:15; 4:11, 26, 30; 9:1, 47; 10:14, 15, 23, 24, 25; 12:34; 14:25; 15:43.

with the return of God to reign over his people (see Isaiah 40:9–10; 52:7). To a people long under Roman occupation this news was good indeed, but it was too easily understood as simply a political reign. This is not to say that politics and religion could easily be disentangled in the ancient world – they could not – but it does mean that the focus could all too easily fall upon simply expelling the Romans and restoring a Jewish monarchy. What was in mind in this Gospel was something of a greater scale: the restoration of the rule of God which had been rejected when Israel demanded a king so that they could be like 'all the other nations' (1 Samuel 8:5). This demand was regardless of the warnings of the prophet Samuel, who gave a telling description of the tyranny of a monarch, a warning that we might see fulfilled in the reign of Solomon. In passing, we might note that this desire to be like the others can bring tyranny in the personal realm too. The life of others might look enticing but is all too often hollow. Richness only comes where God, not self or culture, is king.

The word translated as 'kingdom' actually refers to the act of ruling rather than a geographical area. 'Kingship' or 'reign' would be better translations, and more fully capture what was intended. The 'kingdom' was not a geographical location but a group of people who had all submitted themselves to the rule of God. This will, of course, affect the place in which they live, but it is not their task to build the kingdom of God, which is a work of the Holy Spirit and not of humans. It is a kingdom begun by the coming of the King at the incarnation and brought to fulfilment by his return in glory. It may be quiet, or it may be marked by an outpouring of the reviving Spirit. It is manifested in the church, but not entirely contained by the church. It grows and changes societies, as yeast grows and causes bread to rise, but it should not be thought of simply as a form of government. This is the kingdom presented to us by Mark.

The chronology of the crucifixion

Over the years there has been much debate about the precise timing of the Last Supper and the crucifixion, with some suggesting that the Synoptic Gospels and the Gospel of John contradict each other.[39] This is a suggestion with far-reaching implications: if the Gospels are contradictory, can they be trusted? Which Gospels are more trustworthy? Rather than simply a debate over dates, this question cuts to the heart of the doctrine of the inspiration of Scripture. These issues boil down to a simple question: on what day did Jesus die? On the fourteenth day of Nisan, known as the Day of Preparation, or on the day of Passover itself (Nisan 15)?[40]

Alongside the biblical regulations regarding the Passover, there are other texts that describe the festival.[41] Some of these, like the Book of Jubilees (written in the second century BC), predate the New Testament, and others were written soon after. Of particular interest is the Mishnah, which describes the practice of the Passover in more detail. Although this dates to almost two hundred years after the crucifixion, it is a compilation of earlier oral traditions dating back to the Exile many centuries before.[42]

The timetable of the Passover is summarised in the Book of Jubilees, and it is important to bear in mind that Jewish days ran from sunset to sunset (rather than the midnight to midnight timing

---

[39] 'Sometimes the arguments on both sides tend to cancel each other out; at other times, the balance of probability must be very finely weighed. The reasoning of some critics appears circular; but circularity in such arguments may be to a certain degree inescapable, granted the paucity of our data. The best one can hope to do is to ask which of the possible scenarios seems the most probable.' John P. Meier, *A Marginal Jew, Rethinking the Historical Jesus: Volume 1, the Roots of the Problem and the Person* (New Haven; London: Yale University Press, 1991), 395

[40] Nisan is the first month of the Jewish calendar.

[41] See Exodus 12–13; Leviticus 23:4–8; Numbers 9:1–14; 28:16–25; 33:3; Deuteronomy 16:1–8.

[42] The Mishnah is a collection of rabbinic sayings from the first two centuries AD, compiled to preserve them after the loss of Temple and land. As Neusner notes, 'Behind the Mishnah lay the ruins of half a millennium of continuous, orderly, and systematic Israelite life which had been centered on the regular and reliable offering of the produce of the field and flock upon the Temple altar in Jerusalem – the ordering of society around that Temple, the rhythmic division of time in response to that cult, and the placing of people and things into their proper station in relationship to that center. One disastrous war had ended in the destruction of the Temple. Three generations later, a second war had made certain the Temple would not be rebuilt in the foreseeable future or, as it now appears, ever.' Jacob Neusner, *The Mishnah: Introduction and Reader* (Eugene: Wipf and Stock, 2004), 7.

of the Roman and modern world):[43]

> Remember the commandments that the Lord gave you
> regarding the Passover so that you may celebrate it at its time
> on the fourteenth of the first month, that you may sacrifice
> it before evening, and so that they may eat it at night on the
> evening of the fifteenth from the time of sunset.[44]

This gives us the following timetable:

Nisan 14 – *the Day of Preparation*

Sunset	Clear leaven from the house.[45]
Morning	Clear leaven from the house.
Afternoon	The sacrifice of the Passover lambs at the Temple

Nisan 15 – *Passover*

Sunset	The Passover meal
Morning	The Solemn Assembly

It is worth bearing in mind that the words used in the Passover
festival can carry a range of meanings. The word 'Passover' may refer
to the Passover lamb itself, the Passover meal, the peace offering
(*hagigah*) or the entire festival, including the following week. There
can be a similar confusion over the term 'Festival of Unleavened
Bread', which at times strictly referred to the festival following the
Passover (from Nisan 16 to 21), at other times the festival including
the Passover (Nisan 15 to 21) and even, at yet other times, included
the Day of Preparation (Nisan 14 to 21).[46]

---

[43] In this they followed the pattern set out in the opening chapters of Genesis:
'And there was evening, and there was morning – the first day' (Genesis 1:5).
[44] Jubilees 49:1–2. Translation from James C. VanderKam, *Jubilees: A Commentary*
(Minneapolis: Fortress Press, 2018), 1166.
[45] For the clearing of the leaven, see Mishnah *Pesachim* 1. For the sacrifice of the
lambs, see Mishah *Pesachim* 5.
[46] See, for example, Josephus, *Jewish War*, 5.3.1; 6.9.3.

John and the date of the crucifixion

The apostle John stated that the Last Supper took place 'before the Passover'[47] (John 13:1) and that it was the fear of becoming ritually unclean for the Passover that kept the Jewish leaders from entering the Gentile Pilate's palace (John 18:28). Eleven verses later, Pilate himself offered to release Jesus since it was the Jewish custom 'for me to release to you one prisoner at the time of the Passover' (lit: 'at the Passover'), which suggests that the Passover had not yet arrived. If it had, a prisoner would already have been released.

Jesus's trial took place at about noon on 'the day of Preparation of the Passover' (John 19:14), and John noted that it was because 'it was the day of Preparation, and the next day was to be a special Sabbath' that the Jewish leaders did not wish the bodies to remain on the crosses (John 19:31). When Joseph of Arimathea took Jesus's body, he laid it in a nearby tomb 'because it was the Jewish day of Preparation' (John 19:42). The writings of John, then, clearly suggest that Jesus died on Nisan 14, the Day of Preparation. This, of course, would have fulfilled the desire of the chief priests and the teachers of the law who wanted to arrest and kill Jesus, 'but not during the festival' (Mark 14:2).

When it comes to the Last Supper itself, it is notable that John nowhere described the meal as a Passover, nor did he describe any of the elements of a Passover meal.

The Synoptics and the date of the crucifixion

In the Synoptic Gospels there are a number of references to the Passover, mainly surrounding the Last Supper.

a) The chief priests and teachers of the law desired to arrest and kill Jesus, 'but not during the festival . . . or the people may riot' (Mark 14:2, see Luke 22:1–2).

b) On 'the First Day of the Festival of Unleavened Bread' the disciples asked Jesus where they should make preparations

---

[47] The Greek does not contain the word 'Festival'.

to eat the Passover (Matthew 26:17; Mark 14:12). Luke omitted the disciples' question and simply stated that Jesus sent Peter and John to make the preparations (Luke 22:8). Mark added that this was the day 'when it was customary to sacrifice the Passover lamb' (Mark 14:12)

c) In answering the question about preparations, Jesus told the disciples to ask a certain man, 'Where is my guest room, where I may eat the Passover with my disciples?' (Mark 14:14; Luke 22:11). In Matthew, the disciples were simply to say: 'I am going to celebrate the Passover with my disciples at your house' (Matthew 26:18).

d) After this, the disciples 'prepared the Passover' (Matthew 26:19; Mark 14:16; Luke 22:13).

e) At the Last Supper itself, Jesus said, 'I have eagerly desired to eat this Passover with you before I suffer. For I tell you, I will not eat it again until it finds fulfilment in the kingdom of God' (Luke 22:15–16).

f) All three Synoptic Gospels go on to state that the crucifixion fell on 'Preparation Day' (Matthew 27:62; Mark 15:42; Luke 23:54), and Mark and Luke both state that the Sabbath was about to start as Jesus was buried (Mark 15:42; Luke 23:54).

The issue, simply put, is that the Last Supper appears to have been a Passover meal (and so, it is assumed, was eaten on Nisan 15). That means that the 'day of preparation' referred to in the crucifixion accounts cannot be for the Passover but rather, some suggest, must be a day of preparation for a Sabbath which therefore would have fallen on the following day.

There are problems with this view, though.

a) If the Last Supper was indeed eaten on Nisan 15, the Sanhedrin would not have been able to hold their trial of Jesus since work was forbidden that day (Leviticus 23:7). While they might have done so unlawfully, this is unlikely, and the text suggests no actions contrary to the Law.

b) How could the Sanhedrin have conducted such an arrest

and trial if they were eating the Passover in their own homes?[48]

c) For the same reason, it is unlikely that Simon of Cyrene was travelling on Nisan 15 (Mark 15:21), and it would make better sense that he was coming in from the fields on the Day of Preparation prior to Nisan 15 beginning at sunset.[49]

d) The release of a prisoner at the Passover (Mark 15:6) makes best sense if its purpose was to allow the freed person to participate in the Passover meal.[50] If this is the case, why would Barabbas have been freed *after* the Passover meal had been eaten?

e) The meal, as described, contained no elements of the Passover (such as the lamb or the ritual), and the liturgy of the Passover meal was designed for a family setting with children asking questions. Frankly, as Meier noted, without the references to Passover in Mark 14:1 and 12–16, 'it would never cross the mind of the reader that this meal was supposed to be taken as a Passover meal'.[51]

Paul, Quartodecimans, astronomers and the date of the crucifixion

Looking outside the Gospels, we find the apostle Paul, in 1 Corinthians 5:7, referring to Jesus as 'our Passover lamb', a phrase that finds its echoes in John's Gospel where Jesus is described as the 'Lamb of God' (John 1:29, 36). The phrase is also present in the Book of Revelation where, for instance, Jesus is referred to as 'the Lamb, who was slain' (Revelation 5:12). Gordon Fee noted that 'this

---

[48] Meier, *Marginal 1*, 396.

[49] Gerd Theissen, *The Gospels in Context: Social and Political History in the Synoptic Tradition* (London: T&T Clark, 2004), 167.

[50] Meier, *Marginal 1*, 400. It is possible that this custom is referred to in Mishnah *Pesach* 8:6, which refers to 'one whom they have promised to free from prison'. See also John 18:39, and the discussion in France, *Mark*, 629–30.

[51] Meier, *Marginal 1*, 397.

is a direct application of the death of Christ to the slaughter of the Paschal lambs on the first day of Unleavened Bread'.[52]

Aside from the evidence in the writings of John and Paul, there are later writings that would support the view that the crucifixion took place on Nisan 14. In the earliest years of the church, many of the bishops in what is now Turkey, Syria and Israel kept the feast of 'Pascha' on Nisan 14. For them, the crucifixion was the central element of the Easter celebration (after all, 'Pascha' means suffering), and they held that it was on the cross that Jesus's glory was most deeply made manifest.[53] Their insistence on not celebrating Easter on the following Sunday (which is now the norm) led to a synod being called at the end of the second century, and in their defence these Eastern bishops claimed to be following the practice of the apostles John and Philip, as well as such prominent early Christians as Polycarp.[54] They also pointed to other Eastern churches that followed the same practice.

This practice (which goes by the wonderful title of Quartodecimanism) demonstrated that from the earliest times it was understood that the crucifixion occurred on Nisan 14. The debates were concerned with the proper day to break the Lenten fast (Good Friday or Easter) rather than the date of the crucifixion itself, which would appear not to have been questioned. In addition to this early Christian evidence, the Babylonian Talmud, a later Jewish work, stated, 'On the eve of the Passover Yeshu was hanged.'[55] This too would have been on Nisan 14.

Turning from the history of the church to astronomy, the date of the Passover was also the subject of some research by a physicist and

---

[52] Gordon D. Fee, *The First Epistle to the Corinthians* (Grand Rapids: Eerdmans, 1987), 218.

[53] Melito of Sardis, *On Pascha: With the Fragments of Melito and Other Material Related to the Quartodecimans*, trans. Alistair C. Stewart (New York: St. Vladimir's Seminary Press, 2017), 28.

[54] Eusebius, *Ecclesiastical History*, 5.24. Eusebius, *History*, 335.

[55] Babylonian Talmud, *Sanhedrin*, 43a. Translation from Jacob Neusner, *The Babylonian Talmud: A Translation and Commentary* (Peabody: Hendrickson Publishers, 2011), 16:220. He notes, 'Schachter, p. 281–2, supplies a full translation of the following, which is omitted in censored editions of the Talmud and is not found in the standard printed text, translated here. What follows is verbatim Schachter's translation.'

an astrophysicist who, using astronomical calculations, reconstructed the Jewish calendar for the period between AD 26 and AD 36 and demonstrated that Nisan 15 only once fell on a Friday. That was in AD 27, a date too early for the crucifixion. However, Nisan 15 did fall on a Saturday twice, in AD 30 and AD 33, both of which would be suitable years for the crucifixion.[56] That would also make the date of crucifixion Nisan 14, coinciding with the slaughter of the lambs for the Passover meal.

Putting it all together

Having surveyed all the relevant data – the Gospels, Paul, the early church, Jewish records and astronomical research – we should conclude that the Last Supper, arrest, trial and crucifixion all fell on Nisan 14. Jesus, knowing that his death was near, wanted to eat a meal with his disciples to prepare them for his death. This meal was probably a Passover celebrated a day early, and in it Jesus introduced elements of such significance that they became the foundation for the church's celebration of Communion. Some describe this new meal as the 'Jesus Passover', a reinterpretation of the Passover in light of the coming crucifixion.[57]

This would also make sense of Jesus's words in Luke 22:15–16: 'I have eagerly desired to eat this Passover with you before I suffer. For I tell you, I will certainly not eat it until it is fulfilled in the kingdom of God.'[58] He longed to eat a final Passover with the

---

[56] Colin J. Humphreys and W. Graeme Waddington, 'The Jewish Calendar, a Lunar Eclipse and the Date of Christ's Crucifixion', *Tyndale Bulletin* 43, no. 2 (1992). They conclude that Jesus was crucified on 3 April 33.

[57] Augustyn Jankowski, 'Eucharystia Jako "nasza Pascha" (1 Kor 5, 7) W. Teologii Biblijnej Nowego Testamentu', *Ruch Biblijny i Liturgiczny* 28, no. 3 (1975); R. Bartnicki, 'Ostatnia Wieczerza Nową Paschą Jezusa (Mark 14, 22–25)', *Warszawskie Studia Teologiczne* 33, no. 10 (2015). See the helpful (English) discussion by a third Polish scholar, Mariusz Rosik, 'The Dispute Over the Date of the Last Supper. Its Chronology Revisited', *Verbum Vitae* 38, no. 1 (2020), 189–91.

[58] I have here made the translation more literal. The NIV translation inserts the word 'again' after 'eat it' in verse 17. This word is not found in the earlier manuscripts (the KJV, ESV, GNB, NRSV and NKJV all omit the word). Also, the word translated 'will not' contains two negative words which combine to make the phrase emphatic. I have shown this by changing the translation to read 'certainly not eat it'.

disciples but could not as he would be killed before it arrived. Instead, he ate a meal that would form the basis of the remembrance of his death as the Lamb of God. The Passover was fulfilled as Jesus, the Lamb of God, was killed and the symbol was replaced by the reality.

So, then, returning to Mark's Gospel, we can start to reconstruct the chronology that began 'on the first day of the Festival of Unleavened Bread', described as the day on which the lambs were sacrificed for the Passover. This must refer to Nisan 14 (the day on which lambs were to be killed), which was also known as the Day of Preparation. The reference to the Festival of Unleavened Bread must be the rather looser term that covered the entire proceedings (see the note above) rather than the strict usage of Nisan 16 to Nisan 21. No one argues that Jesus was crucified *after* the Passover.

We then get the following chronology:

Nisan 14 – the Day of Preparation

Sunset	Disciples asked Jesus where to prepare the Passover (Mark 14:12). This was the time when leaven would be cleared from the house.[59]
Evening[60]	Jesus arrived at the house with the Twelve, including Judas (Mark 14:17). He celebrated an early Passover meal, during which he reinterpreted its symbolism. Judas left to betray Jesus, before the Passover festival properly began (see Mark 14:2).
Night	Jesus and the disciples went to the Mount of Olives (Mark 14:26). Jesus prayed at Gethsemane (Mark 14:32–42).

---

[59] Mishnah *Pesachim* 1. See Jacob Neusner, *The Mishnah: A New Translation* (New Haven: Yale University Press, 1988), from page 229.

[60] The word translated 'evening' can cover a wide range of times, and we can see a consequence of this earlier in the Gospel. When Mark wished to indicate that an event happened in the early evening, he wrote 'that evening *after sunset*' (1:32, my emphasis).

Jesus was betrayed by Judas and arrested (Mark 14:43–52).
Jesus was tried before the Sanhedrin (Mark 14:53–65).
Peter disowned Jesus (Mark 14:66–72).

Early morning Jesus was brought to Pilate (Mark 15:1–5).

Morning The crowd was offered Jesus's release for the Passover (Mark 15:6–15).
The soldiers prepared Jesus for crucifixion (Mark 15:15–20).
Simon of Cyrene, travelling back for Passover, was forced to carry Jesus's cross (Mark 15:21).

9 a.m. Jesus was crucified (Mark 15:22–32).

Noon Darkness fell (Mark 15:33). The daily whole offering began at the Temple, followed by the sacrifice of the Passover lambs.[61]

3 p.m. Jesus cried out and died. The Temple veil was torn in two (Mark 15:34–41).

Late afternoon Joseph went to Pilate, asked for Jesus's body and placed it in a tomb (Mark 15:42–7).

Nisan 15 – Passover

All day Jesus remained in the tomb.

---

[61] This practice is set out in the Mishnah, which reads, '[If, however,] the eve of Passover coincided with the eve of the Sabbath [Friday], it [daily whole offering] was slaughtered at half after the sixth hour [12:30 p.m.] and offered up at half after the seventh hour [1:30 p.m.], and [then] the Passover offering [was slaughtered] after it.' Neusner, *Mishnah*, 236–7. See also Exodus 12:6.

Nisan 16

Morning   The three women discovered the empty tomb (Mark 16:1–8).

The structure and narrative of Mark's Gospel

In all, we might identify six main sections in Mark's Gospel.

Part 1: The Prologue (1:1–15)

Although short, this is a significant part of the Gospel. Here Mark sets out Jesus's identity and his place in the scriptural history of Israel. John the Baptist heralds Jesus's arrival, and at his baptism Jesus's divine sonship is disclosed. Following the baptism, Jesus goes into the wilderness and his resistance to temptation is demonstrated.

Part 2: Ministry in Galilee (1:16–6:29)

Jesus's ministry begins in his northern homeland, far from the religious authorities in Jerusalem. His spiritual authority is recognised by those who hear him, he is known by the demons he casts out and his healings attract crowds. There then follow several conflicts over the Law or, more particularly, the traditions that have grown up around the Law. Jesus forgives sins, heals on the Sabbath and chooses twelve disciples. His actions bring condemnation from the teachers of the law who have made the journey from Jerusalem.

Following his dispute with the authorities, Jesus begins to use parables to teach about the kingdom of God. He starts to demonstrate his true nature to the disciples by calming a storm and goes into a Gentile area where he proves his mastery over a legion of demons. Returning to Galilee, he raises the daughter of a synagogue leader and heals a haemorrhaging woman. He has mastery over death, demons, disease and deadly peril. A simple touch of his cloak can bring healing. Who is this?

Opposition starts to grow as local people begin to take offence at this local man. The Twelve are sent out, and the cost of discipleship is shown by the account of John the Baptist's execution at the hands of Herod.

Part 3: From Jew to Gentile (6:30–8:21)

Even if those in his home town are taking offence, many others do not, and Jesus feeds five thousand who have gathered to hear him. After the feeding of this multitude, as the disciples are on the Sea of Galilee, he walks on the water and once more displays his divine mastery over nature.

At this stage, the attention moves from the Jews to the Gentiles. Jesus first reproaches the teachers of the law and Pharisees for their commitment to tradition rather than the commands of God and then goes into Gentile regions. He heals a Syrophoenician woman's daughter and a deaf and mute man: the Gentiles can now hear and speak of the gospel. He then feeds another multitude, this time four thousand Gentiles rather than five thousand Jews. The gospel has expanded from Jew to include Gentile.

Part 4: The Christ and His Followers (8:22–10:52)

Returning to Jewish territory in Bethsaida, Jesus heals a blind man, but curiously he does so in two stages, which sets up a two-stage revelation of Jesus himself: first Peter declares Jesus to be the Messiah, but when Jesus talks about his path of suffering the disciple baulks at the prospect. The second revelation follows: that of Jesus as the glorified Son of God at the transfiguration.

If this is the divine Messiah, then what of those who follow him? They are to rely on prayer, and not be like the disciples who seek to cast out an impure spirit without coming to God. They are to be servants of all, and not seek the place of the greatest. They are not to determine who might be followers, but to allow all who are for Jesus to follow him. Jesus sets the boundaries of faith, not his followers. His are the borders we observe. In fact, a dire punishment awaits those who cause any of these little ones to stumble.

They are to follow the commands of God regarding divorce, and not follow the easy divorce culture of their day. Sexual purity is important. They are to welcome the little children but be wary of being too attached to money. They are to follow a Messiah who is to be killed, a fate many of them will share. Once again, some disciples seek honour, but they have missed the point. The disciple is one who serves.

At the end of this section dealing with discipleship, we have the ultimate example of the disciple: the blind beggar who throws aside his cloak – probably all that he has – to respond to the call of Jesus. The section ends as it begins: with the blind gaining their sight.

Part 5: The Messiah and the Temple (11:1–13:37)

After this, the Messiah finally comes to Jerusalem and is greeted as an entering king. He goes to the Temple – the LORD has finally returned to Zion! – but, after looking around he departs. The next day, as he walks to the Temple, he sees a fig tree which looks as if it is bearing edible buds. Finding none, he curses it. On entering a bustling Temple, which also looks as if it is bearing fruit, he finds only traders and drives them out. The Temple is cursed. The following day the disciples note that the cursed fig tree is withered and dead. A few days later, as the Temple veil is torn, the Temple will suffer the same fate.

There follows a protracted debate between Jesus and the various parties within Judaism who challenge his authority. He tells a parable, not lost on the authorities, pointing to his mission and the fact that they will reject him. They respond by plotting his death and ask several questions designed to trick him: should tax be paid to Caesar; what about marriage in the resurrection; what is the greatest commandment? He responds with a question of his own: whose son is the Messiah? Jesus then warns the delighted crowds about the teachers and their love of pomp, contrasting them with a poor widow who gives out of her poverty.

As they depart, Jesus sits with his disciples on the Mount of Olives and speaks of the destruction of the Temple (which will take place in AD 70) and his later return to gather the elect.

Part 6: The Victory of the Messiah (14:1–16:8)

Left behind in the Temple, the authorities are plotting Jesus's death but are fearful of the crowds. They determine that he should not be killed during the Passover festival. Meanwhile, a woman anoints Jesus in nearby Bethany, as if for his death. Judas slips out to betray Jesus to the chief priests.

The next day, as the sun sets, the Day of Preparation begins. Jesus celebrates a Passover supper with his disciples but does so a day early, since this is the day when the lambs are to be slaughtered in preparation for the great feast. As dusk turns to night he goes to the Mount of Olives and warns the disciples that they will betray him. Peter protests. Jesus withdraws to pray at Gethsemane, but the disciples sleep rather than keep watch. Judas comes with a crowd, and Jesus is betrayed with a kiss. He goes to the Sanhedrin.

At his trial, he keeps silent until he is asked if he is 'the Messiah, the Son of the Blessed One'. He responds, 'I am,' and speaks of his place at the right hand of the 'Mighty One' (Mark 14:61–2). This is enough for the charge of blasphemy, and he is beaten.

As this is underway, Peter, who alone has followed Jesus this far, is in the courtyard outside. As predicted, he denies he knows Jesus and, as predicted, the cock crows.

The Jews have no authority to execute, so they go to Pilate to lay before him charges of treason. Jesus refuses to respond to the charge that he has claimed to be King of the Jews. Pilate seeks to free him – it is customary to release a prisoner at Passover – but the crowd calls for Barabbas instead. After being flogged, Jesus is mocked by the soldiers who enact a mock coronation. Weakened by his beatings, he fails to carry his cross to the site of execution and another is pressed into service.

Even as he is executed, the mocking continues from those executed with him. Jesus is crucified as the Passover lambs are slain. The true Lamb is slain, and the true sacrifice is enacted. As he dies, with the words of Psalm 22 on his lips, the Temple veil is ripped in two. There is no more need for the old sacrificial system. It is fulfilled. The heavenly Passover Lamb is dead.

His body is laid in a borrowed tomb, with no time for formal burial preparations. The sun is setting, the Passover is at hand and work has to stop. Returning after the festival with the traditional spices for burial, three women are surprised to find the tomb empty, save for a white-robed young man. He sends them off to tell the disciples that Jesus has risen and gone ahead to Galilee where they will meet him. Bewildered, they head off, and the Gospel closes. The question hangs in the air for the reader: will you go to meet the Jesus who has gone ahead of you?

I

The Prologue

MARK 1:1–15

1. The beginning and the herald • Mark 1:1–8

The beginnings, or Prologues, of the Gospels set up all that follows. They introduce us to key people and key themes, and also place the text in the context of the Scriptures as a whole.[1]

We are given the privileged role of an insider, and as we go through the remainder of the Gospel, *we* know who Jesus really is: he is 'the Messiah, the Son of God'. We can read with an understanding that escaped nearly all those with whom Jesus came into contact. We can join the dots. We can read with faith.

Mark's Prologue is made up of the first fifteen verses of chapter one, a section that begins, 'The beginning of the *good news* . . .' and then finishes with, 'Repent and believe the *good news*' (my emphasis). As we will see, Mark is keen on the literary device known as an *inclusio*, a way of marking a section of text by repeating a phrase or theme at the beginning and at the end. Everything between the repeats is meant to fit together, and so this device is sometimes known as 'sandwiching'. The 'bread' and the 'filling' go together and interpret each other.

The bread of this particular sandwich is 'the good news', sometimes translated as 'gospel'. The filling is the prophetic message of verse 2, which begins to be fulfilled in the ministry of John the Baptist and Jesus's baptism with its accompanying voice from heaven. This section, then, is the introduction to all that follows in the Gospel.

---

[1] Elizabeth Struthers Malborn, 'Ending at the Beginning: A Response', *Semeia* 52 (1991), 177–81. This approach is also seen in wider classical literature. Peter Phillips, *The Prologue of the Fourth Gospel: A Sequential Reading* (Edinburgh: T&T Clark, 2006), 42.

John the Baptist prepares the way

1 The beginning of the good news about Jesus the Messiah,[a] the Son of God,[b] 2 as it is written in Isaiah the prophet:

'I will send my messenger
    ahead of you,
  who will prepare your way'[c] –
3 'a voice of one calling in the
    wilderness,
  "Prepare the way for the Lord,
    make straight paths for him."'[d]

4 And so John the Baptist appeared in the wilderness, preaching a baptism of repentance for the forgiveness of sins. 5 The whole Judean countryside and all the people of Jerusalem went out to him. Confessing their sins, they were baptised by him in the River Jordan. 6 John wore clothing made of camel's hair, with a leather belt round his waist, and he ate locusts and wild honey. 7 And this was his message: 'After me comes the one more powerful than I, the straps of whose sandals I am not worthy to stoop down and untie. 8 I baptise you with[e] water, but he will baptise you with[e] the Holy Spirit.'

---

[a] 1 Or *Jesus Christ. Messiah* (Hebrew) and *Christ* (Greek) both mean *Anointed One.*
[b] 1 Some manuscripts do not have *the Son of God.*
[c] 2 Mal. 3:1
[d] 3 Isaiah 40:3
[e] 8 Or *in*

The Old Testament foundation (1:1–3)

Straight away, Mark puts Jesus at the forefront of his Gospel. Christ is the heart of all that follows and is the good news that is to be proclaimed. The church has often been tempted to offer some other thing to the world – prosperity, self-fulfilment, morality, good works, wholeness – but none of these is the gospel. A gospel without the life, death and resurrection of Jesus is mere morality. A Christless church is no church at all.

This Jesus is then presented to us as both Messiah and Son of God, and here we discover that we are dealing with no mere teacher: we have a figure who is both divine and human. Yet once more we find the church tempted to offer something less – a teacher, a moralist, an example – a Jesus who is all too human, who simply had a presence of the divine within him. A godless saviour who has no power to save. B. B. Warfield (1851–1921) is surely correct when he states, 'The doctrine of the Incarnation is the hinge on which the Christian system turns. No Two Natures, no Incarnation; no Incarnation, no Christianity in any distinctive sense.'[2]

Having established who Jesus is, Mark then places him into the history of redemption. Jesus is no Plan B, but the fulfilment of God's plan of redemption which springs from Genesis 3:15.[3]

The quote from Isaiah is, in fact, a compound one, with the first two lines coming from Malachi 3. A puzzling question arises: why did Mark announce a quote from Isaiah and then begin by citing words from Malachi? While some might suggest that Mark made a mistake, this is a rather simplistic response. Given that the quotation from Isaiah, which speaks of the way of the LORD, is the main focus of the hybrid quote, and given the importance of Isaiah for Mark's Gospel as a whole, it is more likely that Mark was referring to that prophecy. The quotation from Malachi simply served to introduce us to the one who heralded the fulfilments of Isaiah's prophecy, and so was secondary in importance. It was Isaiah who was in focus here.

This introduction from Malachi prepares us for the forerunner, the messenger who would announce this return of the LORD.[4] Later, in the penultimate verse of the Old Testament – Malachi 4:5 – this messenger was identified: 'See, I will send the prophet Elijah to you

---

[2] Benjamin B. Warfield, 'The "Two Natures" and Recent Christological Speculation: I. The Christology of the New Testament Writings', *The American Journal of Theology* 15, no. 3 (1911), 337.

[3] 'And I will put enmity between you and the woman, and between your offspring and hers; he will crush your head, and you will strike his heel' (the words of God to the serpent). This verse was, from early times, seen as a prophecy of Christ. See, for example, the fifth century Jacob of Serug who imagined Mary as saying: 'the babe who is in me will crush the head of the great serpent; by Him Adam having been expelled is restored to his heritage'. *Homilies*, 679. Translation from Jacob of Serug, *On the Mother of God*, trans. Mary Hansbury (Crestwood: St Vladimir's Seminary Press, 1998), 82.

[4] It is worth noting that Elijah's return is to herald the day of the LORD and *not* the Messiah. In the literature that survives from this era, there is no linking of the return of Elijah with the coming of a Messiah. For a discussion of this, see Morris M. Faierstein, 'Why Do the Scribes Say That Elijah Must Come First', *Journal of Biblical Literature* 100, no. 1 (1981); Dale C. Allison, 'Elijah Must Come First', *Journal of Biblical Literature* 103, no. 2 (1984); Joseph A. Fitzmyer, 'More About Elijah Coming First', *Journal of Biblical Literature* 104, no. 2 (1985). The imagery of Elijah, then, points to something greater than a mere Messiah: the coming of the LORD himself.

before that great and dreadful day of the LORD comes,' and it is in this context that, a few verses on, Mark introduced us to John the Baptist. That John is equated to Elijah was hinted at in Mark 9:13 and made explicit in Matthew 11:14 where Jesus declared, 'if you are willing to accept it, he is the Elijah who was to come' (see also Luke 7:27).

Malachi's prophecy echoed Exodus 23:20, and the prophet re-applied this promise to the community who had returned from the Exile.[5] He promised not only a re-entry to the Promised Land but also a return of the LORD to the Temple, something we will see fulfilled in Mark 11.[6]

So much for the messenger; what of the message? Here Mark turned to Isaiah 40:3:

> a voice of one calling in the wilderness,
> 'Prepare the way for the Lord,
>   make straight paths for him.'

This was a direct engagement with Isaiah: the hoped-for return of the LORD was about to begin. Centuries had elapsed, and patience is often required in the providence of God. We all too readily come up with swift and easy solutions when God has richer purposes in mind. The old Scottish hymn writer put it well:

> Smooth let it be or rough,
> it will be still the best;
> winding or straight, it leads
> right onward to thy rest.[7]

---

[5] In Greek and Hebrew, the word translated 'angel' can also be translated 'messenger'.
[6] In Exodus we read, 'See, I am sending an angel ahead of you to guard you along the way and to bring you to the place I have prepared. Pay attention to him and listen to what he says. Do not rebel against him; he will not forgive your rebellion, since my Name is in him' (Exodus 23:20–2). This is echoed in Malachi, which reads, '"I will send my messenger, who will prepare the way before me. Then suddenly the Lord you are seeking will come to his temple; the messenger of the covenant, whom you desire, will come," says the LORD Almighty' (Malachi 3:1).
[7] Horatius Bonar (1808–89), 'Thy Way, Not Mine, O Lord'.

The way was finally to be prepared, an event so significant that one early name for Christianity was simply 'the Way' (Acts 24:14).

The wilderness was the starting point for this return, which was a place charged with spiritual significance. It was from the wilderness that the people of God had entered the Promised Land, and there was an expectation that it was from the wilderness that a spiritual return would take place.[8] How often it is the case that spiritual renewal follows a period of barrenness, as all is stripped away except our reliance upon God.

Jesus, as the LORD leading his people, was to be the one who would bring about an exodus from this spiritual exile, and John the Baptist was to be the one to prepare the way: the 'voice' comes before the 'Word'. The preaching comes before repentance. Here Gregory the Great (*c.* 540–604) is perceptive:

> The Lord follows his preachers. Preaching comes first, and then the Lord comes to the dwelling places of our hearts; words of exhortation precede, and by means of them Truth is received by hearts. This is why Isaiah addresses preachers: Prepare the way of the Lord, make straight the paths of our God.[9]

The ministry of the herald (1:4–8)

In verse 4, John appeared in the wilderness and began heralding the way of the LORD: he preached a baptism of repentance.[10] This repentance is a key step on the 'way', and evidence of faith — no cheap grace

---

[8] The Dead Sea Scrolls, drawing upon this same verse of Isaiah, taught that the holy will go into the wilderness to 'prepare the way of truth'. *The Community Rule (IQS)* col. viii:14. Wise, Abegg and Cook, *DSS*, 129.

[9] Gregory the Great, *Forty Gospel Homilies*, 19. Translation from Gregory the Great, *Forty Gospel Homilies*, trans. David Hurst (Kalamazoo, Michigan: Cistercian Publications, 1990), 134–5.

[10] We know from the other Gospels that John was the son of elderly parents: Zechariah, who served in the Temple, and Elizabeth, who was a relation of Mary the mother of Jesus. He was some months older than Jesus and, given the fact his father was linked to the Temple, it is likely that he was brought up near to Jerusalem rather than at Nazareth.

here.[11] The first step to receiving forgiveness of sins is acknowledging that you have sins to forgive. As William Perkins (1558–1602), one of the fathers of English Puritanism, put it, 'the needle goes before and draws in the thread which sews the cloth, so the law goes before and makes a way that grace may follow after and take place in the heart'.[12]

This begs the question: what is repentance? Nothing less than an acknowledgment of the reality of sin, and its offence to God. Any sin is putting my desires above my loyalty to God and loving myself more than I love God. I become the one to set the limits of right and wrong and, fundamentally, I defy God. At its core, sin is a turning away from God and towards yourself. Martin Luther (1483–1546) captured this nicely in his *Lectures on Romans*:

> Due to original sin, our nature is so curved *in* upon itself at its deepest levels that it not only bends the best gifts of God toward itself in order to enjoy them (as the moralists and hypocrites make evident), nay, rather, 'uses' God in order to obtain them, but it does not even know that, in this wicked, twisted, crooked way, it seeks everything, including God, only for itself.[13]

Repentance begins as you look at yourself from a God's-eye perspective and therefore obtain a proper diagnosis of yourself. It is acknowledging that God is the judge, and not yourself or the wider society. It is looking upward rather than looking inward or around.

Repentance, then, continues by acting on what is found. We might use the analogy of a speed limit. It is one thing to notice that there is a speed limit, and quite another to think it applies to you. It is still another thing to actually apply the brakes. True repentance involves all three steps: accepting God has a law; acknowledging that

---

[11] 'Cheap grace is the grace we bestow on ourselves. Cheap grace is the preaching of forgiveness without requiring repentance, baptism without church discipline.' Dietrich Bonhoeffer, *The Cost of Discipleship* (New York: Touchstone, 1995), 44.

[12] William Perkins, 'Exposition of Galatians 1–5, Chapter 2, Verses 17–21', in *The Works of William Perkins, Volume 2*, ed. P. M. Smalley, J. R. Beeke and D. W. H. Thomas (Grand Rapids: Reformation Heritage Books, 2015), 129.

[13] Martin Luther, *Lectures on Romans*, trans. Wilhelm Pauck (London: Westminster John Knox Press, 1961), 159.

his law applies to you; then keeping his law. After all, there is no point standing up in a law court and saying that you thought that the judge really wouldn't mind if you broke the law.

Far from this being an off-putting message, it drew crowds to John, from both the city and the rural hinterlands, who sought this baptism of repentance. This was an event recorded decades later by Josephus (a Jewish priest and historian, born in AD 37) who described 'John, that was called the Baptist' as someone who:

> . . . commanded the Jews to exercise virtue, both as to right-eousness towards one another, and piety towards God, and so to come to baptism; for that the washing [with water] would be acceptable to him, if they made use of it, not in order to the putting away [or the remission] of some sins [only], but for the purification of the body; supposing still that the soul was thoroughly purified beforehand by righteousness.[14]

The baptism of John was a symbolic washing, an action born of repentance. It is to be distinguished from Christian baptism, as can be seen from Acts 19:1–7 where those who have only received the baptism of John are baptised by Paul in the name of Jesus. Whereas John's baptism symbolises repentance, baptism in the name of Christ is linked to the reception of the Holy Spirit. Christian baptism is both a repenting of sin *and* a turning to Christ.

Aside from his message, John the Baptist's clothing would also have drawn comment. We have seen the expectation that Elijah would return, and here is one who, like that great prophet, 'had a garment of hair and had a leather belt round his waist' (2 Kings 1:8, see also Zechariah 13:4). His diet, startling to modern western eyes, would not have been so odd to a Jew in the first century. Locusts were declared clean, and able to be eaten (Leviticus 11:22), and the Promised Land was a place 'flowing with milk and honey'.[15]

---

[14] Josephus, *Jewish Antiquities*, 18.5.2 §§116–17. Translation from Flavius Josephus, *The Works of Josephus*, trans. William Whiston (Hendrickson Pub, 1987), 484.
[15] Exodus 3:8, 17; 13:5; 33:3; Leviticus 20:24; Numbers 13:27; 14:8; 16:13–14; Deuteronomy 6:3; 11:9; 26:9, 15; 27:3; 31:20; Joshua 5:6; Jeremiah 11:5; 32:22;

John's message was one that befitted his status as a forerunner. He pointed to the one coming after, the one for whom he was not worthy to carry out even the most menial task. This figure would baptise with the Holy Spirit, a strongly messianic act which fulfils the promise of a future outpouring of the Spirit.[16]

In our day, the job of the preacher is precisely the same: to be a herald. The herald carries the authority of a monarch but speaks only the message that is to be delivered. The authority of the herald is derived from the King. We, like John, point to Christ and preach repentance. The message of the gospel is not ours to change or trim to suit the tastes of the day. We only speak with authority when we speak the words of Christ and echo what is to be found in the Scriptures. Sidney Greidanus is perceptive:

> By whose authority do preachers preach? Whose word do they bring? If preachers preach their own word, the congregation may listen politely but has every right to disregard the sermon as just another person's opinion. . . . The only proper authority for preaching is divine authority – the authority of God's heralds, his ambassadors, his agents. Heralds and ambassadors, we have seen, do not speak their own word but that of their sender. Contemporary preachers, similarly, if they wish to speak with divine authority, must speak not their own word but that of their Sender.[17]

2. The Messiah • Mark 1:9–15

It is at this stage that Jesus entered the narrative of the Gospel. He was baptised by John and declared to be the Son of God by a voice from heaven. He was then driven into the wilderness where he faced, and resisted, temptation before returning to Galilee to begin his ministry with a call to repentance.

Ezekiel 20:6, 15.

[16] See Isaiah 32:14–15; 44:1–5; Ezekiel 11:19; 36:25–7; 37:14; 39:29; Joel 2:28–32.

[17] Sidney Greidanus, *The Modern Preacher and the Ancient Text: Interpreting and Preaching Biblical Literature* (Grand Rapids: Eerdmans, 1988), 12.

The baptism and testing of Jesus

9 At that time Jesus came from Nazareth in Galilee and was baptised by John in the Jordan. **10** Just as Jesus was coming up out of the water, he saw heaven being torn open and the Spirit descending on him like a dove. **11** And a voice came from heaven: 'You are my Son, whom I love; with you I am well pleased.'

12 At once the Spirit sent him out into the wilderness, **13** and he was in the wilderness for forty days, being tempted**f** by Satan. He was with the wild animals, and angels attended him.

Jesus announces the good news

14 After John was put in prison, Jesus went into Galilee, proclaiming the good news of God. **15** 'The time has come,' he said. 'The kingdom of God has come near. Repent and believe the good news!'

---

f 13 The Greek for tempted can also mean tested.

The baptism of the Messiah (1:9–11)

Jesus came to John from Nazareth, where he had been raised. Galilee was not an area that was well regarded by the Jews, and it had a mixed history. It had been the home of some of the northern tribes of Israel, but in 722 BC was conquered by the Assyrians, who had a policy of resettling their conquered nations. The Israelites were moved to other parts of the Assyrian Empire, and Gentiles were in turn relocated to Galilee and the surrounding areas. This meant that for centuries Galilee was Gentile country, until Aristobulus (High Priest and King of Judea from 104 to 103 BC) adopted a policy of forced conversion to Judaism. However, the question lingered: how Jewish is Galilee? To make things worse, about ten miles north of Nazareth the landscape became more barren and was home to bandits and groups of anti-Roman rebels.

Nazareth itself was a small town on a ridge overlooking the Jezreel Valley and was not on a through route.[18] It was on the way to nowhere. The valley itself was fertile and contained one of the

---

[18] Barry Beitzel, *Lexham Geographic Commentary on the Gospels* (Bellingham: Lexham Press, 2018), 34.

main highways through Israel, which thronged with military and trade traffic, but Nazareth was up and off to the side. The valley was also the site of many famous battles in the Old Testament, as well as the contest between the prophets of Baal and Elijah (1 Kings 17–18). A young Jesus would have looked over that valley and no doubt pondered all this rich history.[19]

We should note that there are no backwaters in the kingdom of God and no place or person is too small or despised for God. Rather, as Paul notes:

God chose the foolish things of the world to shame the wise; God chose the weak things of the world to shame the strong. God chose the lowly things of this world and the despised things – and the things that are not – to nullify the things that are, so that no one may boast before him. (1 Corinthians 1:27–9)

Jesus came to John for baptism, but this does not imply that Jesus was in need of being washed from sins. Rather this was an external act that reflected his internal righteousness, and he submitted to baptism as an act of obedience. Jesus's entire life and ministry were in obedience to the Law and to the Father. As our substitute, he did that which we cannot do: fully obey God. He was the lamb with no blemish of sin.

As Jesus emerged from the water, he saw the heavens 'torn' open, a word that is repeated at the end of the Gospel when the temple veil was torn (Mark 15:38). God had torn the heavens and his Spirit descended upon Jesus as a dove (Isaiah 64:1; see also Ezekiel 1:1). Here was a fulfilment of the messianic hope of Isaiah 11:2 where the 'Spirit of the LORD will rest' upon a descendent of Jesse, the father of King David.[20]

This, of course, is not to suggest that the Spirit was incarnate as a dove. The word 'like' also describes people 'like sheep without a shepherd' (Mark 6:34) or people looking 'like trees walking around'

---

[19] For a very helpful discussion on Nazareth, see Beitzel, *Geographic Commentary*, chapter 4.
[20] On this, see Irenaeus, *Against Heresies*, 3.17.1–3.

(Mark 8:24). What is in mind is a comparison: as a dove descends and lands, so did the manifestation of the Spirit of God.

Within ancient Judaism there was a tradition, recorded in the Babylonian Talmud, that at creation the Holy Spirit hovered like a dove,[21] and it is tempting to see the baptism of Christ echoing this.[22] Here the new creation is begun (see 2 Corinthians 5:17; Galatians 6:15), with Jesus emerging from the waters to be greeted by a voice from heaven.

There is more to this than simply a fulfilment of messianic hope. The voice from heaven declared Jesus to be the Son of God, 'whom I love; with you I am well pleased' (see Psalm 2:7). This is a strong echo of the first 'Servant Song' of Isaiah:

> Here is my servant, whom I uphold,
>   my chosen one in whom I delight;
> I will put my Spirit on him,
>   and he will bring justice to the nations.
> (Isaiah 42:1)

As we see in the later Servant Songs, this servant would follow a path of suffering. To be the Son of God, the one who is loved, does not mean that suffering cannot follow. Rather, the very fact that this suffering servant is loved by God will be of comfort to Christ when he is soon tempted.

There is comfort in this for us too: the Christian can face suffering knowing that he or she is beloved by God. To simply equate suffering with God's displeasure is false.

It should be noted that this passage does not imply that Jesus *became* the Son of God at this moment, or that the Holy Spirit somehow conferred divinity upon Christ. Rather, God declared who Jesus *already* was. This was a declarative act, not a defining act. The love of the Father for the Son is eternal, without a beginning. In John 17, Jesus asserted that the Father 'loved me before the creation of the world' (John 17:24). A little earlier Jesus had spoken of 'the

---

[21] Babylonian Talmud, *Hagigah*, 15a.
[22] For a very thorough discussion of this, see Davies and Allison, *Matthew 1*, 1:331–4.

glory that I had with you before the world began' (John 17:5). He was 'in the beginning' (John 1:1). Jesus is, to quote Hebrews 13:8, 'the same yesterday and today and for ever'. The Father has eternally been the Father, and the Son eternally the Son. God is without change. Jesus is eternally God.

It should also be noted that in this passage we see a demonstration of the Trinity, since all three persons were present: the Father spoke to the Son on whom the Spirit rested. There is no room here for the erroneous belief that God somehow operates in different 'modes': at one time being Father, at another being Son and at yet another being Spirit. No. Here, all three persons were present at the same time. God is eternally a Trinity.

The temptation of the Messiah (1:12–13)

No sooner did the Spirit rest upon Jesus than he was sent into the wilderness, where he remained for forty days. In fact, the word translated 'sent' is rather more forceful and is elsewhere translated as 'driven out' or 'expelled' (e.g., Mark 1:39; 3:22; 11:15). How often a spiritual 'high point' is followed by a time of testing. Temptation is not a sign that somehow God is out of control; rather, testing is a means of strengthening our faith. The path of discipleship is often scattered with temptation when obedience is attacked by the desire for self-gratification.

The forty days of testing is a symbolic number. The spies sent into Canaan were there for forty days before filing their fearful report, and the fact that the Hebrews then failed to enter the Promised Land earned them forty years of wandering in the wilderness (Numbers 14:34). During the flood, the rain fell for forty days and forty nights (Genesis 7:4), Moses was on mount Sinai for forty days (Deuteronomy 9:11), and Elijah fasted for forty days and nights before encountering God at Horeb (1 Kings 19:8). Of course, symbolic does not mean untrue: that is a false dichotomy. Rather, it is a mechanism to help us make connections with other passages in the Bible.

Temptations come from two sources: from within and from outside, from our heart or from some external source. Jesus taught that it is from the heart that evil thoughts proceed (Matthew 15:19; Mark

7:21), and the evil thoughts of which Jesus spoke are, in themselves, sinful. To look at someone lustfully is to commit adultery in the heart (Matthew 5:27–8), which is a sobering thought in our pornography-saturated age. When Paul spoke of judgment, he commented that the Lord 'will bring to light what is hidden in darkness and will expose the motives of the heart' (1 Corinthians 4:5). The Word of God 'judges the thoughts and attitudes of the heart' (Hebrews 4:12), and Peter urged Simon the Sorcerer to 'pray to the Lord in the hope that he may forgive you for having such a thought in your heart' (Acts 8:22). To suggest that thoughts, fantasies and temptations are only sinful when they are acted upon is to ignore the teachings of Jesus, Peter, Paul and the author of Hebrews.[23]

However, since Jesus is sinless, it cannot be that his temptations arose from his sinful heart (Hebrews 4:15). They must have come from an external source, and so it is that we read that this testing was carried out by Satan (literally 'the Accuser'). Here is an important point: these temptations were external to Jesus; they came from outside. To deny the reality of Satan means that we would have to conclude that these temptations instead came from Jesus's heart, which would leave us with a sinful Saviour, which is nonsense. A Satan who is merely a metaphor leaves us with a Jesus who had sinful thoughts arising from a fallen heart, one as fallen as the rest of us; one who cannot save since he is not a spotless sacrifice.

Mark noted that Jesus was among the wild animals, which has messianic overtones. Isaiah, when writing about the Davidic Messiah, looked forward to his time as one where:

> The wolf will live with the lamb,
>   the leopard will lie down with the goat,
> the calf and the lion and the yearling together;
>   and a little child will lead them.
> The cow will feed with the bear,

---

[23] This inward desire is known as concupiscence and is widely held as having the nature of sin in the Reformed confessions. So, for example, the Thirty-Nine Articles of the Church of England contain the following: 'And although there is no condemnation for them that believe and are baptized, yet the Apostle doth confess, that concupiscence and lust hath of itself the nature of sin' (Article IX).

their young will lie down together,
and the lion will eat straw like the ox.
The infant will play near the cobra's den,
and the young child will put its hand into the viper's nest.
(Isaiah 11:6–8)

Having demonstrated his obedience through this time of temptation, we then see the beloved Son being ministered to by the angels. Here we witness the supernatural nature of these events, something that comes to the fore in the next section of the Gospel.

Many struggle with all this talk of angels, yet to have any belief in God is to acknowledge the existence of a supernatural realm and to acknowledge that not all of reality is intelligible to human beings. To reject the supernatural is to claim that the human race is the centre of all existence, such that if a human cannot detect something, it cannot exist (which is nonsensical and arrogant in equal measure). Why should it be that all of reality centres itself around the human? To claim, as the atheist does, that something cannot exist unless a randomly evolved organism on the edge of the known universe says so seems rather unlikely.

The Bible consistently refers to angels which, unlike God, are created beings (Psalm 148:2–5; Colossians 1:16) and are capable of doing wrong (2 Peter 2:4; Jude 6). They are rational (Matthew 24:36; 1 Peter 1:12; 2 Peter 2:11) and many in number (Matthew 26:53; Revelation 5:11). Their purpose is both to announce the will of God (as Gabriel did to Mary) and to protect the believer (Psalms 34:7; 91:11; Matthew 18:10). At the temptation, as on the Mount of Olives (Luke 22:43), they ministered to Jesus.

What are we to make of all this supernatural activity? Neither too little nor too much. To dismiss it through either unbelief or by ignoring the whole issue is to reduce the world to our own understanding and to reject what is revealed through Scripture. To swing to the opposite extreme and to hold that everything is supernatural and the natural order is somehow inferior or evil is to ignore the fact that all creation was seen as 'good' by God,[24] and that Jesus himself

---

[24] Genesis 1:4, 10, 12, 18, 21, 25, 31.

took human flesh. In the end, the supernatural realm, as the natural, is under the control and command of God, so it is not to be feared, nor should we think we can bend it to our will.

The ministry of the Messiah (1:14–15)

Upon the arrest of John the Baptist, the ministry of the herald ended and the one to whom he pointed stepped onto the stage. This is the hinge between the hopes of Isaiah and the prophets and their fulfilment, yet Jesus did not begin by travelling south to Jerusalem. Rather, he turned to the region around his home: Galilee. This was to be the setting of Jesus's early ministry, and it was some time before he travelled to the religious heartland of the nation. Beware being quick to despise the small and remote regions in favour of the big cities, or of trying to rush the providence of God.

Jesus proclaimed the good news of God, and there is some debate as to whether the 'good news' is *about* God or *from* God. In the end, both are true: the good news is both from God and about God. The good news set forth in Isaiah was that 'the Sovereign LORD comes with power' (Isaiah 40:10), and this hope was heightened as Jesus began to preach that the 'time has come' and 'the kingdom of God has come near'. These two statements are, of course, related to the person of Jesus himself. The time had come because he had begun to preach. The kingdom was near since the King had arrived.

The response to this good news was to be twofold: repentance and belief. It is hard to overstress the importance of this. Christianity makes a demand on every part of life. Repentance is a change not only of thinking but also of action. It is a change of heart that brings with it remorse over past actions. It is a change of mind and a new manner of thinking and behaving. It is both a consequence of a faith truly held and a mark of grace. Christianity is no mere veneer, something added to one's life. Rather, it is a change of heart and a turning around. It is following Christ as King with a renewed mind (Romans 12:2). It is being 'born again' (John 3:3).

Repentance also acknowledges the reality of sin and its abhorrence to God. In Romans 1:18 Paul refers to the 'wrath of God' being poured out against 'all the godlessness and wickedness of people', and Jesus taught that it would be better to 'gouge out' your eye than have it lead you to sin (Matthew 5:29, speaking in the context of lust). In the wider world there is a great desire for 'justice', yet this often sits alongside a rejection of any sense of absolute moral standards, or at least the standards of God. This, of course, makes any sense of justice impossible. It is not for the defendant to tell the judge what is right and wrong. Justice demands absolute standards.

Sin is a word that is offensive, since it speaks of those absolutes. It challenges the modernist view that it doesn't really matter what you do, as long as it doesn't hurt anyone else. The problem is, though, that the seriousness of sin lies at the heart of the Christian faith. If you remove it, then the rest unravels. After all, as Paul wrote in 1 Timothy 1:15, Christ came to save sinners. Remove sin and you remove the need for Christ. A church that rejects sin can only offer a purposeless Christ.

A rejection of sin also leads to a misunderstanding of what it is to be human. None of us is perfect; our motives are mixed and at times we regret our actions even as we do them. It is healthy to acknowledge this. Also, when we understand that we've done wrong, the forgiveness of Christ is an even richer experience. There is nothing more annoying than someone saying, 'I forgive you,' when you've done nothing wrong. There is nothing more comforting than someone forgiving you when you know you were in the wrong.

Sin is a concept of which the church should not be bashful. It is not a word or idea we should hide. Rather, to acknowledge sin is to be honest about yourself and then to glory in God's forgiveness. To confess your sin makes the grace of God all the more amazing. Grace is deepened where transgression is fully acknowledged. Grace shines all the more brightly against the ink-black backdrop of sinfulness.

It is, therefore, no wonder that when those who heard Peter's sermon at Pentecost asked, 'What shall we do?', the apostle replied, 'Repent and be baptised, every one of you, in the name of Jesus Christ for the forgiveness of your sins' (Acts 2:38). Or, when preaching in the Temple portico, he urged his hearers, 'Repent, then, and turn to

God, so that your sins may be wiped out' (Acts 3:19). Here are the twin emphases of repentance and good news that lay at the heart of Jesus's teaching ministry and formed the core of the preaching in the Acts of the Apostles. The call to repent of sin comes with the good news that Christ has come to deal with the effects of that sin.

2

Ministry in Galilee

MARK 1:16–6:29

1. The spiritual authority of Christ • Mark 1:16–39

In any ministry, the issue of authority looms large. On whose authority do you speak? What are your credentials? For the reader of Mark, this question has already been answered at Jesus's baptism where he was revealed to be the Son of God. We read as privileged insiders, but those who first heard him did not share our knowledge.

As Jesus embarked upon his ministry, he did so by calling a band of followers and then teaching in a synagogue. Teaching was to be the hallmark of his ministry, and it was with teaching that he began. This teaching demonstrated his authority and brought about wonder from his hearers and opposition from the impure spirits. Here was a spiritual authority indeed, and the miracles he worked only served to underscore that authority.

Authority to call disciples (1:16–20)

Jesus calls his first disciples

16 As Jesus walked beside the Sea of Galilee, he saw Simon and his brother Andrew casting a net into the lake, for they were fishermen. 17 'Come, follow me,' Jesus said, 'and I will send you out to fish for people.' 18 At once they left their nets and followed him.

19 When he had gone a little farther, he saw James son of Zebedee and his brother John in a boat, preparing their nets. 20 Without delay he called them, and they left their father Zebedee in the boat with the hired men and followed him.

Having proclaimed the kingdom of God, Jesus now sought out its subjects. He called Simon and Andrew to follow him, reversing the usual pattern of the student seeking out a rabbi. To issue a call is to require a response, and 'at once' they did. It should be noted that to 'fish for people' suggests that this is an all-consuming, hard pattern of work. Fishing in the first century was often carried out at night when it was cooler and the boats would not cast shadows into the water below and scare off the fish. This was arduous work. The days were often filled with processing the fish and mending nets.

Later, Jesus saw James and John, whom he also called. As we will see throughout the Gospel, such is the authority of Jesus that he speaks, and things happen. Echoes here of the words spoken at creation. That James and John left their father with hired hands would suggest that their family fishing enterprise was of a reasonable size.

These four were called by Jesus just as they were. They did not earn their calling, nor did they need to meet certain criteria. The call of Christ is simply that: Christ's call. He calls whom he will, and none is beyond his power to call. The disciples were not the obvious choice for leading a worldwide movement of God, being lowly fishermen from a backwater of the Roman Empire, but the message they bore had power enough. It is the gospel that is glorious, not the messenger (see 1 Corinthians 1:18–31), and God equips his heralds. Jesus took these unlikely men and, as Eusebius of Caesarea wrote, 'breathed into them His divine power, He filled them with strength and bravery, and like a true Word of God and as God Himself, the doer of such great wonders, He made them hunters of rational and thinking souls'.[1]

Herman Bavinck (1854–1921) noted that these followers received two callings: first as disciples; and second as apostles in Mark 3:14, where they were given the preaching task.[2] Not all are called to be preachers, but all are called to be disciples and live out their faith in

---

[1] *The Proof of the Gospel*, 3.7. Eusebius of Caesarea, *The Proof of the Gospel: Being the Demonstratio Evangelica of Eusebius of Cæsarea*, trans. W. J. Ferrer (London: The Society for Promoting Christian Knowledge, 1920), 1:156.

[2] Herman Bavinck, *Reformed Dogmatics Volume 4: Holy Spirit, Church, and New Creation*, trans. John Virend (Grand Rapids: Baker Academic, 2008), 333.

the wider world as well as in the church. Note also that the primary calling of the two sets of brothers was to 'fish for people'. Evangelism was the first calling received by the apostles, but unfortunately is often the first lost by the church.

The call to preach came later, and was a vital one, since all who would dare to teach or preach will be judged more strictly (James 3:1). In today's internet age it is all too easy to set up a self-appointed ministry, but the call to preach is something discerned by the wider church. Authority is given, not demanded. It is servant-hearted, not domineering. It derives from the call of Christ, not the character of the individual.

It is sadly true that in many parts of the world, particularly where the church has both money and power, corruption can creep in. It should not be forgotten that Christ is the head of the church, which is his body (Ephesians 1:22–3). No individual should usurp that position, nor think themselves to be above the church. The authority of the minister or elder derives from Christ, and once that person departs from the way of Christ, their authority ebbs.

All four disciples were called to follow, and follow they did. John the Baptist had prepared the 'way for the LORD' (Mark 1:3), and now these disciples followed the LORD along that way.

Authority over impure spirits (1:21–8)

Jesus drives out an impure spirit

21 They went to Capernaum, and when the Sabbath came, Jesus went into the synagogue and began to teach. 22 The people were amazed at his teaching, because he taught them as one who had authority, not as the teachers of the law. 23 Just then a man in their synagogue who was possessed by an impure spirit cried out, 24 'What do you want with us, Jesus of Nazareth? Have you come to destroy us? I know who you are – the Holy One of God!'

25 'Be quiet!' said Jesus sternly. 'Come out of him!' 26 The impure spirit shook the man violently and came out of him with a shriek.

27 The people were all so amazed that they asked each other, 'What is this? A new teaching – and with authority! He even gives orders to impure spirits and they obey him.' 28 News about him spread quickly over the whole region of Galilee.

Capernaum sits on the north-west shore of the Sea of Galilee and occupies a strategic spot on the road to Damascus. Given its location, the Romans made their presence felt, and recent excavations have unearthed a Roman milestone. A centurion was based here with his troops, and it was a centre for the collection of taxes. It was here that Jesus focused his early mission, and the foundations of the synagogue in which he taught can still be seen forming the base of a later building.

Jesus went into the synagogue on the Sabbath which, following the Jewish pattern of measuring days, began at sundown on Friday.[3] Services in the synagogues would follow a pattern of prayers, readings, a sermon and a benediction, which reflected the primacy of Scripture. Hearing his teaching, the congregation were amazed 'because he taught them as one who had authority, not as the teachers of the law'. This theme of authority is important in Mark, and the contrast drawn between Jesus and the 'teachers of the law' would not have been pleasing to the latter. Jesus spoke on his own authority as the Son of God, whereas their authority was second-hand and derived from the Law.

It was at this stage that a man possessed by an impure (literally 'unclean') spirit cried out, 'What do you want with us, Jesus of Nazareth?' Although the man was speaking, it is clear that these were the words of the spirit, and the plural 'us' has caused some discussion. It might be that the spirit was referring to the others in the synagogue (William Lane thinks this 'distinctly possible'[4]), but it is more likely that the 'we' refers to other spirits.[5] This, then, is best viewed as a cry from the spiritual realm from those who recognised Jesus as 'the Holy One of God'.

This identification of Jesus is significant. As we progress through Mark's Gospel it will become apparent that the unclean spirits knew precisely who Jesus was, even when others did not. The singular

---

[3] In the account of creation in Genesis chapter 1, we read, 'And there was evening, and there was morning – the first day' (or second day, third day and so on).

[4] William L. Lane, *The Gospel of Mark* (Grand Rapids: Eerdmans, 1974), 73.

[5] See the discussion in Simon J. Gathercole, *The Preexistent Son: Recovering the Christologies of Matthew, Mark, and Luke* (Grand Rapids; Cambridge: Eerdmans, 2006), 150–51.

title 'Holy One' is widely used in the Old Testament to refer to God, especially in Isaiah, with the vast majority of uses of the term occurring in the phrase, 'Holy One of Israel'. However, we should not conclude that this was the meaning here: if the spirits were referring to Jesus as God, then we would expect some outrage from the synagogue crowd, and there is none reported.

The plural 'holy ones' is also used in the Old Testament to refer to heavenly beings or angels, but the unclean spirit addressed Jesus in the singular and used the definite article ('the'). Jesus was identified as a heavenly being above all others, *the* Holy One, and was recognised by those in the spiritual realm. Simon Gathercole is surely correct in stating that 'the demons refer in their question to the advent of the pre-existent holy one of God into the realm of human and demonic existence on earth'.[6]

Jesus first silenced the spirit – here we see the beginning of the secrecy that is a feature of Mark's Gospel – and then ordered it out. This was no supernatural struggle between equals, though: Jesus cast out the spirit simply by speaking.

The assembled crowd was astonished, but note it was the teaching that had impressed them along with the authority with which Jesus spoke. The casting out of the spirit bore witness to his authority but wasn't the cause of the amazement. As in all small rural communities, the news spread quickly.

NOTE: IMPURE SPIRITS AND DEMONS

Many will dismiss all this talk of spirits out of hand, thinking belief in then is naïve. They dismiss the possibility of the supernatural, and so find none. The great rejection of the supernatural, following Immanuel Kant (1724–1804), has left us ill-equipped to consider much beyond the reach of human senses or the equipment of the laboratory. However, as we noted earlier, to believe in God is already to believe in the supernatural. To hold to the existence of the soul, or consciousness, is already to believe in the existence of things undetectable. To believe that Jesus is the Son of God is to place your faith in one who himself believed in spirits.

---

6 Gathercole, *The Preexistent Son*, 152.

At this point, a person might argue, 'But Jesus was just using the language of the time, and while he spoke of spirits he really knew that he was dealing with mental illness.' That is to suggest Jesus misled others and was happy to leave them in their ignorance, yet Jesus described himself as 'the truth' (John 14:6). To hold to this line of reasoning is to leave us with a Jesus who cannot be trusted.[7] In the end, the modern person must accept that dealing with spirits or demons was very much part of Jesus's ministry. That we, with rationalistic presuppositions, are likely to dismiss things we cannot define does not mean that they do not exist.[8]

On the other hand, some might imagine a degree of horror such as that portrayed on the cinema screen and fear they are caught up in a battle of good and evil, two equal and opposite forces fighting over the human soul. This is not the case. It is remarkable how low-key Jesus's dealings with demons were. He spoke and cast them out. There was no battle, no struggle between equals. No need to create drama; simply an assertion of the authority of Christ over all things. The evil spirits are to be acknowledged, but not feared.

Authority over sickness (1:29–34)

Jesus heals many

29 As soon as they left the synagogue, they went with James and John to the home of Simon and Andrew. 30 Simon's mother-in-law was in bed with a fever, and they immediately told Jesus about her. 31 So he went to her, took her hand and helped her up. The fever left her and she began to wait on them. 32 That evening after sunset the people brought to Jesus all who were ill and demon-possessed. 33 The whole town gathered at the door, 34 and Jesus healed many who had various diseases. He also drove out many demons, but he would not let the demons speak because they knew who he was.

---

[7] While the identification of the impure spirit is made by Mark in this passage, Jesus refers to spirits in Mark 5:8 and 9:25.

[8] For an interesting discussion of this from the perspective of Ghanian Christians in London, see Emmanuel Frimpong, 'Reading the Gospel of Mark with African Eyes: A Fresh Look At the Exorcism and Healing Passages in Mark', *Ghana Bulletin of Theology* 4 (2012): 146–72.

In the ancient world, as in many parts of the world today, it was common for extended families to live in the same house. From time to time, extensions were built on homes to accommodate a growing family, and as a result familial bonds would be strong. Here we find a home for two brothers, as well as Simon Peter's mother-in-law. Given Peter's marriage, it is not unreasonable to imagine children as part of this household. Andrew may too have been married, but the text is silent.

Not far from the foundations of the first-century synagogue in Capernaum can be found the remains of a house of the same date, which has long been held to be the house of Simon and Andrew.[9] The disciples did not have to walk far from synagogue to home.

When told of the woman's illness, Jesus simply took her by the hand and helped her up. There was no need for a great display and there was an ease about Jesus's actions, as we have noted with the casting out of the impure spirit. His compassion may also be seen in his gentle actions, and he commonly took people by the hand when restoring them (see Mark 1:41; 5:41; 8:23). Here the tenderness of Isaiah 40:11 is displayed:

He tends his flock like a shepherd:
  He gathers the lambs in his arms
and carries them close to his heart;
  he gently leads those that have young.

Here we have a saviour to whom we can fly, confident of his gentle compassion.

Peter's mother-in-law responded to the healing by beginning to serve them, giving us a model of discipleship. To serve others is a key component of the Christian life and a fitting response to Christ's mercy. We follow the Christ who came 'to serve' (Mark 10:45).[10]

---

[9] Virgilio C. Corbo, 'Capernaum', in *The Anchor Bible Dictionary*, ed. David Noel Freedman (New Haven: Yale University Press, 1992), 1:867–8.
[10] The great twentieth-century Russian theologian Bulgakov (1871–1944) notes, 'For Scripture it is not the institution of the primacy of Peter, or the apostolic primacy of the episcopate, but service, determined by the place of each member in the Church, that represents the fundamental norm of universal priesthood. This

Both the healing and the woman's act of service took place upon the Sabbath, and the question of the Sabbath becomes a point of dispute in chapter 3. Jesus astonished his synagogue hearers with the authority of his teaching, and here he demonstrated his authority over the Law. It is important to note that Jesus was not setting the Law aside, but rather he was keeping its true intent. As we will see, a multitude of traditions had risen up around the Old Testament Law, and these robbed it of its mercy.

Once the sun had set and the Sabbath was over – around 6 p.m. – crowds came to the house seeking healing. Mark gave no details but emphasised the scale of the gathering ('the whole town'). Jesus's actions in the synagogue had drawn attention, but it was healing they were seeking and not his teaching.

Here we find a common danger: we seek the benefits of Jesus rather than Jesus himself. We desire healing, wealth and salvation rather than Christ. It is true that to believe in Christ is to find salvation, but this salvation cannot be separated from Christ himself. True faith brings a change so deep it may be described as a new birth (John 1:13; 3:3, 7–8; James 1:18; 1 Peter 1:23, 1 John 2:29, 3:9, 4:7, 5:1, 18) or 'new creation' (2 Corinthians 5:17). The apostle Paul repeatedly described the believer as being 'in Christ', which suggests a deep connection, a union with Christ. Christianity is no bolt-on, an improvement to our lifestyle, but a radical change. The Christian faith is a person: 'Jesus Christ and him crucified' (1 Corinthians 2:2).[11]

Many were healed by Jesus, and many demons were cast out (Mark is careful to distinguish between demon possession and illness). Once again, the demons were silenced and not allowed to speak of Jesus's identity. The Messianic Secret was maintained (see introduction).

---

is the authentic "apostolic succession" in the Church, and denies any basis for clerical absolutism or "monarchic episcopatism" as manifestations of ecclesiastical hierarchism.' Sergius Bulgakov, *Bride of the Lamb*, trans. Boris Jakim (Grand Rapids: Eerdmans, 2001), 279.

[11] For a very helpful investigation into this theme, see Sinclair B. Ferguson, *The Whole Christ: Legalism, Antinomianism, and Gospel Assurance – Why the Marrow Controversy Still Matters* (Wheaton: Crossway, 2016), especially chapter 2.

Authority to preach (1:35–9)

Jesus prays in a solitary place

35 Very early in the morning, while it was still dark, Jesus got up, left the house and went off to a solitary place, where he prayed. 36 Simon and his companions went to look for him, 37 and when they found him, they exclaimed: 'Everyone is looking for you!'

38 Jesus replied, 'Let us go somewhere else - to the nearby villages - so that I can preach there also. That is why I have come.' 39 So he travelled throughout Galilee, preaching in their synagogues and driving out demons.

Having spent much of the previous evening, and perhaps night, dealing with the townspeople of Capernaum, Jesus rose before sunrise and went off to seek solitude in order that he might pray. It is notable that Jesus gave such an emphasis to prayer and made it such a high priority. In our rather pragmatic age, with how-to books and off-the-shelf solutions, it is easy to neglect prayer in favour of activity.

Jesus's practice of seeking solitude in prayer is one he commended to his disciples (Matthew 6:6). Prayer is a means of ensuring that God is given the glory for his work and a sign that we do not take his providence for granted. Prayer is the engine that drives the church, and a sign of reliance upon God. If Jesus felt the need for regular prayer in isolation, how much more do those who follow him need it? The question posed by Thomas Watson (*c.* 1620–86) is a good one: 'Do we pray in the morning as if we were to die at night?'[12]

The disciples were concerned and went to seek him out (the verb means 'hunt' or 'search eagerly'). When they did find him, they informed him that everyone else was also looking for him. Jesus's reply was somewhat telling. Rather than courting popularity or seeking to engage with the crowd, he instead suggested they went elsewhere so that he could preach in the surrounding villages. This was the purpose of his ministry. The crowds were seeking healing, but Jesus was looking to preach.

It is important to note the priority Jesus gave to preaching. While his miracles grabbed the attention of the crowds, he saw it as far

---

[12] Thomas Watson, *The Christian Soldier, or Heaven Taken by Storm* (New York: Robert Moore, 1816), 110.

more important to ensure they had a correct view of God. We should be wary of simply presenting a therapeutic God whose sole intent is to make us well and give us a sense of worth. The purpose of the preacher is to point to the Christ who was crucified so that *he* might bring about a deep change.

Jesus went on throughout the region and brought his teaching to new areas. He had been popular in Capernaum but did not want to return; rather, he wanted to reach new people and go to places that had not yet heard him teach. The gospel was to be spread widely – his was an itinerant ministry, often preaching outdoors or in houses – but he was also happy to make use of the existing network of synagogues. He did not favour one setting over the other. Alongside his preaching, Jesus also cast out demons, which suggests that his teaching also provoked a supernatural response. Jesus taught no mere human morality, but rather he spoke of deeper things that brought about a spiritual response.

2. The Christ and the Law • Mark 1:40–3:12

As Jesus began his ministry, the people were astonished at the authority with which he taught: 'a new teaching – and with authority' (Mark 1:27). This authority was contrasted with that of the teachers of the law (Mark 1:22), and in this section of the Gospel we see a number of disputes over the Old Testament Law itself.

It is important to note that at no point did Jesus seek to set the Law aside or suggest that it no longer applied. Throughout his ministry he lived in obedience to the Law, fulfilling its requirements (John 4:34; Galatians 4:4; Philippians 2:8; Hebrews 4:15; 7:27–8). Rather, the issue was the regulations that had grown up around the Law, regulations having their origin in a pious tradition but not in the Scriptures themselves.

So it was that Jesus debated the traditions that had grown up around ritual cleanliness (Mark 2:13–17), the Sabbath (Mark 2:23–8; 3:1–6) and fasting (Mark 2:18–22). The section begins, though, with the healing of a man with leprosy who is then urged to fulfil the regulations of the Law.

The leper and the law (1:40–45)

Jesus heals a man with leprosy

40 A man with leprosy^g came to him and begged him on his knees, 'If you are willing, you can make me clean.'

41 Jesus was indignant.^h He reached out his hand and touched the man. 'I am willing,' he said. 'Be clean!' **42** Immediately the leprosy left him and he was cleansed.

43 Jesus sent him away at once with a strong warning: **44** 'See that you don't tell this to anyone. But go, show yourself to the priest and offer the sacrifices that Moses commanded for your cleansing, as a testimony to them.' **45** Instead he went out and began to talk freely, spreading the news. As a result, Jesus could no longer enter a town openly but stayed outside in lonely places. Yet the people still came to him from everywhere.

---

g 40 The Greek word traditionally translated *leprosy* was used for various diseases affecting the skin.

h 41 Many manuscripts *Jesus was filled with compassion*

Among diseases, leprosy held a particular place in the Law: it made a person unclean. In modern usage leprosy refers to Hansen's disease, but in the ancient world the word covered a range of skin conditions (as can be seen in Leviticus 13–14). This was not simply a medical matter, but one with religious significance, so the afflicted man knelt before Jesus – a posture of humility – and begged him not just for healing, but also for ritual cleanliness. Both body and soul were to be restored.

It is important to note that the man did not demand his healing. He rather said, 'If you are willing . . .' He did not seek to impose his will upon Christ, but rather prayed that Christ's will was to heal him. Here was an acting out of the Lord's Prayer: 'your will be done'.

Jesus's reaction is unexpected: he was indignant.[13] What might

---

[13] If you were to look at other translations of this passage you would find a very different phrase. For example, the English Standard Version has 'moved with pity' and the King James Version has 'moved with compassion'. What causes this difference is that fact that while the majority of the early manuscripts have 'angry', a few have 'had compassion'. The Greek words are utterly different, and this is no copying error. So why not simply go with the majority of manuscripts, as most English translations of the Bible do? It is normally assumed that ancient scribes would not change a manuscript to make it more off-putting. If you have two manuscripts

have provoked this response in Jesus? Given his reactions elsewhere, it would seem unlikely that it was the approach of the leper; after all, the leper was on his knees and was not demanding anything of Jesus. We should also note that Jesus did in fact heal the man, which would be a strange response if Jesus were indignant at him. Better to see this anger directed at the leprosy itself, which was a consequence of the fall (see, for example, Romans 8:22f). This was similar to the emotion we see at the raising of Lazarus (John 11:38).

This indignation does not imply that Jesus was consumed with the uncontrolled rage of a man overcome, but rather experienced sorrowful anger at the damage done to a fallen creation. This was Jesus, in whom 'all things were created' (Colossians 1:16), lamenting the disfiguring damage wrought by sin on his creation. Paul wrote that 'the whole creation has been groaning as in the pains of child-birth right up to the present time' (Romans 8:22), and here we see an example of that pain of creation.

Within the Psalms we find many places where the psalmist cried out, 'Why?' to God, and we might imitate this cry when we, too, face serious illness. Often the path to peace winds through mysti-fied distress, and a deep trust in the providence of God is won by long-anguished prayer.

Jesus touched the leper, something that would have rendered Jesus ritually unclean, but here we find the normal state of affairs reversed. In the Old Testament sacrificial system, both the sin offering (Leviticus 6:24–30) and the altar (Exodus 29:37) make holy those who touch it. Elsewhere in the New Testament Jesus is depicted as the atoning sacrifice for sin (Hebrews 10:8–14), and also as the place of sacrifice (Romans 3:25, NIV footnote). Since Jesus is both these things, he would make holy that which was unclean, simply by touch.[14] As we

---

that differ in one word, then they would tend to accept the one with the more difficult wording. This is the principle known as *Lectio Difficilior Potior*, which translates as 'the more difficult reading is preferable'. The complicating issue in this instance is that the *Lectio Difficilior* comes in a fifth-century manuscript known as D, whose scribe had a habit of making significant changes. On balance, it would seem most sensible to dismiss D at this point, but since the NIV adopts this reading – and in other places we do see Jesus having this type of reaction – we will deal with D here.

[14] See Mark 1:40–45; 5:35–43; 6:1–6; 7:31–7; 8:22–6. For those who are healed as

will see in chapter 5, he even brought healing to those who reached out to touch his cloak without his knowledge. In Leviticus, we read of the sin offering that 'whatever touches any of the flesh will become holy' (Leviticus 6:27), and Mark shows us that Christ, the offering for our sin, makes holy those whom he touches. Here is righteousness indeed!

In all of this, we have a precursor of what was achieved on the cross when Jesus's righteousness was 'imputed' to those who place their faith in him. In a passage overwhelmed with praise, John Calvin (1509–64) captured the wonder of all this:

> This is the wonderful exchange which, out of his measureless benevolence, he has made with us; that, becoming Son of man with us, he has made us sons of God with him; that, by his descent to earth, he has prepared an ascent to heaven for us; that, by taking on our mortality, he has conferred his immortality upon us; that, accepting our weakness, he has strengthened us by his power; that, receiving our poverty unto himself, he has transferred his wealth to us; that, taking the weight of our iniquity upon himself (which oppressed us), he has clothed us with his righteousness.[15]

After the healing, Jesus sent the man away (the Greek means 'cast out') with a twofold 'strong warning': don't tell anyone and go to the Temple. This insistence on following the process set out by Moses was especially significant, and we should be careful to note that Jesus was keen to ensure all the laws surrounding ritual purity were kept. Jesus was not setting aside the Old Testament Law, but rather embodying it.

This might also be seen as pointing to the authority of the Scriptures that contain those laws. As Matthew Barrett has pointed out, 'By looking to the manner in which Jesus accomplishes redemption – that is, his self-conscious covenant obedience to the Scriptures

---

they touch Jesus see Mark 3:7–12; 5:24–34; 6:53–6.
[15] John Calvin, *Institutes of the Christian Religion*, 4.17.2. J. Calvin, *Institutes of the Christian Religion*, trans. F. L. Battles (2011), 1362.

– one also discovers Jesus' own attitude towards the Scriptures.'[16] The Law is not to be overturned but is to be fulfilled. That Jesus understood himself to be bound by the Old Testament Law underlines the authority he gave to the Scriptures.

But what of us? Are we still under this Old Testament Law? In answering this question, it is important to distinguish between the three types of law we find in the Old Testament.[17] The first, known as the ceremonial law, dealt with the sacrificial system and the associated rounds of feasts, as well as circumcision and dietary laws. This law was fulfilled by Jesus's death and resurrection (Ephesians 2:14f; Hebrews 10:1–18). His was the once-and-for-all sacrifice for sin (Romans 3:25; Hebrews 9:26), the 'Lamb of God, who takes away the sin of the world' (John 1:29). His was the New Covenant which 'has made the first one obsolete' (Hebrews 8:13).

The second type of law – the moral law – encompasses those laws that speak to our behaviours and morality. These are global and eternal in application, since they reflect the character of God and apply to all peoples. We might think here of the Ten Commandments, and their applicability to non-Jewish nations is demonstrated by the fact that it was defilement that led to the Canaanites being driven out of the Promised Land.[18] These laws are just and reflect God's wisdom. Moses, speaking of these 'decrees and laws' given to him, said to the Hebrews, 'Observe them carefully, for this will show your wisdom and understanding to the nations, who will hear about all these decrees and say, "Surely this great nation is a wise and understanding people"' (Deuteronomy 4:6). We might think of these as creation ordinances, as a moral 'rightness' arising from the character of the creator himself. As we will see, when Jesus spoke

---

[16] Matthew Barrett, *Canon, Covenant and Christology: Rethinking Jesus and the Scriptures of Israel* (Downers Grove: IVP Academic, 2020), 7.

[17] This threefold division is common in Reformed literature (e.g., Article 7 of the Articles of Religion of the Church of England). For a thorough discussion of this categorisation and its biblical roots, see Philip S. Ross, *From the Finger of God: The Biblical and Theological Basis for the Threefold Division of the Law* (Ross-shire: Mentor, 2010).

[18] 'Do not defile yourselves in any of these ways, because this is how the nations that I am going to drive out before you became defiled. Even the land was defiled; so I punished it for its sin, and the land vomited out its inhabitants' (Leviticus 18:24–5).

of marriage, he began by referring back to the opening chapters of Genesis. These laws *do* still apply.

A third type of law might be identified: civil law. Ordinarily, this is understood as laws tied to the ancient state of Israel and now redundant. For example, the requirement to wear tassels on clothing (Numbers 15:38) or to refer mould in a house to a priest (Leviticus 14:33–57). There is no longer a Levitical priesthood, and the tassels were a command given to the men of Israel. Principles may still be helpful (e.g., the tassels were to remind the men of the commands of God), but the practice is no longer necessary.

Before leaving the subject of the Law, we might also consider the three main functions that the Law continues to play. Classically, the Reformed churches have taught that the Law serves to restrain evil in wider society, reveal to individuals their sinfulness and lead believers into patterns of living acceptable to God.

We can see Jesus's attitude to the Law illustrated in the strong command given to the man to go to the Temple and fulfil the ritual requirements. This was not only a matter of obedience but was also to be a 'testimony' to the priests. This passage sits at the beginning of a section where Jesus and the authorities clashed over the Law, and at the outset of his ministry Jesus sent a signal that his intention was not to overturn the Law. The man was to perform the prescribed sacrifices (an eight-day process is laid out in Leviticus 14), and so be reintegrated into the wider society. The priests were to witness not only the miracle but also Jesus's attitude to the Temple and the sacrificial system. He left it to the priests to declare the leper clean.

The healed leper could not, however, keep it to himself. He spread the news, with the result that Jesus could not enter a town without being known. What an example this is of the power of simply talking to others about your experience of Jesus. As a result, Jesus remained in the lonely places (literally 'wilderness'), but even there he was found by the crowds.

The authority to forgive sins (2:1–12)

Jesus forgives and heals a paralysed man

2 A few days later, when Jesus again entered Capernaum, the people heard that he had come home. **2** They gathered in such large numbers that there was no room left, not even outside the door, and he preached the word to them. **3** Some men came, bringing to him a paralysed man, carried by four of them. **4** Since they could not get him to Jesus because of the crowd, they made an opening in the roof above Jesus by digging through it and then lowered the mat the man was lying on. **5** When Jesus saw their faith, he said to the paralysed man, 'Son, your sins are forgiven.'

6 Now some teachers of the law were sitting there, thinking to themselves, **7** 'Why does this fellow talk like that? He's blaspheming! Who can forgive sins but God alone?'

8 Immediately Jesus knew in his spirit that this was what they were thinking in their hearts, and he said to them, 'Why are you thinking these things? **9** Which is easier: to say to this paralysed man, "Your sins are forgiven," or to say, "Get up, take your mat and walk"? **10** But I want you to know that the Son of Man has authority on earth to forgive sins.' So he said to the man, **11** 'I tell you, get up, take your mat and go home.' **12** He got up, took his mat and walked out in full view of them all. This amazed everyone and they praised God, saying, 'We have never seen anything like this!'

Jesus returned home to Capernaum[19] and the news quickly spread, with the result that the locals crowded into a house – possibly Peter's – to see him. A typical house of the time would be around seven metres square, with a first-floor mezzanine covering about half of the ground floor. Upstairs would be the living and sleeping area, with a kitchen, stores and animals on the lower floor.[20] Such was the crowd that the house was full, and the doorway well and truly blocked. Jesus took advantage of this gathering to preach 'the word' to them.

This is an interesting phrase and one that has strong echoes in the Old Testament. The 'word' is authoritative (Psalm 119:160) and is the mechanism by which the prophets prophesied (2 Samuel

---

[19] See Matthew 9:1.
[20] Beitzel, *Geographic Commentary*, from page 16.

23:2). 'The word of the LORD' came repeatedly to the patriarchs and prophets, being the means of revelation for them. It was this 'word' that gave Jesus his authority: he spoke from divine revelation, and this was recognised by those who thronged around him.

As we have seen previously, while Jesus's ministry was primarily one of preaching, the people looked to him for healing. This pattern repeats itself here. Four men brought a paralysed man and found the house too crowded to enter.[21]

First-century houses in this area tended to be capped by roof beams covered in a thatch topped off with compacted soil. With access via exterior steps, they were useful places for storage, work or even sleeping. The four climbed up, dug through the roof and lowered the sick man. This would have been no easy task and bears witness to their strong desire to bring this man before Christ.

Jesus 'saw their faith', and we should note that it is not simply the paralysed man's faith in view here, but that of the group. From this we might draw two conclusions. First of all, faith is demonstrated by action: Jesus '*saw* their faith'. True faith results in actions, not just feelings; it changes behaviour and gives a fresh perspective on life. Jesus commented that we can judge people by their fruit (Matthew 7:16–20), and James taught that 'faith by itself, if it is not accompanied by action, is dead' (James 2:17). That old Anglican bishop J. C. Ryle (1816–1900) put it pithily: 'In short, where there is no sanctification of life, there is no real faith in Christ.'[22]

Second, we might view the action of the friends as an enacted parable dealing with prayer. As often takes place in Mark's Gospel, one person brings another's needs to Christ (see also Mark 5:21–43; 7:24–30), and Christ responds. We should never grow weary of interceding for others, or tire of prayer. Prayer may involve a tenacious struggle or long hours of tears, but it is a deep honour to bring others into the very throne room of God. As the widow persisted with the judge, so must we be tireless in bringing our petitions before a gracious God (Luke 18:1–8). There are no shortcuts in prayer.

---

[21] The Greek simply means 'lame', but the fact that the man was carried to the house on a mat suggests some level of paralysis.

[22] J. C. Ryle, *Holiness: Its Nature, Hindrances, Difficulties and Roots* (London: William Hunt and Company, 1889), 26.

Jesus responded to the startling actions of the four by declaring the paralysed man's sins to have been forgiven. However, this should not lead to the conclusion that somehow the man was saved by the faith of his friends. It seems unlikely that the four would have brought the paralysed man to Jesus against his will, and forgiveness of sins comes in response to personal faith, not second-hand faith.

In the previous passage the leper had been made clean, and here sins are forgiven. Both these functions belonged properly to the Temple and to the work of God. It was therefore not surprising that the teachers of the law thought Jesus was blaspheming. Even though Jesus made no claim to have forgiven the sins himself, none-theless the implication seemed clear enough to the teachers of the law. Blasphemy is no small matter: 'Anyone who curses their God will be held responsible; anyone who uses the name of the LORD blasphemously is to be put to death' (Leviticus 24:15–16). This was no blasphemy, though. This was a demonstration of Jesus's divinity. He proclaimed the forgiveness of God.[23]

We might note that the teachers of the law, in their zeal to follow God, ended up opposed to God. Zeal for Christ must always be held up to the light of Scripture or we run the risk of confusing our own prejudices with the will of God. It is sobering to think that those opposing Jesus were convinced they were following God's purposes.

Mark stated that Jesus knew the thoughts of the teachers of the law 'in his spirit'. Throughout the Gospel, Mark demonstrated that Jesus *in his human nature* had limited knowledge. In Luke 2:52 we read that 'Jesus grew in wisdom and stature, and in favour with God and man' (see also Luke 2:40), and in his human nature Jesus shared the limitations of all humans (except, of course, sin). In many passages in Mark's Gospel, Jesus asked for information or sought it out (Mark 5:30; 6:38; 9:21; 11:13), and in Mark 13:32 he acknowledged that he did not know the timing of all that he described. We find it easy to accept that Jesus's body was fully human – he got tired, he thirsted,

---

[23] This should not be thought to indicate that a public, or specific, confession of sin is a necessary precursor to healing. For an interesting discussion of this in a Ghanian context, see Daniel Nii Aboagye Aryeh, 'An Exegetical Discussion of Mark 2:1–12: Lessons for Forgiveness and Healing in Contemporary Christianity in Ghana', *Conspectus* 25, no. 1 (2018).

he died – and it is important to confess that his mind was also fully human. Jesus's humanity and his divinity were both entirely complete. They were not mixed up together, nor were they capable of being divided. They were unchangeable and could not be separated. Jesus was (and is) a single person, but also one having two natures.

Throughout the history of the early church, attempts to make Jesus less human or less divine were rejected. At the Council of Nicaea, in AD 325, Jesus's full divinity was defended against Arianism, and at the Council of Constantinople, in AD 381, the notion that Jesus had only a divine mind or soul (Apollinarianism) was rejected. Later, in AD 431, in Ephesus, the notion that Jesus's human nature could be divided from his divine nature (Nestorianism) was condemned, and in AD 451 the Statement of Chalcedon was produced as the definitive statement of orthodoxy on the person of Christ.

The statement of Mark that Jesus knew 'in his spirit' suggests that the Holy Spirit imparted this knowledge to him. The Holy Spirit dwelt within the humanity of Jesus without measure and imparted the strength for holiness and the gifts of wisdom and knowledge.[24] This knowledge was something that Jesus had 'immediately' and was not the product of a process of deduction. His response to this knowledge was to issue a challenge: is it easier to say that sins are forgiven, or to heal the man? The implication was that actions are harder than words. In order that they may be convinced that he could forgive sins, he healed the man. Note that he said he had the authority to forgive sin 'on earth'. The implication is that the Father has authority in heaven, but while the Son was on earth, he had authority on earth.

The miracle is both instant and public, and also brings with it praise to God (the Son always points to the Father). This was something new to the congregation, a theme that would be developed when Jesus would teach on the new wineskins. The curse and decay brought about by Adam's sin were being overturned by the presence and ministry of Christ.

---

[24] See John Owen's *Pneumatologia*, Chapter 4. John Owen, 'Πνευματολογια or, a Discourse Concerning the Holy Spirit', in *The Works of John Owen, Volume 3*, ed. William H. Goold (Edinburgh: T&T Clark, 1862), from page 168.

The mission of Jesus to sinners (2:13–17)

Jesus calls Levi and eats with sinners

13 Once again Jesus went out beside the lake. A large crowd came to him, and he began to teach them. 14 As he walked along, he saw Levi son of Alphaeus sitting at the tax collector's booth. 'Follow me,' Jesus told him, and Levi got up and followed him.

15 While Jesus was having dinner at Levi's house, many tax collectors and sinners were eating with him and his disciples, for there were many who followed him. 16 When the teachers of the law who were Pharisees saw him eating with the sinners and tax collectors, they asked his disciples: 'Why does he eat with tax collectors and sinners?'

17 On hearing this, Jesus said to them, 'It is not the healthy who need a doctor, but those who are ill. I have not come to call the righteous, but sinners.'

As Jesus went to the lake, once more a crowd gathered and – as was his practice – he taught them. It would seem that Jesus was walking as he taught, and as he did so he came across Levi, who was collecting taxes. Customs duties were collected by the Romans on goods and, given Capernaum's location, is it unsurprising that there was a tollbooth there. Levi probably collected taxes on fish, and his name implies he was a Levite.[25] Strauss notes that the fact that he was a Levite in a tollbooth in Capernaum, and not ministering in the Temple, would have only added to his unpopularity.[26] That he collected taxes on fish would not have endeared him to Peter, Andrew, James and John. There was not a large pool of friends for tax collectors in the ancient world.

There has been a lot of discussion about the precise identity of this Levi, son of Alphaeus. He appears here and in the parallel passage in Luke 5:27–32, but not elsewhere in the New Testament. In Matthew's Gospel, the tax collector is named Matthew rather than Levi (Matthew 9:9), and Levi is not listed among the disciples later in Mark's Gospel (whereas Matthew is, Mark 3:16–19). A son of Alpheus does appear in those lists, but he is named James, not Levi.

---

[25] Ben Witherington III, *The Gospel of Mark: A Socio-Rhetorical Commentary* (Grand Rapids: Eerdmans, 2001), 120.

[26] Mark L. Strauss, *Mark* (Grand Rapids: Zondervan, 2014), 130.

The most satisfactory solution to this problem is that Levi was also known as Matthew, something supported by the different names in the parallel texts. It may be that his name was changed by Jesus in the same manner that Simon was renamed Peter, or that Matthew was his birth name and Levi a nickname because of his tribe. If this is correct, it would also suggest that James and Matthew were another pair of brothers, along with James and John, and Peter and Andrew.

On seeing Levi, Jesus told him, 'Follow me.' And so he did, an act that underscores true discipleship. Mark's Gospel opens with the prophetic call to 'prepare the way for the Lord' (Mark 1:3), and in John's Gospel Jesus described himself as 'the way' (John 14:6). Later, in the Acts of the Apostles, we see that 'the Way' had become a very early name for Christianity (Acts 9:2; 19:9; 19:23; 24:14). True repentance, which is a core component of Jesus's ministry (Mark 1:15), always issues in action. To say that you have repented of something and then to carry on behaving in the same way is to demonstrate that you have not repented at all. Christianity from its inception was a faith that issued in a way of life, a change in direction. Levi was called out of his own situation, gave up everything and followed Jesus. You cannot become a Christian and then stay the same.

There is great encouragement in this. That fact that Christianity was called 'the Way' demonstrates that it is the destination that is important, not the starting point. To follow on 'the Way' is to move from one place to another, from the start to the finish. Levi might have been an outcast, but by following Jesus he walked into the kingdom of God. Jesus calls us *as we are* and then leads us into glory. James and John were called from their fishing boat and Levi from his tollbooth. We all join 'the Way' at different points but we are all heading in the same direction.

This was clearly demonstrated when Jesus went to dine with Levi. Strauss notes that within the rabbinic tradition, if a tax collector entered a house, everything within it was rendered unclean.[27] It was not a place for a nice, respectable rabbi. To dine at the house of a tax collector, with many other tax collectors and sinners present, was to risk uncleanness. The Greek translated 'having dinner' literally reads

[27] Strauss, *Mark*, 130. He refers to Mishnah *Tohorot* 7:6.

'reclining at table' and suggests this was a formal affair, not simply a meal. Why would Jesus be present at a place of such ritual impurity?

The Pharisees among the teachers of the law were puzzled by this. They sought a fuller observance of the Old Testament Law and placed a high value on purity, particularly in matters of food. While they have become the villains of the Gospels in the popular imagination, in their day they were respected by the general population.[28] They were an observant, lay movement who sought to keep God's commands. Why, they wondered, was Jesus not doing the same?

Jesus heard the question, either directly or it was relayed to him by the disciples, and his answer was profound. The path to righteousness is not the sort of separation advocated by the Pharisees, but rather an active reconciliation of sinners to God. Jesus had come to call sinners to himself, not those who thought themselves righteous. Why was he eating with sinners? The answer was simply that this was where he was needed. 'It is not the healthy who need a doctor, but those who are ill. I have not come to call the righteous, but sinners.'

There are two main implications that follow from Jesus's words. First of all, in all communities there are those who are outcasts, who live on the edges of society, but none is beyond the reach of Christ. The gospel is not simply for those 'like us', and we should be diligent in ensuring that it is preached to all in society, even if that means we run the risk of becoming outcasts ourselves. All are to be called to repentance and to follow Christ.

Second, Jesus came to save *sinners*, something the apostle Paul was also keen to stress (1 Timothy 1:15). While many seem to shy away from the language of sin, it was central to Jesus's mission. It is only those who are willing to admit that they are sinners who reach out their hands so they can be saved. Those who deny their sinfulness will look for no help. It is only those who accept they are sick who look to a doctor. The love of God is not demonstrated by turning a blind eye to sin, but rather by offering a remedy. 'For we cannot know the magnitude of Christ's grace unless we first recognize our malady.'[29]

---

[28] Josephus, *Jewish Antiquities,* 13.298; 18.15, 17.
[29] Philip Melanchthon, *Apology of the Augsburg Confession* (1531), Article 2 (33).

The law, the disciples and the bridegroom (2:18–22)

Jesus questioned about fasting

18 Now John's disciples and the Pharisees were fasting. Some people came and asked Jesus, 'How is it that John's disciples and the disciples of the Pharisees are fasting, but yours are not?'

19 Jesus answered, 'How can the guests of the bridegroom fast while he is with them? They cannot, so long as they have him with them. **20** But the time will come when the bridegroom will be taken from them, and on that day they will fast.

21 'No one sews a patch of unshrunk cloth on an old garment. Otherwise, the new piece will pull away from the old, making the tear worse. **22** And no one pours new wine into old wineskins. Otherwise, the wine will burst the skins, and both the wine and the wineskins will be ruined. No, they pour new wine into new wineskins.'

While it is clear that the practice of fasting was at the heart of the controversy in this passage, it is less easy to answer the question, why? Within the Old Testament, fasting was only commanded on one day in the year – the Day of Atonement – and there is no suggestion that this debate was taking place on that day.[30] It would seem therefore that this was more a debate about fasting in general, and in order to gain an understanding of the debate it is worth spending a little time considering the role of fasting in Judaism.

Within the Scriptures we can see that over time fasting developed into a penitential act, usually associated with prayer. King Saul, for instance, instructed his troops to fast in an attempt to bring about victory in battle (1 Samuel 14:24), and David fasted, even for his enemies when they were sick (Psalm 35:13). In Jeremiah 36:6 the prophet instructed Baruch the scribe to 'go to the house of the LORD on a day of fasting', which suggests that by the sixth century BC several fasts throughout the year were commonly observed in Israel.

By the time of the return from the Exile, a pattern of national fasts had arisen, possibly in Babylon, and there is evidence for this in the

---

Translation from Robert Kolb, Timothy J. Wengert and Charles P. Arand, *The Book of Concord: The Confessions of the Evangelical Lutheran Church* (Minneapolis: Fortress Press, 2000), 117.

[30] See Leviticus 16:29–31; 23:27–32; Numbers 29:7.

words of the prophet Zechariah: 'This is what the LORD Almighty says: "The fasts of the fourth, fifth, seventh and tenth months will become joyful and glad occasions and happy festivals for Judah. Therefore love truth and peace"' (Zechariah 8:19). Zechariah was speaking to those who had come from Bethel (Zechariah 7:2), and the fasts he mentioned were held to mark the fleeing of the Judean leadership and the breaching of Jerusalem's walls, the destruction of the Temple, the assassination of Gedaliah and the beginning of the siege of Jerusalem (bringing with it the end of the Davidic rule).[31] The question raised by the delegation from Bethel was whether, in light of the rebuilding of the Temple, the fast associated with its destruction should continue to be kept.

The answer given by the prophet is important for the passage we are considering. In the future, he said, all these fasts would be replaced by feasts, but this was not simply because of the rebuilding of the Temple. There was something greater that would occur, as we can see from the words proclaimed by Zechariah earlier in the same chapter: 'This is what the LORD says: "I will return to Zion and dwell in Jerusalem. Then Jerusalem will be called the Faithful City, and the mountain of the LORD Almighty will be called the Holy Mountain"' (Zechariah 8:3). The LORD would return, and this was the reason given for the replacing of fasts by feasting.

Later in chapter 8, Zechariah went on to expand the prophecy: 'In those days ten people from all languages and nations will take firm hold of one Jew by the hem of his robe and say, "Let us go with you, because we have heard that God is with you"' (Zechariah 8:23). So it was that not only would these fasts end when the LORD returned, but also all the nations would seek him. Here, then, was the eschatological edge to fasting and the promise of its fulfilment. In Jesus, this fulfilment had taken place. The LORD had returned. Soon the Gentiles would be called in.

Jesus's reply contained imagery of a bridegroom, and R. T. France noted that in ancient Judaism there does not appear to be any use of

---

[31] Carol L. Meyers and Eric M. Meyers, *Haggai, Zechariah 1–8. A New Translation with Introduction and Commentary* (New York: Doubleday & Company, 1987), 434; Elizabeth Rice Achtemeier, *Nahum – Malachi* (Atlanta: Westminster John Knox Press, 1986), 134.

bridegroom imagery for the Messiah. However, he pointed out that there was frequent use of the bridegroom metaphor for God himself (Isaiah 61:10; 62:4–5; Hosea 2:14–20), and this was the allusion Jesus made.[32] While he – the LORD – was with the disciples they would feast. Yet, Jesus continued, the bridegroom would be taken from the disciples (one assumes at the crucifixion, or maybe the ascension), and then fasting would be restored.

Fasting remains very much a part of some Christian traditions, particularly Eastern Orthodoxy and Roman Catholicism. There the emphasis is both repentance and the idea that denying the flesh renders one stronger in resisting temptation. It is a training of the body, a spiritual exercise regime. It should be noted that fasting is not a means of gaining blessings – that is for God alone to determine – nor does it mechanically obtain forgiveness of sins. That is the role of faith and repentance. Nonetheless, many find it useful in battling the sinful flesh that envelops us all.

The question arises: should we imitate Jesus in this practice? While fasting is a practice commended in the New Testament (in Matthew 6:16 Jesus says, 'When you fast,' not, 'If you fast'), we should be careful to understand that it is not some sort of mechanism to unlock blessings. Throughout the Old Testament, the people of Israel were chastised for thinking that a bare keeping of rituals such as fasts would earn them God's favour (for example, Isaiah 58:6–11; Jeremiah 6:20; Amos 5:21–3). To fast in an attempt to gain some personal spiritual benefit is to miss the point.

So to return to the question, should the Christian fast? The short answer is yes. As we have seen, Jesus certainly assumed Christians would do so and we have evidence that the New Testament church did so.[33] The practice endured. The Didache is a very early collection of teachings, headed 'An Instruction of the Lord Given to the Heathen by the Twelve Apostles'. Most scholars date it to the first century, with the earliest date being around AD 60–70. It may well, therefore, be contemporary to the Gospels themselves, and it states, 'Your fasts should not coincide with those of the hypocrites. They

---

[32] France, *Mark*, 139.
[33] See Acts 13:2–3; 14:23.

fast on Mondays and Tuesdays; you should fast on Wednesdays and Fridays.'[34] Again, fasting is assumed.

This is not to say that fasting is a requirement of salvation; rather, it is simply a path to holiness. It weakens the sinful desires of the flesh and is part of the spiritual exercise of the believer. It recognises that the body and the spirit are intertwined. It should not be an exercise of bare duty or an act done for the praise of others, but a path to prayer. The great preacher and medic, Martyn Lloyd-Jones (1899–1981) is characteristically balanced:

> We should not do these things mechanically. We must discipline our lives, but we must do so all the year round, and not merely at certain stated periods. I must discipline myself at all times, and must fast only when I feel led by the Spirit of God to do so, when I am intent on some mighty spiritual purpose, not according to rule, but because I feel there is some peculiar need of an entire concentration of the whole of my being upon God and my worship of Him. That is the time to fast, and that is the way to approach the subject.[35]

Jesus then continued with a pair of short parables dealing with the incompatibility of the new and the old. In the first parable, the unshrunk cloth will tear away if used to patch an old garment. When it is washed, or simply gets wet, the patch will shrink and tear itself away from the garment. The second parable deals with an old and inelastic wineskin. If such a skin is filled with fresh wine which is still fermenting and expanding, it will inevitably burst.

In both parables the lesson is clear: the old and the new simply cannot co-exist. But what is the old, and what is the new? This passage is often used to justify some new practice or teaching, but just because something is new does not necessarily mean it is good. Any innovation in the church or in the interpretation of

---

[34] *Didache*, 8. Translation from *The Didache, the Epistle of Barnabas, the Epistles and the Martyrdom of St. Polycarp, the Fragments of Papias and the Epistle to Diognetus*, trans. James A. Kleist (New York: The Newman Press, 1948), 19.

[35] D. Martyn Lloyd-Jones, *Studies in the Sermon on the Mount, Second Edition* (Leicester: InterVarsity Press, 1976), 357.

Scripture is to be held up to the light of Christ who is 'the same yesterday and today and for ever' (Hebrews 13:8). Nor does this passage suggest that the Old Testament has simply been replaced by the New Testament. The New Testament embraces, fulfils and transforms the Old Testament. They sit together as revelations of the one eternal God and must not be separated.

Rather than novelty or innovation, Jesus was dealing with the contrast between what Paul would later refer to as the letter and the Spirit (2 Corinthians 3:1–6). The Christian is filled with the living Spirit of God and so cannot inhabit a rigid religion bound by regulation. In the kingdom of God, ethics is a spiritual matter and not one to do with external rules of behaviour. The Spirit transforms the person from the inside out, and our ethics – the 'fruit of the Spirit' (Galatians 5:22–3) – is evidence of that work of the Spirit. The English Puritan John Preston (1587–1628) described it well:

A woman many times thinks she is with child, but if she finds no motion or stirring, it is arguable she was deceived. So, when a man thinks he has faith in his heart, but yet he finds no life, no motion, no stirring, or there is no work proceeding from his faith, it is arguable he was mistaken, he was deceived in it. For if it is a right faith it will work, there will be life and motion in it.[36]

This has implications for the life of the individual believer. Repentance brings a renovation of the whole heart and person, and there can be no half measures. You cannot be a little bit Christian: either you are or you are not.

---

[36] John Preston, *The Saint's Qualification; or, a Treatise of Humiliation and Sanctification,* 3rd ed. (London: I. D. for Nicholas Bourne, 1639), 332. Cited in Joel R. Beeke, *The Quest for Full Assurance: The Legacy of Calvin and His Successors* (Edinburgh: Banner of Truth, 1999), 119. I have updated the spelling and grammar for the purposes of clarity.

The disciples and the Lord of the Sabbath (2:23–8)

Jesus is Lord of the Sabbath

23 One Sabbath Jesus was going through the cornfields, and as his disciples walked along, they began to pick some ears of corn. 24 The Pharisees said to him, 'Look, why are they doing what is unlawful on the Sabbath?'

25 He answered, 'Have you never read what David did when he and his companions were hungry and in need? 26 In the days of Abiathar the high priest, he entered the house of God and ate the consecrated bread, which is lawful only for priests to eat. And he also gave some to his companions.'

27 Then he said to them, 'The Sabbath was made for man, not man for the Sabbath. 28 So the Son of Man is Lord even of the Sabbath.'

In the previous passage, we saw Jesus's disciples drawing comments owing to their lack of fasting. In this passage, it was their activity on the Sabbath that offended. We would do well to note that Jesus was being judged by the actions of his disciples. Those who profess to follow Christ have a weighty responsibility since others will judge the merits of Christianity by the actions of Christians. This is something particularly true for those who hold office within the church, and high-profile scandals leave much damage in their wake. No wonder James warned that 'we who teach will be judged more strictly' (James 3:1). Integrity is a prize to be valued highly and serves to glorify God. 'For we are taking pains to do what is right, not only in the eyes of the Lord but also in the eyes of man' (2 Corinthians 8:21).

The Pharisees did not object to the fact that the disciples were taking the grain, since this was an action permitted in the Old Testament Law: 'If you enter your neighbour's cornfield, you may pick the ears with your hands, but you must not put a sickle to their standing corn' (Deuteronomy 23:25). The issue was that this took place on the Sabbath. This was a debate over the correct interpretation of the fourth commandment.

In the first century, the Sabbath was an important sign of Jewish identity and one that was scorned by the Romans. For example, Augustine noted that the Roman philosopher Seneca (4 BC–AD 65) took a dim view of the practice: 'The Jews, he said, served no good purpose by resting every seventh day, since they lost nearly a seventh part of their whole lives and must neglect many matters calling for immediate attention.'[37] Philo (c. 20 BC–c. AD 50), a Jewish scholar, related the amazement of a Roman prefect and governor in Egypt when the Jewish population refused to bow to his threats of violence and continued to keep the Sabbath.[38]

All of this demonstrates that the Sabbath not only carried the weight of the Old Testament Law but also was at the core of Jewish self-identity. It was one of the things that marked them out as different from the surrounding peoples in the ancient world. Unsurprisingly, these markers became particularly important when Israel was under Gentile occupation, and therefore much effort was made to ensure they were kept.

This effort, however, led to the development of a number of other regulations that were not found in the Bible. These were designed to ensure that there would be no unintentional breaking of the Sabbath. They were seen as safeguards and clarifications of the biblical mandate. For instance, in the Dead Sea Scrolls there is a prohibition on the making of music on the Sabbath, and even the private reading of Scripture.[39] The Book of Jubilees, commonly dated to the second century before Christ, reads:

> Any person who does work: who goes on a trip; who works farmland whether at his home or in any (other) place; who lights a fire; who rides any animal; who travels the sea by ship; any person who beats or kills anything; who slits the throat of an animal or bird; who catches either a wild animal, a bird, or a fish; who fasts and makes war on the Sabbath day – a person who does any of these things on the Sabbath day is to die.[40]

---

[37] Augustine, *City of God*, 6.11. Translation from Augustine, *The City of God, Books I–VII*, trans. Demetrius B. Zema and Gerald G. Walsh (Washington: The Catholic University of America Press, 1950), 355.

[38] *On Dreams that they are God-Sent*, 2.123. See Philo, *The Works of Philo: Complete and Unabridged*, trans. C. D. Yonge (Hendrickson, 1993), 396–7.

[39] Vered Noam and Elisha Qimron, 'A Qumran Composition of Sabbath Laws and Its Contribution to the Study of Early Halakah', *Dead Sea Discoveries* 16, no. 1 (2009).

[40] Jubilees 50:12–13. Translation from VanderKam, *Jubilees*, 1192. On the Sabbath more generally, see Jubilees 2.

External compliance became vitally important, and the regulations just quoted serve to illustrate the seriousness with which this was viewed.[41] This was no small matter, and Jesus here was swept into these controversial debates.

In answering the Pharisees, Jesus ignored the debates of the day and returned to first principles: the Scriptures. Here is an example to be followed when controversies escalate and traditions harden. Often we lose sight of what is *actually* written in the Bible, and by so doing we confuse our own thinking with the Scriptures. Jesus did not turn to the Ten Commandments, but rather to a passage in 1 Samuel, and in so doing he illustrated an important principle: the best interpreter of Scripture is Scripture. The Bible acts as a whole and should be read as a whole. One part illuminates the other, and as we trace themes or doctrines through the Bible we gain a clearer understanding of their intent. If we find our own particular interpretation of a passage contradicted elsewhere in the Bible, that should be enough to cause us to rethink. Thomas Watson puts it well: 'The scripture is to be its own interpreter, or rather the Spirit speaking in it; nothing can cut the diamond but the diamond; nothing can interpret scripture but scripture.'[42]

So it was that Jesus referred to the actions of David and his companions in 1 Samuel 21:1–6. They entered the Tabernacle and ate the bread of the Presence, which was surely a worse transgression than picking ears of corn in a field. Yet David was a man after God's own heart (1 Samuel 13:14), and the verdict of Scripture is that he 'had done what was right in the eyes of the LORD and had not failed to keep any of the LORD's commands all the days of his life – except in the case of Uriah the Hittite' (1 Kings 15:5). There was no judgment upon David for this transgression.

France shrewdly noted that the point here is that it was David – the greatest of the kings, and a man on whom God bestowed great favour – who carried out this act, and the Scriptures would appear to approve. If David could act in such a way, how much more the

---

[41] See also Exodus 31:14.
[42] Thomas Watson, *A Body of Divinity: Contained in Sermons Upon the Westminster Assembly's Catechism* (Edinburgh: Banner of Truth, 1965), 25.

followers of the greater David, the Son of Man, the Lord of the Sabbath?[43]

In their laudable concern to keep the Sabbath law, the Pharisees had lost sight of the purpose of the regulation. It was for the benefit, not the oppression, of people: 'The Sabbath was made for man, not man for the Sabbath.' It is part of the creation purposes of God. God rested on the seventh day of creation, and so also should those who are made in his image. It is part of God's good design for his people. It is a gift, and we should beware of confusing external behaviour with an attitude of the heart. This leads to bare ritualism, a cold-hearted faith.

There are, for instance, many parts of the world where the economy operates throughout the week, and those in the workplace – especially home-based or shift workers – have no option but to work on Sundays. In those circumstances, the answer should not be legalism – demanding a certain behaviour on a certain day (see Colossians 2:16–18) – but an appeal to creation principles. Weekly rest should be part of our pattern of life. A day of rest is a pattern of creation (see Genesis 2:1–2; Hebrews 3–4), and so is to be part of our Christian life. Clergy have long worked on Sundays, but then another day should be taken and made holy. In doing this we not only imitate the pattern of God but also enter into his rest (Hebrews 4:9–10).[44] This is a challenge in a technologically driven world, where communication is instant and the cycle of consumerism endless. To mark a Sabbath and keep it holy is a countercultural act, but it is one that is not only part of our faith but also a gift and a blessing. It is a weekly reset, and a chance to engage with the things of God.

NOTE: ABIATHAR AND THE RELIABILITY
OF THE SCRIPTURES

Before leaving this passage, it should be noted that there is a rather tricky problem in the text: Jesus refers to Abiathar as the high priest,

---

[43] France, *Mark*, 145.

[44] The Christian marks Sunday and not Saturday since Sunday is the day of resurrection, the day on which Jesus entered into his rest. It is the Lord's Day (Revelation 1:10). That this was a widely followed practice by the second century can be seen in the writings of Ignatius of Antioch (*c.* 35–*c.* 107), the Epistle of Barnabas (end of first century) and Justin Martyr (*c.* 100–*c.* 165).

whereas the text of 1 Samuel 21 refers to Ahimelek (who was the father of Abiathar). Some early scribes (particularly those in the West) omitted the reference to Abiathar, but the overwhelming majority have his name. Others amended the text to add a 'the' so that it could read 'in the time of Abiathar the [one who became] high priest', but this is also a minority tradition.

Some suggest that it might mean 'in the passage of scripture dealing with Abiathar the high priest'. Chapter and verse numbering did not exist until many centuries after the time of Christ, and it was not unusual to refer to passages by their main content. You can see an example of this in Mark 12:26 when Jesus says, 'Have you not read in the Book of Moses, in the account of the burning bush . . .?'

Some commentators have gone as far as to suggest a mistake in the text, made by Jesus, Mark or a later scribe. The first two options are the most troubling since they undermine either the perfection of Christ or the reliability of the Scriptures. If the Scriptures are not reliable, how are we to know for certain anything about God? More than that, unreliable Scriptures also bring into question the character of God, something neatly put by Iain Murray:

> Are we to suppose that God sent his Son to live and die in this world and left us with no dependable revelation of his words? Or are we to believe the disciples had to make up words they attributed to Christ because his promise that the spirit 'will guide you into all truth' (John 16:13) was untrue? Were the apostles without revelation and simply dependent upon their own thoughts and memories? Close to the argument against inspiration lies unbelief in everything miraculous.[45]

The third possible source of a mistake is a later scribe who made the error when copying an earlier manuscript. Should this be the case, this would not be a challenge to the classic evangelical view

---

[45] Iain H. Murray, *Evangelicalism Divided: A Record of Crucial Change in the Years 1950 to 2000* (Edinburgh: Banner of Truth, 2000), 201, note 2.

of the inspiration of Scripture set out by A. A. Hodge (1823–86) and B. B. Warfield (1851–1921), who argued that the Scriptures 'are without any error, when the *ipsissima verba* [the very words] of the original autographs are ascertained and interpreted in their natural and intended sense'.[46] In this argument, Mark's original manuscript (the original autograph) is correct but later scribes made an error. Scripture remains without error since the mistake was not in the original manuscript.

Other options have been proposed. For instance, Robert H. Gundry suggested that Jesus intentionally embellished the text from 1 Samuel to make a point: 'To strengthen his argument, Jesus adds a number of features not found in the OT passage.'[47] In making this assertion, Gundry argues that Jesus is employing the Jewish technique of midrash, yet, as one Jewish scholar pointed out, Jesus's arguments in this passage would not be considered valid from a rabbinic point of view.[48] Gundry's suggestion seems unlikely.

The most likely suggestion, and the one followed by the New International Version and the English Standard Version, among others, is to translate the passage as either 'in the days of Abiathar' or 'in the passage dealing with Abiathar'. The Greek word *epi* may be translated as 'when' or 'during' (among many other options). '*When* Abiathar was high priest' could equally well be translated as, '*During the period when* Abiathar was high priest'.[49]

---

[46] A. A. Hodge, and B. B. Warfield, 'Inspiration', *The Presbyterian Review* 2, no. 6 (1881), 238.

[47] Robert H. Gundry, *Mark: A Commentary on His Apology for the Cross* (Grand Rapids: Eerdmans, 2000), 141. He goes on to list seven features.

[48] Rabbi D. M. Cohn-Sherbok, 'An Analysis of Jesus' Arguments Concerning the Plucking of Grain on the Sabbath', *Journal for the Study of the New Testament* 1, no. 2 (1979).

[49] This is the translation favoured by the standard New Testament Lexicon. F. W. Danker W. Baur, W. F. Arndt, F. W. Gingrich, *A Greek-English Lexicon of the New Testament and Other Early Christian Literature (3rd Edition)* (Chicago: University of Chicago Press, 2000; hereafter BDAG), 367, 18.a.

The withered arm and the Sabbath (3:1–6)

Jesus heals on the Sabbath

3 Another time Jesus went into the synagogue, and a man with a shrivelled hand was there. **2** Some of them were looking for a reason to accuse Jesus, so they watched him closely to see if he would heal him on the Sabbath. **3** Jesus said to the man with the shrivelled hand, 'Stand up in front of everyone.'

4 Then Jesus asked them, 'Which is lawful on the Sabbath: to do good or to do evil, to save life or to kill?' But they remained silent.

5 He looked around at them in anger and, deeply distressed at their stubborn hearts, said to the man, 'Stretch out your hand.' He stretched it out, and his hand was completely restored. **6** Then the Pharisees went out and began to plot with the Herodians how they might kill Jesus.

In the previous passage, Jesus came into conflict with the Pharisees over the observance of the Sabbath, and here we see this dispute escalating (it is likely that the 'they' of verse 2 refers to the Pharisees who are identified in verse 6). The presence of a man in need of healing in the synagogue gave the Pharisees an opportunity to entrap Jesus. The issue was not healing, but rather the Sabbath. It may well be that they knew Jesus had healed on the Sabbath before, casting out an unclean spirit in Mark 1:21–8 and healing Peter's mother-in-law later that same day (Mark 1:29–31). Rather than confronting Jesus directly, the Pharisees simply watched to see how he reacted to this man in need of healing in the synagogue. Could they catch him red-handed?

There is, of course, a great irony here. The service in the synagogue was supposed to be one of worship, with God being the focus, but the Pharisees in their zeal had subverted this and were instead treating it as an opportunity for entrapment. The unfortunate man with the withered arm was not so much an opportunity for the demonstration of God's grace and restoration, but rather bait. Athanasius (*c.* 295–373) puts it well: 'If he was withered in his hand, the ones who stood by were withered in their minds.'[50]

---

[50] Athanasius, *Of the Seed* 28; see TLG 2035.069, 28.165.829; PG 28:165; see E. A. W. Budge, *Coptic Homilies in the Dialect of Upper Egypt* (London: British Museum, 1910). Cited in Thomas C. Oden and Christopher A. Hall, *Mark (Revised)* (Downers Grove: InterVarsity Press, 1998), 35.

Jesus asked the man to 'stand up in front of everyone', perhaps to elicit some sympathy from the Pharisees: he was, after all, a man in need. Jesus was also bold to act publicly and to openly confront the issue. He posed the question, 'Which is lawful on the Sabbath: to do good or to do evil, to save life or to kill?'[51] His hearers were put on the spot.

In raising this question, Jesus returned to the issue of the Law and its intention, something seen in the previous passage. What was the point of the Sabbath? Was it something restrictive (so that we are made for the Sabbath) or a blessing (so that the Sabbath is made for us)? There was no answer to his question, only silence – a hostile silence.

Jesus's response was strong: 'He looked around at them in anger' and was 'deeply distressed at their stubborn hearts'. It is telling that Jesus's distress was a response to the 'stubborn hearts' of his opponents, their settled opposition to the presence of God's grace (the 'Lord of the Sabbath') in their midst. There are echoes here of Psalm 81:

But my people would not listen to me;
   Israel would not submit to me.
So I gave them over to their stubborn hearts
   to follow their own devices.
(Psalm 81:11–12)

Jesus's anger is commonly viewed as evidence of his human nature, but it should also be noted that this anger (*orgē*) is also manifested by God as an aspect of his holiness. This is not uncontrolled anger, but rather an aspect of his pure righteousness. We shouldn't think that Jesus had lost control. Stephen Charnock (1628–80) made the point that without this context of purity, 'his patience would be an indulgence to sin, his mercy a fondness, his wrath a madness, his power a tyranny, his wisdom an unworthy subtlety'.[52] This righteous

---

[51] There was a tradition, later recorded in the Mishnah, that a person's life could be saved on the Sabbath: 'And any matter of doubt as to danger to life overrides the prohibitions of the Sabbath.' Neusner, *Mishnah*, 278.

[52] Stephen Charnock, 'Discourse on the Existence and Attributes of God: A Discourse on the Holiness of God', in *The Complete Works of Stephen Charnock*

anger is directed at sin, yet the mercy of God calls the sinner to repentance.

This should be a comfort to those of us who are sinners (which is to say all of us). God is not composed of parts so that part of him is loving and another part is wrathful. Rather, he is one. His wrath is loving *and* holy. We cannot catch him on a bad day. We should never fear to repent, thinking that we will be rejected. The crucifixion stands as a witness both to God's wrath at sin (it is 'the sheathing the sword of his wrath in the heart of his Son'[53]) and to his merciful grace.

Jesus then asked the man to stretch out his hand, and when the man did so he found it restored. The great irony is that Jesus did not in fact perform any visible work on the Sabbath: he did not touch the man's hand or even command the healing. The healings recorded for us in the Bible are notable for their lack of drama. At creation, God simply spoke and things came into being. Here Jesus spoke and creation was restored. He had managed to neatly sidestep the trap laid so carefully.

Nonetheless, the Pharisees took offence and went off to plot Jesus's death with the Herodians. Jesus had asked the question, 'Which is lawful on the Sabbath: to do good or to do evil, to save life or to kill?' Here the Pharisees had taken the option of doing evil and, on the Sabbath itself, plotted to kill. A dark work to carry out on a day holy to the LORD. How we need to watch our hearts even as we are zealous for God. Is our zeal truly for God, or for our own interpretations?

That the Pharisees plotted with the Herodians demonstrates the depth of the threat they felt from Jesus. They, who strongly resisted the Roman influence in Judea, were willing to align themselves with those who represented the Rome-backed ruling party. Their hatred of Jesus was strong enough to overcome other enmities.

(Edinburgh: James Nichol, 1864), 2:193.
[53] Stephen Charnock, 'Discourse on the Existence and Attributes of God: A Discourse on the Wisdom of God', in Charnock, *Works*, 2:63.

From Holy One to Son (3:7–12)

Crowds follow Jesus

7 Jesus withdrew with his disciples to the lake, and a large crowd from Galilee followed. **8** When they heard all he was doing, many people came to him from Judea, Jerusalem, Idumea, and the regions across the Jordan and around Tyre and Sidon. **9** Because of the crowd he told his disciples to have a small boat ready for him, to keep the people from crowding him. **10** For he had healed many, so that those with diseases were pushing forward to touch him. **11** Whenever the impure spirits saw him, they fell down before him and cried out, 'You are the Son of God.' **12** But he gave them strict orders not to tell others about him.

This passage comes at the end of the section of Mark's Gospel that focuses on the authority of Jesus. At the beginning of his public teaching ministry, he was recognised by the impure spirits as 'the Holy One of God', and here they acknowledged him as 'the Son of God'. As Jesus had taught and healed he had earned the enmity of various Jewish parties, but the demons had a clearer idea of his identity. His was a spiritual authority, and so the spirits recognised him first. Yet, as before, he commanded them to silence.

Jesus withdrew, which he often did at moments of great popularity, and went off with his disciples to the lake. Again we see that Jesus was not seeking celebrity or status. He had great faith in his ministry and accordingly had great patience in its timing. His was no quick fix or off-the-shelf ministry. It may well have been that he sensed that his teaching was becoming obscured by the attention the healings brought.

Undeterred, a great crowd followed not only from Galilee but also from all of Israel, as well as from the Gentile areas of Tyre and Sidon. Many wanted healing, and so Jesus was reduced from a teacher to a healer. They sought the benefits of Christ rather than Christ himself. They sought healing and not the healer. Those with diseases were crowding forward, and while we might sympathise with them in their desperation, they did not recognise who it was that was before them. How often do we see Christianity – or Jesus – as something for our benefit (see John 6:26)? Jesus was one who brought deep and lasting change, but a healer is one who simply restores someone to their prior condition.

In much modern evangelism we are quick to present the benefits of Christ, and not Christ himself. We might speak of a sense of purpose, inner peace or escape from hell. Some may go as far as to speak of healing, wealth and status. Yet the apostle Paul is clear on what is the core of the gospel: 'we preach Christ crucified' (1 Corinthians 1:23). Jesus, not his gifts. Jesus, not his benefits. These may well follow, but we should be careful to ensure we offer Christ the Son of God, and not simply pander to the very human desire for personal fulfilment. We are 'to strike up beams of his glory in a dark world, and commend him and his way before and to others'.[54]

Such were the crowds seeking healing that Jesus could not teach them and bring lasting change. What great irony there is in this.

3. The kingdom and the subjects • Mark 3:13–5:43

The previous section of Mark's Gospel tackled the issue of authority and the interpretation of the Law. While the teachers of the law failed to recognise his authority, Jesus was known by the impure spirits. His is a spiritual realm, and there now follows a section where we are introduced to the first subjects of the kingdom of God – the appointed apostles – before Jesus delivers a series of parables dealing with the kingdom. The heir to the throne of David is claiming his kingdom.

After these parables, Jesus demonstrates that his rule extends to the created realm (he calms a storm), Gentile areas, the spiritual realm (the casting of demons from Legion) and eventually over death itself (Jairus's daughter is raised).

We also discover that Christ's kingdom is not simply the province of Judea or any other land with geographical bounds. His reign is eternal, and his kingdom is all-encompassing. Whereas some simply thought the Messiah would cause Israel to shrug off the occupation of the Romans, there is something deeper afoot in the reign of Christ. The kingdom of God sees the fulfilment of the promises of God.

---

[54] Thomas Boston (1676–1732), 'The Peculiar Mercy and Business of Life, Opened Up, and Applied. Preached At Ettrick, in the Year 1727', in *The Whole Works of Thomas Boston, Volume 7*, ed. S. M'Millan (1850), 548.

The apostles Called (Mark 3:13–19)

Jesus appoints the Twelve

13 Jesus went up on a mountainside and called to him those he wanted, and they came to him. 14 He appointed twelve[a] that they might be with him and that he might send them out to preach 15 and to have authority to drive out demons. 16 These are the twelve he appointed: Simon (to whom he gave the name Peter); 17 James son of Zebedee and his brother John (to them he gave the name Boanerges, which means 'sons of thunder'), 18 Andrew, Philip, Bartholomew, Matthew, Thomas, James son of Alphaeus, Thaddaeus, Simon the Zealot 19 and Judas Iscariot, who betrayed him.

a 14 Some manuscripts *twelve - designating them apostles -*

At this stage of his ministry, Jesus had called just five disciples: Peter, Andrew, James, John (Mark 1:16–20) and Levi (Mark 2:14). He now added seven more to bring the total to a significant twelve. Twelve were the tribes of Israel (Genesis 49:28), twelve spies were sent into the Promised Land (Numbers 13:1–15) and the priestly breastplate carried a dozen stones (Exodus 39:8–14). In the previous chapter, the Gentiles had crowded around him, and here Jesus symbolically restored the tribes of Israel, an act of the true servant of the LORD:

It is too small a thing for you to be my servant
    to restore the tribes of Jacob
    and bring back those of Israel I have kept.
I will also make you a light for the Gentiles,
    that my salvation may reach to the ends of the earth.
(Isaiah 49:6)

However, before issuing the call, Jesus ascended a mountain. Mountains are significant places in the Bible and often serve as places of revelation and divine encounter. Eden itself was located on a mountain (see Ezekiel 28:13–15), and Abraham took Isaac up a mountain in Moriah (Genesis 22:1–14). It was on Mount Horeb, the 'mountain of God', that Moses encountered the burning bush (Exodus 3:1–2) and met with God in the giving of the Law (Exodus

19–20, Deuteronomy 9–10).[55] Elijah met with God at the same place (1 Kings 19:8–18), and later in Mark's Gospel it is on a 'high mountain' that Jesus is transfigured (Mark 9:2–8). He also went up a mountain to pray before walking on the water (Mark 6:45–52).

This going aside to pray is a practice that Jesus himself taught (Matthew 6:6), but it is a going aside in order to return. There is a balance to be sought between time in prayer and time in proclamation. All too often we want to *do* something and we neglect prayer. Activity replaces intercession, and the plans that consume so much energy are simply products of our own thinking. It is sobering to ask quite why this might be. Do we not *really* have faith in God's ability to hear prayer, or to answer? Is God *really* to be seen as irrelevant in our planning? Is prayer only to be treated as the last resort? Better to do less and to pray more.

> The more we pray, the more we shall want to pray; the more we pray, the more we can pray; the more we pray, the more we shall pray. He who prays little will pray less, but he who prays much will pray more; and he who prays more, will desire to pray more abundantly.[56]

Once on the mountain, Jesus called others to himself. There was a strong sense of Jesus's initiative in all of this: he 'called to him those he wanted . . . He appointed twelve. . . These are the twelve he appointed'. As with the calling of the first five disciples, those whom Jesus called came to him. These were the actions of the ruler of the kingdom of God, and there was a strong sense of Jesus's sovereignty in his actions. It is not clear if only the twelve he later appointed as apostles were called up to him, or whether a wider group was assembled so that they might witness the appointing of the Twelve.

The apostles were appointed to be his companions and were also commissioned to preach and drive out demons. We note again the priority of preaching, which will result in the need to cast out

---

[55] It is widely held that Mount Sinai and Mount Horeb are the same mountain.
[56] C. H. Spurgeon, 'Golden Vials Full of Odours', in *The Metropolitan Tabernacle Pulpit Volume XVIII* (London: Passmore & Alabaster, 1872), 288.

demons. The apostles were not to expect any less opposition than that experienced by Jesus.

In passing, we might note that the call to a preaching ministry is something that comes from Christ. The authority of the Twelve came from Jesus, and so it should be for all who dare engage in the ministry of the word. There is no such thing as a self-appointed ambassador or herald, and any calling to ministry is something to be tested by the church. 'Where the call is manifest, the promise is assured, "Certainly I will be with thee." But if we run unsent, our labours must prove unblest.'[57]

The NIV notes that some manuscripts add 'designating them apostles' (see NIV footnote), and the weight of evidence for this longer reading is strong. We might also note that the phrase is included in the parallel passage in Luke 6:12–16, and Matthew's parallel (Matthew 10:1–4) refers to the twelve 'apostles'. In recent years there has been a rise in the desire to name others in the New Testament as 'apostles', and so, for example, some name Mary Magdalene as an 'apostle' since at the resurrection she was sent to the disciples to give them the news. While it is true that Paul and Barnabas were called apostles (Acts 14:4, 14), this was done in response to a formal setting-aside by the church (see Acts 13:1–2), and their work was seen as a continuation of the work of the Twelve.[58] The

---

[57] Charles Bridges, *The Christian Ministry: With an Inquiry Into the Causes of Its Inefficiency* (New York; Boston: Jonathan Leavitt; Crocker & Brewster, 1831), 1:120.

[58] Andrew Clark helpfully comments, 'What then did Luke expect his readers to make of Acts 14:4, 14? It is often neglected that in the immediate context Luke has shown Paul applying the words of Isaiah 49:6 to himself and Barnabas (13:47). He is thus claiming that they have a significant role to play within salvation-history. The phrase "to the end of the earth" provides a clear echo of the words of the commission given to the eleven apostles in Acts 1:8. It would not, therefore, be too surprising if Luke expected his readers to understand by his use of "apostles" in Acts 14:4, 14 for Barnabas and Paul that they were fulfilling with respect to the nations the commission originally given to the eleven apostles. This verdict is supported by the clear verbal parallel, generally ignored by scholars, between 14:3 ("signs and wonders done by their hands") and 5:12 ("signs and wonders done by the hands of the apostles"). Thus it is better to see the designation "apostles" in 14:4, 14 as not merely denoting "missionaries", or even indicating an almost grudging recognition of the fact that Paul claimed to be an apostle and was recognized as such by others, but a clear hint by Luke that he himself saw Paul and Barnabas as playing a role similar to that of the twelve apostles.' Andrew C. Clark, 'The Role of

word is a title, not a description of a task. Not all whom Jesus told to 'go' are apostles.

May we still find apostles today? While the title faded, in recent years it has come again into prominence, with some church leaders claiming the designation. This would seem unwise, since this makes the implicit claim to an equal authority with those who were sent out by Jesus. The twelve apostles had a particular, foundational role in the formation of the church that was built on their teaching (Ephesians 2:20; 3:5; 4:11; see also Revelation 21:14). They echoed the twelve tribes of Israel, and their role is uniquely symbolic. Their role of eyewitnesses was crucial to their authority (see Luke 24:48; Acts 1:8, 21–2; 2:32; 3:15; 4:33; 5:32; 10:41). We should not expect those who claim that title today to have such a foundational ministry, nor would they carry the authority of those who were both taught by Christ himself and were chosen by him to build his church.

In the list of those whom Jesus called, Simon is renamed Peter ('rock'). At that time, 'Peter' did not exist as a personal name, so this is to be viewed as more of a nickname.[59] From now on in Mark's Gospel Simon is referred to as Peter, except at Gethsemane when Jesus rebuked the sleeping disciple (Mark 14:37). James and John are nicknamed 'sons of thunder', which is probably a reference to their fiery character (see Luke 9:54), but unlike Peter, they are called by their existing names throughout the remainder of the Gospel. Levi is referred to as Matthew (see discussion at 2:14) and may well be the brother of James 'son of Alphaeus'.

In Luke's disciple lists (Luke 6:12–16 and Acts 1:13–14), Thaddeus does not appear and is replaced by Judas the son of James. This may well be another example of a person being known by two names since Thaddeus is a name with Greek roots, and it was fairly common for Jews to have both Jewish and Greek names.[60] Given the connotations of the name 'Judas' in the New Testament, it would

---

the Apostles', in *Witness to the Gospel: The Theology of Acts*, ed. I. Howard Marshall and David Peterson (Grand Rapids: Eerdmans, 1998), 184–5.

[59] Witherington, *Mark*, 151.

[60] 'The name Thaddaeus (Greek *Thaddaios*) is an example of a Greek name (it could be *Theodosios, Theodotos,* or *Theodoros*) which has first been turned into a Semitic shortened version, *Taddai*, and has then been Graecized again as *Thaddaios*.'

not be surprising that Judas the son of James was referred to by his other name.

The list of twelve ends with Judas. It is not entirely clear what the term 'Iscariot' signifies. Some suggest it might indicate that Judas come from Kerioth in Judah (or Kerioth in Moab). If that is the case, then Judas is the sole non-Galilean in the group. More likely is the suggestion that 'Iscariot' is derived from *sikarios*, which is defined as 'one who is intent on killing someone as part of an organized subversive political program' and refers to a group of Judean nationalists who carried out assassinations.[61]

This list, then, begins with the 'rock' and ends with the betrayer. It contains a tax collector, those who paid taxes and those who violently opposed the Romans. It was a mixed group. It is a common purpose and renewal of the mind (Romans 12:2) that will bring true unity, not background or upbringing. The church should be no less diverse than the apostles whom Jesus sent to found it.

Who is the true family of faith? (3:20–35)

Jesus accused by his family and by teachers of the law

20 Then Jesus entered a house, and again a crowd gathered, so that he and his disciples were not even able to eat. **21** When his family[b] heard about this, they went to take charge of him, for they said, 'He is out of his mind.'

22 And the teachers of the law who came down from Jerusalem said, 'He is possessed by Beelzebul! By the prince of demons he is driving out demons.'

23 So Jesus called them over to him and began to speak to them in parables: 'How can Satan drive out Satan? **24** If a kingdom is divided against itself, that kingdom cannot stand. **25** If a house is divided against itself, that house cannot stand. **26** And if Satan opposes himself and is divided, he cannot stand; his end has come. **27** In fact, no one can enter a strong man's house without first tying him up. Then he can plunder the strong man's house. **28** Truly I tell you,

---

Richard Bauckham, *Jesus and the Eyewitnesses: The Gospels as Eyewitness Testimony* (Grand Rapids: Eerdmans, 2017), 99.
[61] BDAG, 923.

people can be forgiven all their sins and every slander they utter, **29** but whoever blasphemes against the Holy Spirit will never be forgiven; they are guilty of an eternal sin.'

30 He said this because they were saying, 'He has an impure spirit.'

31 Then Jesus' mother and brothers arrived. Standing outside, they sent someone in to call him. **32** A crowd was sitting round him, and they told him, 'Your mother and brothers are outside looking for you.'

33 'Who are my mother and my brothers?' he asked.

34 Then he looked at those seated in a circle round him and said, 'Here are my mother and my brothers! **35** Whoever does God's will is my brother and sister and mother.'

---

b 21 Or *his associates*

Much of Jesus's ministry occurred in a domestic setting. He was often among the people rather than simply in places of power, and being in houses allowed everyone to be present – men, women and children. There is an important principle here: the gospel is to be taken to people where they are, and we should not simply rely upon people to come to church buildings. Jesus, the 'one who came from heaven' (John 3:13), was sent by the Father, and the apostles are those sent by Jesus. The one who was sent in turn sent others out, and this outward motion is at the heart of the mission of the church.

The domestic setting of much of Jesus's teaching also emphasises the importance of the home in the practice of the faith. In many parts of the world it is common to find devotional items in the home, but the rejection of statues and images at the Reformation meant that this practice was heartily discouraged. However, that is not to say that the Reformers and their heirs thought the home to be irrelevant to the practice of the faith. Far from it. There was a desire that the home was seen as a place of worship, almost a domestic monastery, with prayers taking place in the home. Richard Baxter (1615–91) is a fine example of this way of thinking: 'Holy families are the seminaries of Christ's church on earth,' he wrote.[62] Elsewhere he commented on the importance of families: 'if we suffer

---

[62] Richard Baxter, 'The Poor Man's Family Book', in *The Practical Works of the Rev. Richard Baxter, Volume 19*, ed. William Orme (London: James Duncan, 1830), 484.

the neglect of this, we undo all'.[63] The home is a vital engine of the church, and whether we live alone or with others, we would do well to treat it as a place of worship.

The crowds formed around the house, and there was not even room to eat. His family, who were presumably nearby, learned what was happening and came to take control, since they thought he was 'out of his mind'.

The NIV footnote suggests that the phrase translated 'his family' might also be rendered 'his associates'. This is because the Greek is not specific and simply means 'those along with him'. The phrase could refer back to the Twelve who were called in the previous passage, or it could be seen as a reference to his family who arrived in verse 31. In context, 'his family' would seem to be the best translation.

Jesus's family thought him 'out of his mind' and so sought to 'take charge of him'. Their desire was to save Jesus from himself, but in so doing they had become his opponents. There are many Christians who find themselves in a similar situation, whose families – through a loving concern – are opposed to their faith. This opposition may be sharp, and may even be motivated by antagonism, and to be a lone Christian in a family is often a far-from-easy calling.

Also present were the teachers of the law who had made their way down from Jerusalem. Whereas his family thought him mad, the teachers of the law thought Jesus was bad: 'He is possessed by Beelzebul! By the prince of demons he is driving out demons.' This was a fundamental shift, since Jesus was now accused of being evil and not simply of being wrong. There has been much discussion concerning quite who Beelzebul is, but from the passage it is clear that he was the 'prince of demons'.[64] Jesus would appear to have presumed this to be a reference to Satan (Mark 3:23).

In response to this slur, Jesus taught a parable. In fact, it may be that these attacks caused Jesus to preach by means of parables rather

---

[63] Richard Baxter, 'The Reformed Pastor', in *The Practical Works of the Rev. Richard Baxter, Volume 14*, ed. William Orme (London: James Duncan, 1830), 97.

[64] There is a similar name, Baal-Zebub, in 2 Kings 1:2, 3, 6, 16, but he is not identified here (or elsewhere in Jewish literature) as prince of demons. The name means 'Baal of flies' and is translated in the LXX as *baal muian* which is quite different from the name Mark uses.

than teach directly. The meaning of this parable was clear: why would Satan attack himself? No house or kingdom that is divided can stand. If Jesus were truly possessed by the prince of demons, he would surely not be attacking the demons. Indeed, the very fact that Jesus was able to cast out impure spirits would suggest that he had first overcome Satan, and this we saw earlier in the Gospel in the passage dealing with Jesus's temptation in the wilderness (Mark 1:12–13).

Jesus then said something which has, over the years, caused anxiety to many: 'whoever blasphemes against the Holy Spirit will never be forgiven'. What does it mean to blaspheme against the Holy Spirit? Might one have done so without realising? The judgment passed upon those who do so is severe – they are 'guilty of an eternal sin' – and so it is only natural to fear such a sentence. It is important, however, to note the context of Jesus's words. The teachers of the law had equated a work of the Holy Spirit (the casting out of demons) with the work of an impure spirit. To blaspheme the Holy Spirit is to think he is demonic; it is to equate a work of God with a work of Satan. It is to call good evil, and evil good. It is to reject the witness of the Spirit to Christ. It is to reject God and think of Jesus as one who had 'an impure spirit'.

Christians should never be concerned that they have blasphemed the Holy Spirit in this way. The very fact that they are concerned that they may have committed such blasphemy is an indication that they have not. Such fear is something looked upon with favour by God:

> These are the ones I look on with favour:
>> those who are humble and contrite in spirit,
>> and who tremble at my word.
> (Isaiah 66:2)

The dread words concerning this blasphemy may cause the reader to overlook the deep grace evident in the previous verse: 'people can be forgiven all their sins'. It is blasphemy against the Holy Spirit alone that is unforgivable since such blasphemy leads to a rejection of God himself. The one who heeds the call of the Spirit and repents of sin may have all sins forgiven. None who turns to Christ falls outside the scope of his forgiveness.

Yet this warning should also give pause to those who suggest that, in the end, all will be saved. Such universalism will have to deal with the fact that there are sins that, in the words of Jesus, 'will never be forgiven'.

It was at this point that Jesus's mother and brothers arrived and sent someone in to fetch him. When the message was delivered, Jesus asked, 'Who are my mother and brothers?' This question, surely, would have been baffling to those who heard it, and the answer Jesus gave to his own question was no less surprising: 'Whoever does God's will is my brother and sister and mother.' To do the will of God is to share the same Father. The kingdom of God and the family of God are one and the same. Jesus's true family is based upon obedience, not biology.

We should note the role of obedience in this saying: 'Whoever does God's will'. Faith in Christ issues in action and is not simply a passive affair. We are not saved by our good works, but a saving faith will produce good works. They bear witness to God's working upon our hearts and may be to us a sign of our progress in the faith. To quote the great American theologian Jonathan Edwards (1703–58): 'Christian practice or a holy life is a great and distinguishing sign of true and saving grace.'[65]

To be a follower of Christ is both to become more Christlike and to be able to call him 'brother'. It is to be part of the family of faith.

The seed of the gospel (4:1–20)

The parable of the sower

4 Again Jesus began to teach by the lake. The crowd that gathered round him was so large that he got into a boat and sat in it out on the lake, while all the people were along the shore at the water's edge. ²He taught them many things by parables, and in his teaching said: ³'Listen! A farmer went out to sow his seed. ⁴As he was scattering the seed, some fell along the path, and the birds came and ate it up. ⁵Some fell on rocky places, where it did not have much soil. It sprang up quickly, because the soil was shallow. ⁶But

---

[65] Jonathan Edwards, *Religious Affections* (New Haven: Yale University Press, 2009), 406.

97

when the sun came up, the plants were scorched, and they withered because they had no root. **7** Other seed fell among thorns, which grew up and choked the plants, so that they did not bear grain. **8** Still other seed fell on good soil. It came up, grew and produced a crop, some multiplying thirty, some sixty, some a hundred times.'

9 Then Jesus said, 'Whoever has ears to hear, let them hear.'

Jesus was once more by the lake, and once more the people crowded around him. Such was the size of the crowd and the resourcefulness of Jesus that he climbed into a boat to teach. Here was one who was content to teach both in the Temple and on a boat. There was no place too grand or too humble for him to grace with his life-giving words, and the surrounding shore gave Jesus a natural amphitheatre.[66] Taking a boat as a makeshift platform he began teaching, and we are given an extended example of Jesus's style of parables, along with an explanation given privately to his disciples.

The imagery of sowing seeds would have been familiar in a rural, subsistence economy.[67] Seed was scattered rather than planted, and so some would inevitably fall away from the best soil. This was the fate of the first three groups of seeds in the parable. The fourth group, however, fell into the good soil and went on to produce three different yields. Whether or not these yields were miraculous or simply represented a very good harvest has been a matter of some debate. Assuming that the yield is based on kernels per stalk, and not on the stalks themselves, then a hundredfold return represents a very good year, but is not unachievable. Pliny the Elder records similarly strong yields in Africa.[68] The point is that the return is great.

Those who heard would have readily recognised the scenario. They would have seen birds pecking the seeds lying on top of the paths

---

[66] See Perry G. Phillips, 'Natural Amphitheaters Along the Sea of Galilee', in *Lexham Geographic Commentary on the Gospels*, ed. Barry J. Beitzel and Kristopher A. Lyle (Bellingham: Lexham Press, 2016).

[67] There has been much discussion as to the precise way sowing seed took place. It is generally accepted that the seed was ploughed into the soil after sowing, and some suggest that the soil was also ploughed before the sowing.

[68] Pliny the Elder, *Natural History*, 18.21.95. See also Strabo (63 or 64 BC to *c.* 24 AD), *Geographica*, 15.3.11.

and known the effects of rocks hidden just under the soil, giving quick but short growth. They may have shaken their heads at the thorns, calling to mind Proverbs 24:30–31:

> I went past the field of a sluggard,
>   past the vineyard of someone who has no sense;
> thorns had come up everywhere,
>   the ground was covered with weeds,
>   and the stone wall was in ruins.

They would have been impressed with the yield, even seeing it as a blessing: 'Isaac planted crops in that land and the same year reaped a hundredfold, because the LORD blessed him' (Genesis 26:12).

However, they may not all have understood the point of the parable (to which we will return in the next passage). When Jesus finished with the words, 'Whoever has ears to hear, let them hear,' not all would have truly heard at all. Understanding is a gift of God by his Spirit and a matter for prayer. Not all who turn to the Scriptures find their meaning, and praying before reading the Bible is a wise habit to cultivate. The same Spirit who inspired the Scriptures also illuminates them and applies them to our hearts. Prayer, meditation and obedience lie at the heart of the serious study of Scripture, and with obedience often comes a spiritual struggle. Yet, as Luther commented in 1539, it is these three principles that lie at the heart of 'a correct way of studying theology . . . taught by Holy King David (and doubtlessly used also by all the patriarchs and prophets) in the one hundred nineteenth psalm'.[69]

Not all who cite Scripture do so in a scriptural manner, and not all uses of the Bible are biblical. From its earliest days, the church has struggled against those who misuse Scripture, and the words of Irenaeus of Lyon still ring true:

> They boast rather loudly of knowing more about it than others
> do, citing it from non-scriptural works; and, as people would say,

---

[69] Martin Luther, *Pastoral Writings*, trans. Erik H. Herrmann (Minneapolis: Fortress Press, 2016), 482.

they attempt to braid ropes of sand. They try to adapt to their own sayings in a manner worthy of credence, either the Lord's parables, or the prophets' sayings, or the apostles' words, so that their fabrication might not appear to be without witness. They disregard the order and the connection of the Scriptures and, as much as in them lies, they disjoint the members of the Truth. They transfer passages and rearrange them; and, making one thing out of another, they deceive many by the badly composed phantasy of the Lord's words that they adapt.[70]

Oh, that God would waken our ears![71]

10 When he was alone, the Twelve and the others around him asked him about the parables. 11 He told them, 'The secret of the kingdom of God has been given to you. But to those on the outside everything is said in parables 12 so that,

' "they may be ever seeing
but never perceiving,
and ever hearing but never
understanding;
otherwise they might turn and
be forgiven!" a'

a 12 Isaiah 6:9,10

Later, when the crowds had gone, a smaller group ('the Twelve and others around him') asked about 'the parables'. Since this is in the plural it is best understood that they were asking about parables in general rather than simply the parable of the sower. The answer Jesus gave to this group was startling: they had received the 'secret of the kingdom of God', but he spoke in parables so that others would not receive this understanding, 'otherwise they might turn and be forgiven!' Was this a technique to keep people from repentance? Was Jesus setting up some sort of secret society?

No. In making this point, Jesus alluded to Isaiah 6:9–10 (he did not make a direct quotation), verses dealing with the call of Isaiah:

---

[70] Irenaeus of Lyon, *Against Heresies: Book 1*, 1:8, trans. Dominic J. Unger (New York: The Newman Press, 1992), 41.

[71] See Isaiah 50:4–5.

He said, 'Go and tell this people:

"'Be ever hearing, but never understanding;
    be ever seeing, but never perceiving."
Make the heart of this people calloused;
    make their ears dull
    and close their eyes.
Otherwise they might see with their eyes,
    hear with their ears,
    understand with their hearts,
and turn and be healed.'

These verses speak to what Alec Motyer termed 'the preacher's dilemma'. He described it in this way:

> If hearers are resistant to the truth, the only recourse is to tell them the truth yet again, more clearly than before. But to do this is to expose them to the risk of rejecting the truth yet again and, therefore, of increased hardness of heart. . . . It was at just such a point that Isaiah was called to office. His task was to bring the LORD's word with fresh, even unparalleled clarity, but in their response people would reach the point of no return.[72]

There is more to faith than simply hearing sermons, and hearing the word apart from the activity of the Holy Spirit is simply hearing words.

We can see an example of this in Acts and the response of Lydia to Paul's teaching. Luke described her response in this way: 'The Lord opened her heart to respond to Paul's message' (Acts 16:14). Calvin commented, 'Accordingly we see that not only faith, but also all understanding of spiritual things, is a special gift of God, and that ministers do not accomplish anything by speaking, unless the inward calling of God is added at the same time.'[73]

---

[72] J. A. Motyer, *Isaiah* (Downers Grove: InterVarsity Press, 1996), 79.
[73] John Calvin, *The Acts of the Apostles, Volume 2*, trans. John W. Fraser and W. J. G. McDonald (Grand Rapids: Eerdmans, 1965), 73.

The focus, then, is not on the fact that the word is obscured, but rather that the hearts of those hearing are hardened: some immediately (the path), and some after some growth (the rocky soil and the thorns). Later in Isaiah, we find mention of a sower and the seed (Isaiah 55:10–11), which assures us that the word will do precisely as God wills:

As the rain and the snow
    come down from heaven,
and do not return to it
    without watering the earth
and making it bud and flourish,
    so that it yields seed for the sower and bread for the eater,
so is my word that goes out from my mouth:
    it will not return to me empty,
but will accomplish what I desire
    and achieve the purpose for which I sent it.

Success in evangelism is not to be measured by numbers, nor is the fact that Jesus would be rejected a sign of his failure. Such was the providence of God that the hardening of Pharaoh's heart led to the glorification of God in the Exodus.[74] We should avoid trying to cut out the more uncomfortable parts of Christianity in an effort to make it more palatable. Rather, our task is to explain it more clearly. The herald is to deliver, not edit, the message.

13 Then Jesus said to them, 'Don't you understand this parable? How then will you understand any parable? **14** The farmer sows the word. **15** Some people are like seed along the path, where the word is sown. As soon as they hear it, Satan comes and takes away the word that was sown in them. **16** Others, like seed sown on rocky places, hear the word and at once receive it with joy. **17** But since they have no root, they last only a short time. When trouble or persecution comes because of the word, they quickly fall away. **18** Still others, like seed sown among thorns, hear the word; **19** but the worries of this life, the deceitfulness of wealth

---

[74] Exodus 4:21; 7:3; 9:12; 10:1, 20, 27; 14:4, 8, 17.

and the desires for other things come in and choke the word, making it unfruitful. **20**Others, like seed sown on good soil, hear the word, accept it, and produce a crop – some thirty, some sixty, some a hundred times what was sown.'

After he had discussed the nature of parables in general, Jesus turned to an explanation of the parable of the seeds in particular. Note that there is one interpretation, and it is not left up to the hearer to decide what is or is not true. Truth is situated in the Scriptures themselves, not in our response to the Scriptures. God is his own interpreter, and we must be very wary of imposing our own prejudices onto the text. It is Jesus who is 'the truth' (John 14:6), not us. God is the one who will display his wisdom (Job 38–41), and Jesus reveals the Father (John 14:9). The mark of the true reader of Scripture is humility.

> Blind unbelief is sure to err,
> and scan his work in vain;
> God is his own interpreter,
> and he will make it plain.[75]

In this parable, the seed is the word, and the soils represent types of hearing. In the first instance – the path – the seed had no opportunity to take root, and the hearts of the hearers were as hard as the beaten soil of the path. Satan snatched this seed away at once and it produced no crop. This lack of crop was no fault of the sower, rather the grace of preaching meant that the word was widely spread.

In the second case, the soil was shallow with rocks beneath the surface. The seed quickly sprouted as the word was joyfully received, but as troubles arose the seed died back. Jesus later spoke of the inevitability of persecution (Mark 10:29–30), and a faith that has its roots simply in joy will wither in the face of oppression. The danger of preaching prosperity is that persecution, not prosperity, is a mark of the Christian life. Jesus came to reconcile us to God, not to make us wealthy in this life.

---

[75] William Cowper (1731–1800), 'God Moves in a Mysterious Way'.

The issue of prosperity raised its head once more in the third type of soil. Here it was not persecution but anxiety that caused the problem. The thorns of worldly worries, money and the 'desires for other things' choked the seed, and there was no fruit. Worry is a dogged pursuer of the Christian, particularly in those parts of the world where the faith is accompanied by persecution or where poverty is the norm. For these worries, the caring, sovereign hand of God is the balm applied by the apostle Peter: 'Cast all your anxiety on him because he cares for you' (1 Peter 5:7). We need only look to the cross as an expression of the care of God, and it stands as a witness to his love.

For others, wealth itself brings anxiety. Like a young dog with a bone, the person with wealth may be overwhelmed with concern for its loss. The apostle Paul counselled Timothy, 'Command those who are rich in this present world not to be arrogant nor to put their hope in wealth, which is so uncertain, but to put their hope in God, who richly provides us with everything for our enjoyment' (1 Timothy 6:17).

For some, it was the desire for 'other things' that choked the seed. This may seem rather vague, but there is a tyranny of the 'new' which is driven by the skill of the advertisers. It is tempting to think that life would be better if a particular gadget were owned, or if a new job were found. Hope lies in possible imagined futures rather than in the present reality of the presence of God. Rather than satisfaction with what one has, there is a nagging discontent that there must be something more. The words of Paul are deeply subversive in a market-driven world: 'I have learned to be content whatever the circumstances' (Philippians 4:11). This state of contentment has to be learned and is a deep rest in the providence of God. Should times be turbulent or peaceful, contentment is the response of the Christian. Remember, Paul was writing from prison.

In the final soil, the word was not only *heard* but also *accepted*, and it was the accepting that was crucial. This is the difference between knowledge and faith. Just to hear something is not to have faith in it, any more than simply being present in a church during a service makes you a Christian. Acceptance is the key here, and this acceptance brings with it obedience and a change of heart. The crop is variable, but the point is that the crop occurs at all. Jesus made no attempt to differentiate between the different yields, and we might simply note that this is a fact of discipleship. The point is not the size of the fruitfulness, but the fact that the disciple is bearing fruit.

In all of this, the task of the sower was to sow the seed of the word of God. If the word is not preached, the word is not sown. If the truth is not broadcast, the seed lies unsown. If something other than the word is preached, the sower is no sower at all. We have no responsibility for where the seed falls, but we must ensure it is sown.

The light of the gospel (4:21–5)

A lamp on a stand

21 He said to them, 'Do you bring in a lamp to put it under a bowl or a bed? Instead, don't you put it on its stand? 22 For whatever is hidden is meant to be disclosed, and whatever is concealed is meant to be brought out into the open. 23 If anyone has ears to hear, let them hear.'

24 'Consider carefully what you hear,' he continued. 'With the measure you use, it will be measured to you – and even more. 25 Whoever has will be given more; whoever does not have, even what they have will be taken from them.'

It would appear that this saying followed on directly from the previous passage, which would imply that it was the disciples who were being addressed. The theme of hiddenness and revelation is continued, with a change in imagery such that the word is now a shining light.

It may be that some of the disciples heard the parable of the sower and were discouraged by the fact that so much seed was wasted. There is an almost wasteful grace implied in the parable, and there may be a temptation for a sower to try to identify what constitutes 'good' soil and focus efforts there. However, this parable urged that the work of sowing must continue, and the light should not be hidden. In fact, 'whatever is hidden is meant to be disclosed, and whatever is concealed is meant to be brought out into the open' (verse 22). There is no secret gospel, nor is it the decision of the sower where to sow. The gospel is meant to be proclaimed everywhere.

There is an irony in the wording Jesus used. The word translated as 'bowl' describes a basket used to measure grain. Rather than being used to measure the great harvest of the good soil, the basket was instead being used to hide the light.

There is a question here: what precisely was being hidden? Was it the gospel, the kingdom of God or the Messianic Secret? Was Jesus speaking about things being disclosed in his own ministry, or was this something that would occur after the resurrection?

In answering this question, we would do well to pay heed to the methodology proposed by Geerhardus Vos (1862–1949), which he summarised: 'Without God's acts the words would be empty, without His words the acts would be blind.'[76] God's actions interpret his words, and vice versa. Given the theme of hiddenness in Mark's Gospel (Mark 1:25, 34, 44; 3:11–12; 5:43; 7:36; 8:26, 30; 9:9), it would seem that which is to be disclosed is the precise nature of Jesus's mission. This mission can only be fully understood in light of his crucifixion, resurrection and ascension. These are 'God's acts' which will give full meaning to the words of Jesus, and after that time the Messianic Secret of Mark was to be proclaimed. It is essential, therefore, that an understanding of who Jesus is takes full account of the resurrection and ascension. The Messianic Secret was in place to ensure that Jesus's ministry was taken as a whole, and not simply in part. It was a temporary measure to ensure people did not jump to the wrong conclusion and end up with a Jesus who is merely human.

As well as through the proclamation of the gospel, we might see the light shine through actions. In the parallel passage in Matthew, Jesus goes on to say, 'In the same way, let your light shine before others, that they may see your good deeds and glorify your Father in heaven' (Matthew 5:16). The Christian life is lived out in the midst of the wider world and is not to be hidden in seclusion. It is 'meant to be brought out into the open'.

The disciples were then charged to carefully consider Jesus's teaching. The time taken in contemplation of Scripture is richly rewarded by fruitfulness, and we must beware a shallow theology. We have the great blessing of being part of a church that has pondered Christ's teaching for two thousand years, and there is much benefit

---

[76] Geerhardus Vos, *Biblical Theology: Old and New Testaments* (Eugene: Wipf and Stock, 1934), 9–10.

in visiting its riches. There is also an implied warning not to add to what is heard, nor to tinker with Jesus's teachings (see also Galatians 1:6–10). Better the path of the highly commended Bereans (Acts 17:11).[77]

A less-than-careful listening to Jesus's words, or a tampering with them, lay behind much of the controversy in the early church. A simple faith was made more complicated. In the fourth century, Basil the Great (330–79) wrote words that still resonate:

> If all those upon whom the name of our God and Saviour Jesus Christ had been invoked had preferred not to tamper with the truth of the gospel and to content themselves with the tradition of the apostles and the simplicity of the faith, there would be no need for our present treatise. Instead, we would have maintained even now the complete silence we have honoured from the beginning. But the enemy of truth ceaselessly proliferates evil, adding to the weeds he sowed in the church of God at the beginning.[78]

Jesus then continued, 'With the measure you use, it will be measured to you – and even more. Whoever has will be given more; whoever does not have, even what they have will be taken from them.' Given the context, the measure here is the careful consideration given to Scripture. The more consideration you give, the greater the reward. The more careful study, the richer the understanding. Meditation lies at the heart of the business of reading Scripture: 'I have more insight than all my teachers, for I meditate on your statutes' (Psalm 119:99). This leads to the question: what is mediation? Thomas Watson answered this well: 'Meditation is the soul's retiring by itself, that by a serious and solemn thinking upon God, the heart may be raised up to heavenly affections.'[79] This is no simple emptying of the mind,

---

[77] 'Now the Berean Jews were of more noble character than those in Thessalonica, for they received the message with great eagerness and examined the Scriptures every day to see if what Paul said was true.'

[78] Basil of Caesarea, *Against Eunomius*, 1, trans. M. DelCogliano and A. Radde-Gallwitz (Washington: Catholic University of America Press, 2011), 81.

[79] Thomas Watson, 'A Christian on the Mount; or, a Treatise Concerning

but rather filling it with God. It is allowing the Scriptures to soak into your soul.

The growth of the kingdom (4:26–9)

The parable of the growing seed
26 He also said, 'This is what the kingdom of God is like. A man scatters seed on the ground. 27 Night and day, whether he sleeps or gets up, the seed sprouts and grows, though he does not know how. 28 All by itself the soil produces corn – first the stalk, then the ear, then the full grain in the ear. 29 As soon as the corn is ripe, he puts the sickle to it, because the harvest has come.'

We return once more to the subject of the kingdom of God, and to the imagery of seed. Whereas the parable of the sower was concerned with the yield of the sowing, the focus here was on the growth itself. The farmer scattered the seed, and the seed grew by itself. The farmer had no knowledge of the mechanics of the growth ('he does not know how'), but simply waited until the time of harvest. The responsibility was simply limited to the sowing and the reaping, not the growth itself.

Given the context of this teaching, it is reasonable to see this as a parable concerning evangelism, and we might find a further example of this understanding in the comments of Paul: 'I planted the seed, Apollos watered it, but God has been making it grow. So neither the one who plants nor the one who waters is anything, but only God, who makes things grow' (1 Corinthians 3:6–7). Growth, then, is a work of God and not a human endeavour. The seed needs to be sown, but the yield is in the hands of God.

This is an important principle: the growth of the kingdom of God is a divine and not a human affair. It is not for us to build the kingdom or seek to widen its boundaries through our own good deeds or human effort. While the lives of individual Christians will result in good works being done, the kingdom

---

Meditation', in *A Divine Cordial; the Saint's Spiritual Delight; the Holy Eucharist; and Other Treatises, the Writings of the Doctrinal Puritans and Divines of the Seventeenth Century* (London: The Religious Tract Society, 1846), 33.

itself is of a spiritual nature and a result of divine activity. It is not the result of initiatives, but of God himself. As Herman Bavinck says, 'Scripture knows nothing of a self-sufficient nature and an autonomous man; always it is God who keeps the world in force and who makes history.'[80]

However, it is also important to note that Jesus was not simply suggesting that the seed is sown and then nothing further needs to be done. There is no warrant here for negligence. Once the growth has taken place, the harvest still needs to be carried out and the sickle put to the corn. The work of evangelism is to be done, but there has to be trust in God that the word will bear fruit.

This parable also describes the progressive nature of spiritual growth within the individual and points to the expectation that growth will take place. Here is no static Christianity, but rather one that develops over time. The threefold nature of this growth – stalk, ear, full grain – has led many to develop a similar threefold under-standing of Christian growth, such as we find with Thomas Oden: 'We have been saved from the penalty of sin in justification; we are being saved from the power of sin in sanctification; and we shall be saved finally from the presence of sin in glorification.'[81] Justification is our being put right with God through faith in Christ. Sanctification is our growth in holiness into Christlikeness. Glorification is our eternal dwelling with the Triune God in heaven. Here is the progress of the Christian faith.

The imagery of the growth of the seed also speaks to the experi-ence of sanctification in the Christian life. First of all, sanctification is no simple matter of human effort, and the Christian who – through sheer force of will – seeks to bring about change in his or her life will end up discouraged. As with the growth of the kingdom of God, sanctification is a matter for prayer and faith. It is a work of God through his Spirit in the life of the believer.

Second, the growth is gradual. The one who stands in a field hoping to watch the grain grow will be disappointed, and it is possible to

---

[80] Herman Bavinck, *Our Reasonable Faith* (Grand Rapids: Eerdmans, 2016), 540.
[81] Thomas C. Oden, *Life in the Spirit: Systematic Theology: Volume III* (San Francisco: Harper and Row, 1992), 84.

watch one's own sanctification too closely. This work of the Spirit is better measured in years than days.

Finally, the passage should give pause to those who seek to judge the faith of others. Sanctification is the outworking of justification, but it is not instant. The farmer did not know how the seed grew, and so it is with the work of the Spirit in the believer.

The scale of the kingdom (4:30–34)

The parable of the mustard seed

30 Again he said, 'What shall we say the kingdom of God is like, or what parable shall we use to describe it? 31 It is like a mustard seed, which is the smallest of all seeds on earth. 32 Yet when planted, it grows and becomes the largest of all garden plants, with such big branches that the birds can perch in its shade.'

33 With many similar parables Jesus spoke the word to them, as much as they could understand. 34 He did not say anything to them without using a parable. But when he was alone with his own disciples, he explained everything.

We come to the end of this series of parables describing the kingdom of God and its growth, all using the metaphor of seeds. The focus of this final parable was not so much the fact that growth is the preserve of God, but rather the scale of that growth. It may well be that the kingdom of God had small beginnings, but that did not limit its growth. From the smallest of seeds comes the largest of plants, and the kingdom is present in both.

This parable is a challenge to the culture of 'how to' books and conferences. Once again we see that the kingdom of God grows by the power of God, not by human initiatives. The ordinary means of grace – preaching, sacraments and discipline – is the responsibility of the church. The rest lies with God. The seed is to be sown, but God gives the growth. Small starts should not be a matter of concern since the right seed produces the right growth. The important factor is the seed itself.

The mention of birds in the parable has caused much comment: are they intended to be part of the parable, or are they simply there to emphasize the size of the plant? In Ezekiel 17 we find an empire pictured as a large cedar tree, and in the tree planted by God, 'Birds of every kind will nest in it; they will find shelter in the shade of its branches' (Ezekiel 17:23). Similar imagery may be found in Ezekiel 31:1–14 and in Daniel 4:10–21. The birds finding shade in the mustard plant not only emphasise its size but are also an image of the large range of peoples who will find their place in the kingdom of God.

Having related this parable, this section of the Gospel concludes with a final comment on parables. Using imagery drawn from the parable of the sower, Mark noted that Jesus spoke 'the word' to them. Here was the seed being sown, but it was sown using parables. It was to the disciples alone that Jesus explained things clearly, and here we see the importance of correct interpretation. Most who heard the parables did not fully understand, and so it is that Jesus's words might be misunderstood or – worse – twisted. The postmodern turn in much scholarship, with its willingness to redefine and re-understand the Scriptures in light of modern cultural norms, puts one in mind of *Alice in Wonderland*:

'When *I* use a word,' Humpty Dumpty said in rather a scornful tone, 'it means just what I choose it to mean – neither more nor less.'

'The question is,' said Alice, 'whether you *can* make words mean so many different things.'

'The question is,' said Humpty Dumpty, 'which is to be master – that's all.'[82]

The fact that Jesus explained everything to his disciples demonstrates that his words are to have a particular interpretation. The levels of understanding may vary, but not the meaning. Truth transcends culture and so requires patient enquiry. We cannot simply impose the understanding of a particular society upon the text, but rather Scripture has to have an inner coherence. The Scriptures themselves play an explanatory role in the understanding of God, as Calvin's well-known example of the spectacles illustrates:

---

[82] Lewis Carroll, *Through the Looking-Glass, and What Alice Found There* (London: Macmillan and Co., 1872), 124.

Just as old or bleary-eyed men and those with weak vision, if you thrust before them a most beautiful volume, even if they recognize it to be some sort of writing, yet can scarcely construe two words, but with the aid of spectacles will begin to read distinctly; so Scripture, gathering up the otherwise confused knowledge of God in our minds, having dispersed our dullness, clearly shows us the true God.[83]

Before leaving this section of Mark's Gospel, we would do well to note that the fact that not everyone understood the parables does not imply that the Scripture is not clear. Scripture is God's gracious gift to us and is clear in its content, but that does not mean all will understand it. As Mark Thompson notes, 'The light of the Scriptures shines in the midst of darkness. But in the perversity of our sin, human beings, apart from the regenerative work of God's Spirit, love darkness rather than light (John 3:19).'[84]

The kingdom and the natural realm (4:35–41)

Jesus calms the storm

35 That day when evening came, he said to his disciples, 'Let us go over to the other side.' 36 Leaving the crowd behind, they took him along, just as he was, in the boat. There were also other boats with him. 37 A furious squall came up, and the waves broke over the boat, so that it was nearly swamped. 38 Jesus was in the stern, sleeping on a cushion. The disciples woke him and said to him, 'Teacher, don't you care if we drown?'

39 He got up, rebuked the wind and said to the waves, 'Quiet! Be still!' Then the wind died down and it was completely calm.

40 He said to his disciples, 'Why are you so afraid? Do you still have no faith?'

41 They were terrified and asked each other, 'Who is this? Even the wind and the waves obey him!'

---

[83] John Calvin, *Institute of the Christian Religion*, 1.6.1. 1:70.

[84] Mark D. Thompson, *A Clear and Present Word: The Clarity of Scripture* (Downers Grove: InterVarsity Press, 2016), 104.

Having concluded a section dealing with parables, we now witness Jesus's mastery over the natural world. It was evening, which suggests it was getting dark, and Jesus said to his disciples, 'Let us go over to the other side.'

The word translated 'go over' (*dielthōmen*) is rather unexpected as it normally denotes going *through* something rather than *over*. It is the word used in Mark 10:25 for going through the eye of a needle, and in Mark 5:21 and Mark 6:53 we find the more usual verb *diaperaō* ('cross over'). Mark's use of 'go through' here is significant, since it implies that Jesus was aware that the journey would take them *through* something.[85] It would appear that Jesus was aware of the impending storm.

The disciples left, taking Jesus 'just as he was'. The impression given here is one of simple obedience: Jesus spoke, and the disciples acted. There was no other preparation by either Jesus or the disciples.

It would appear that the group were in the same boat as the one introduced in Mark 3:9, and we certainly know that Jesus had been in the same boat since Mark 4:1.

A first-century fishing boat was discovered in the mud at the north-west shore of the Sea of Galilee in 1986, after severe droughts.[86] Measuring twenty-six feet and six inches long by seven feet and six inches wide, this boat would have comfortably accommodated the Twelve along with Jesus, and the surviving fittings would suggest it could be both rowed and sailed.[87]

There were other boats with Jesus, probably containing some who had come to listen to him, and they too set out. They did not reappear, and it may well be that they simply turned back when they saw the storm. Their lack of perseverance caused them to miss this great sign, which might be seen as a warning to those who seek to turn back too quickly.

---

[85] Gundry, *Mark*, 244.

[86] Shelley Wachsmann, 'The Galilee Boat. 2,000-Year-Old Hull Recovered Intact', *Biblical Archaeology Review* 14, no. 5 (1988).

[87] Wachsmann, using estimates from Joe Zias who was at the time a physical anthropologist at the Israeli Department of Antiquities working with skeletal remains, assumes the average first-century Jew to be five feet and five inches tall and weighing ten stone (140 pounds). Wachsmann, 'Boat', 32.

The severity of the storm should not be underestimated: the phrase could be translated as a 'great whirlwind' or 'large hurricane'. The wind was strong, whipping up the waves such that they almost swamped the boat,[88] something that would cause fear even among those who were well used to fishing in those waters. We should not assume that the fishermen could swim – Peter sank as he cried out to Jesus in Matthew 14:30 – and the danger was existential.

In the midst of all this turmoil, Jesus was asleep in the stern, resting on a cushion. Mark referred to this as *the* cushion, and it may well be that this was the ballast sandbag used for trimming the boat when it was under sail.[89] There are echoes here of Jonah asleep under the deck in a storm as he fled from his call to the Gentiles (Jonah 1:5). Jonah fled from the Gentiles, while Jesus was crossing 'through' to them. His tiredness reflected the exertion of teaching, but also his peaceful trust in God for his safety. With his characteristic turn of phrase, Charles Haddon Spurgeon (1834–92) put it nicely:

> There is no sweeter pillow than providence; and when providence seemeth adverse, believe it still, lay it under thy head, for depend upon it there is comfort in its bosom . . . That great trouble which is to come in thy way in the early part of thy pilgrimage, is planned by love, the same love which shall interpose as thy protector.[90]

The disciples woke him up, and their blunt words reflected their panic: 'Don't you care?'[91] Jesus responded by rebuking the wind and, intriguingly, Mark used the same word as he did in Mark 1:25 and Mark 9:25 where impure spirits were commanded to be quiet. We should be wary of thinking that this implies that the waters were demon-possessed; rather, it would seem that there was a deliberate echo of those Old Testament passages where the LORD rebuked the

---

[88] The recovered Galilean boat was only four and a half feet high.

[89] Wachsmann, 'Boat', 33. Others suggest a helmsman's seat, or a bundle of the sailor's clothes. The latter seems unlikely given Mark's use of the definite article.

[90] C. H. Spurgeon, 'Israel at the Red Sea', in *The New Park Street Pulpit, Vol II* (London: Passmore & Alabaster, 1856), 149.

[91] France, *Mark*, 224.

sea (Psalms 18:15; 104:7; 106:9; Isaiah 50:2; Nahum 1:4). The 'great' whirlwind was replaced by a 'great' calm (the same Greek word appears in both phrases). As at creation, God spoke and brought order out of chaos.

There is a directness to Jesus's speech which is deeply significant. Here was a direct command of Jesus over nature – he did not feel the need to ask in God's name or to pray. The implication was clear: the storm was stilled at the order of Jesus and upon his own authority. He spoke as the master of creation.

Jesus then addressed the disciples, wondering why they were so afraid. He went on to ask, 'Do you still have no faith?' While it is easy to have some sympathy with the disciples – after all, they had been on the verge of sinking – the issue here was clearly identified as their lack of faith. Jesus had said that they would 'go through', and go through they did. Although they had witnessed Jesus's teaching, exorcisms and healings, they had not yet fully understood who he was, and that had resulted in fear. Nor had they been in a position of danger themselves, and so their faith in Jesus was – at that stage – merely theoretical. It is as dangers surge that faith reveals itself.

Thus far we have encountered 'great' winds, and 'great' calm and now we have 'great' fear from the disciples. 'Who is this?' they wondered. 'Even the wind and the waves obey him.'

Within Judaism, the deep waters were associated with primordial chaos and destructive beasts (Job 26:12; Psalms 65:5–7; 74:12–14; 89:9–10; Isaiah 27:1; 51:9), and Jesus demonstrated his mastery over creation with a rebuking word (two imperative words in the Greek text). Here was a divine act (Psalm 89:9), and the whole incident would surely have brought Psalm 107:23–30 to a fisherman's mind.

'Who is this?' they wondered. The irony is that we who have read Mark's introduction know, as do the impure spirits. Although the disciples had been with Jesus and the parables had been explained to them, they only had small glimpses of a full understanding of Jesus's identity. Throughout Mark's Gospel we have disciples who failed to understand Jesus. The disciples were no heroes to be imitated – at least, not as they were prior to the resurrection. Nonetheless, their perseverance with Jesus did result in their coming to a full understanding of the truth, and that is something to be emulated. The resurrection changed everything.

There are many who practise their faith in places of great danger. They pray, and persecution continues, which might lead them to conclude that they have been abandoned; that Jesus is asleep. The way of Christ does not promise to be persecution free. In fact, Jesus himself proclaimed, 'Blessed are those who are persecuted because of righteousness, for theirs is the kingdom of heaven' (Matthew 5:10). The promise of Jesus is that you will go *through*, and you will arrive at the other side.

Legion, demons and the kingdom (5:1–20)

Jesus restores a demon-possessed man

5 They went across the lake to the region of the Gerasenes.[a] **2**When Jesus got out of the boat, a man with an impure spirit came from the tombs to meet him. **3**This man lived in the tombs, and no one could bind him anymore, not even with a chain. **4**For he had often been chained hand and foot, but he tore the chains apart and broke the irons on his feet. No one was strong enough to subdue him. **5**Night and day among the tombs and in the hills he would cry out and cut himself with stones.

6When he saw Jesus from a distance, he ran and fell on his knees in front of him. **7**He shouted at the top of his voice, 'What do you want with me, Jesus, Son of the Most High God? In God's name don't torture me!' **8**For Jesus had said to him, 'Come out of this man, you impure spirit!'

9Then Jesus asked him, 'What is your name?'

'My name is Legion,' he replied, 'for we are many.' **10**And he begged Jesus again and again not to send them out of the area.

11A large herd of pigs was feeding on the nearby hillside. **12**The demons begged Jesus, 'Send us among the pigs; allow us to go into them.' **13**He gave them permission, and the impure spirits came out and went into the pigs. The herd, about two thousand in number, rushed down the steep bank into the lake and were drowned.

14Those tending the pigs ran off and reported this in the town and countryside, and the people went out to see what had happened. **15**When they came to Jesus, they saw the man who had been possessed by the legion of demons, sitting there, dressed and in his right mind; and they were afraid. **16** Those who had seen it told the people what had happened to the demon-possessed man – and told about the pigs as well. **17** Then the people began to plead with Jesus to leave their region.

18 As Jesus was getting into the boat, the man who had been demon-possessed begged to go with him. **19** Jesus did not let him, but said, 'Go home to your own people and tell them how much the Lord has done for you, and how he has had mercy on you.' **20** So the man went away and began to tell in the Decapolis[b] how much Jesus had done for him. And all the people were amazed.

---

[a] 1 Some manuscripts *Gadarenes*; other manuscripts *Gergesenes*

[b] 20 That is, the Ten Cities

Having crossed a storm-tossed lake, they encountered a man with a storm-tossed mind. It is not entirely clear where the region of the Gerasenes was, but it was within the region known as Decapolis and was a Gentile settlement.[92] When Jesus disembarked, a man with an impure spirit came to meet him, almost as if Jesus were expected.

The man was clearly not himself. He lived among the tombs and possessed such strength that even chains could not hold him. He would cry out and cut himself with stones (echoing the action of the priests of Baal who slashed themselves with swords and spears[93]). None had the strength to subdue him. Yet when he saw Jesus in the distance, he ran to him, fell to his knees and called out to him, using both Jesus's name and title. This, we are told, was in response to Jesus's ordering the spirit to leave the man, but it is not clear if Jesus spoke before the man fell to his knees or after.

The word translated as 'fell on his knees' is an interesting one and is commonly translated as 'worshipped'. It is a position of humility and submission to one who has a higher authority. It was a dramatic act.

The title used is unusual and is more pagan in nature (we are now in non-Jewish lands): 'Son of the Most High God'. This recognition speaks to both Jesus's divine nature and the fact that the spirit was aware of the presence of one who is greater.[94] It may be that the

---

[92] See discussion in Witherington, *Mark*, 179f.

[93] 1 Kings 18:28.

[94] See also Acts 16:17.

use of Jesus's name was an attempt to 'bind' him in some sort of demonic exorcism.[95] In the ancient world, knowing a name was viewed as having power over someone, and the spirit did seek to both command/bind Jesus with the formula 'in God's name' and call on his pity: 'don't torture me'. This we might see as an act of desperation.

Jesus then asked the spirit's name, which elicited the strange response: 'My name is Legion . . . for we are many.' Here we have a curious mix of singular and plural. At the beginning of the passage we were told that the man had 'an impure spirit' (singular), and when addressed, the impure spirit cried out, 'What do you want with me?' (singular). Jesus asked him, 'What is your name?' (singular), to which he replied, 'My name [singular] is Legion . . . for we [plural] are many.' We then read that he (singular) begged Jesus not to send them (plural) out of the area, and later read that the demons (plural) begged Jesus to be sent into the pigs, with the result that the impure spirits (plural) came out into the pigs and around two thousand rushed into the lake.

What do we make of all this? Is it the case that the demon was avoiding being named, or were there many spirits within the area and 'Legion' spoke for them all? In Luke's Gospel, it is explicitly stated that 'many demons had gone into him' (Luke 8:30), and later in Mark 5:15 it is said that the man 'had been possessed by the legion of demons'. It would appear, then, that Legion was a spokesman for the many demons who had possessed the man. A full Roman Legion was around six thousand men, but we need not conclude that this is the precise number of demons (later we see that two thousand pigs perished). The point is that there was a multitude, and Legion, apparently now conceding defeat, begged not to be sent out of the area.

At this, the multitude of demons added to their entreaties and begged to be sent into the nearby herd of pigs. Permission was given, and so the pigs rushed down the bank into the Sea of Galilee and perished. We see here an expression of the wideness of Christ's mercy, that he was even willing to listen to the requests of the evil spirits.[96]

---

[95] France, *Mark*, 228.
[96] See Ephrem the Syrian, *Hymns on Paradise,* 12, trans. Sebastian Brock (Yonkers: St Vladimir's Seminary Press, 1990), 163.

We might also note that the presence of pig farmers underlines the very Gentile nature of the region. There was no prohibition on eating pork here.

The pig tenders – who one assumes were not pleased – spread the news, and the residents came to the tombs to see what had happened. There they found the man 'dressed and in his right mind' and were afraid of the apparent power of Jesus. Once they heard what had occurred, they too begged Jesus to leave the area. There are echoes here of the fear of the disciples in the previous passage; Jesus's mastery over nature induced an awe-filled fear in those who observed it.

The final begging comes from the once-demonised man, who wanted to join the disciples and come along with Jesus. This request was refused, but in sharp contrast to his dealings in Israel, Jesus did not urge the man to keep silence. This is somewhat surprising, since he did later command secrecy when he healed a deaf and dumb man in the same region. It is tempting to think that the Messianic Secret was not to be kept in this Gentile area since there was no risk of an erroneous understanding of Messiahship in this non-Jewish area. Perhaps it might be that secrecy was not so important as Jesus was shortly to leave the area (unlike when the deaf and dumb man was healed, Mark 7:31–7), or maybe the very strong confrontation with demons in such a pagan area was to be a sign to them that he was no mere healer.

Obedient to his commission, the man went throughout the region of the Decapolis ('Ten Cities') and bore witness to his experience of Christ. The Greek is a little stronger than simply 'tell' as the NIV translates it: elsewhere the word is translated as 'proclaim' or 'preach'. We have here the first evangelist to the Gentiles, a proto-Paul. The people who heard the preaching were 'amazed', which, in Mark, is a common response to the works of Christ (Mark 1:22, 27; 2:12; 5:42; 6:51; 12:17).

This is a curious passage and represents Jesus's ministry extending into Gentile areas. Rather than simply a Messiah for the Jews, Jesus was revealed as Messiah for the whole world. The darkness of the Gentile area, with its tombs, pigs and legions of demons, now received the light of Christ (Isaiah 49:6), and those who were healed by Jesus were sent out to preach yet further. There is nowhere outside the scope of the kingdom of God: even the demon-inhabited come to Christ.

To those who focus merely on the material things of this world, this sort of exorcism sounds strange, or even alarming. We noted earlier that any belief in God necessarily entails a belief in the supernatural, so we should not be surprised to find it rather more populated than we expected. This is no cause for fear – Jesus was not engaged in an existential struggle with Legion – but rather it is a call for us to ensure we look for the whole picture and deal with the whole person: mind, body and soul.

NOTE: DEMON POSSESSION IN THE BIBLE

Passages such as this have led to fears surrounding demons, something worsened by the portrayals of exorcisms in modern media, but it is worth noting that within the New Testament this incident is unique in its intensity. It may be that the highly pagan nature of the area lay behind the scale of Legion's possession, which was further exacerbated by Jesus's presence. Anecdotally, missionaries speak of heightened spiritual activity in areas barely touched by the gospel.

The phrase 'demon possession' is an unfortunate one. To be 'possessed' suggests that another has control over you, but the biblical language does not carry that meaning. Rather, we see a demon having influence over a person. The Bible contains no clear statement on the nature of demons, and so we are left to piece together an understanding based on a number of narrative passages and the opinions of those recorded in them.

This lack of information has led to a small industry of speculation, and no little fear. However, we should be as wary of going beyond what is revealed in Scripture as we should be in dismissing what is clearly set out. We can see that such spirits may in some way inhabit human bodies (as in the case of Legion) and speak. They have the capacity for understanding and for knowing who Jesus is (Mark 1:24), and shudder at the knowledge of God (James 2:19). They are consistently viewed as evil or impure and seek to lead people away from Christ (1 Timothy 4:1). Given this, we shouldn't be surprised that Jesus's ministry was accompanied by a great activity of forces opposed to him.

What we don't find in Scripture is teaching that the spirits of the dead return to haunt, or that there are territorial spirits, demonic hierarchies, spirits associated with specific diseases, or strongholds. These are all speculations which should be dismissed as unbiblical. We would do well to avoid occultic practices, but we should also avoid giving them too much credence. They are simply 'things taught by demons' (1 Timothy 4:1).

Some might suggest these are simply delusions of an earlier age, but it is worth noting that Jesus himself spent time teaching his disciples concerning demons (e.g., Luke 11:17–26), which would be strange if he felt them to be simply 'nothing else than evil emotions or perturbations which come upon us from our flesh'.[97] We should also note that there is a distinction drawn between those who are ill and those who are demon-possessed in Mark 1:32. In Matthew 4:24 the distinction is even clearer: 'people brought to him all who were ill with various diseases, those suffering severe pain, the demon-possessed, those having seizures, and the paralysed; and he healed them'.

It is notable that there is an ease to Jesus's actions with impure spirits, and in an extreme case he noted that 'this kind can come out only by prayer' (Mark 9:29). Prayer, then, is the correct response to all of this. These are matters for God, and not for human ingenuity. Simple prayer – the treasure of all Christians – is all that we need.

Any conclusion will have to be tentative. We should begin by acknowledging that human beings are fallen, and prone to temptation (see, for example, Matthew 15:19). In Genesis 3 we see an example of such a temptation, but in the end the one who is tempted remains responsible for his or her actions. The witness of Jesus and the New Testament is that one such source of temptation is evil spirits, who may attach themselves to particular persons. These, however, may be cast out (de-attached) through prayer and should not be seen as

---

[97] Calvin, *Institutes*, 1:178. In refuting this opinion, he concluded, 'How meaningless would these expressions be, that the devils are destined for eternal judgment, that fire has been prepared for them, that they are now tormented and tortured by Christ's glory, if devils were nonexistent!'

equal in power to God himself. Not all evil comes from evil spirits (in Matthew 15:19 Jesus lists many that come from the human heart), but some may. The Christian needs to be watchful, but not fearful (1 Peter 5:8–9).[98] The Christian is wise to don the armour of God (Ephesians 6:10–18) and trust in its protection.

King over sickness and death (5:21–43)

Jesus raises a dead girl and heals a sick woman

21 When Jesus had again crossed over by boat to the other side of the lake, a large crowd gathered round him while he was by the lake. 22 Then one of the synagogue leaders, named Jairus, came, and when he saw Jesus, he fell at his feet. 23 He pleaded earnestly with him, 'My little daughter is dying. Please come and put your hands on her so that she will be healed and live.' 24 So Jesus went with him.

A large crowd followed and pressed round him. 25 And a woman was there who had been subject to bleeding for twelve years. 26 She had suffered a great deal under the care of many doctors and had spent all she had, yet instead of getting better she grew worse. 27 When she heard about Jesus, she came up behind him in the crowd and touched his cloak, 28 because she thought, 'If I just touch his clothes, I will be healed.' 29 Immediately her bleeding stopped and she felt in her body that she was freed from her suffering.

30 At once Jesus realised that power had gone out from him. He turned round in the crowd and asked, 'Who touched my clothes?'

31 'You see the people crowding against you,' his disciples answered, 'and yet you can ask, "Who touched me?" '

32 But Jesus kept looking around to see who had done it. 33 Then the woman, knowing what had happened to her, came and fell at his feet and, trembling with fear, told him the whole truth. 34 He said to her, 'Daughter, your faith has healed you. Go in peace and be freed from your suffering.'

35 While Jesus was still speaking, some people came from the house of Jairus, the synagogue leader. 'Your daughter is dead,' they said. 'Why

---

[98] For a more thorough discussion of this, see Robert Duncan Culver, *Systematic Theology: Biblical and Historical* (Ross-shire: Mentor, 2005), chapter 20; Wayne A. Grudem, *Systematic Theology: An Introduction to Biblical Doctrine. Second Edition* (Grand Rapids: Zondervan Academic, 2020), chapter 20.

bother the teacher anymore?'

36 Overhearing[c] what they said, Jesus told him, 'Don't be afraid; just believe.'

37 He did not let anyone follow him except Peter, James and John the brother of James. **38** When they came to the home of the synagogue leader, Jesus saw a commotion, with people crying and wailing loudly. **39** He went in and said to them, 'Why all this commotion and wailing? The child is not dead but asleep.' **40** But they laughed at him.

After he put them all out, he took the child's father and mother and the disciples who were with him, and went in where the child was. **41** He took her by the hand and said to her, *'Talitha koum!'* (which means 'Little girl, I say to you, get up!'). **42** Immediately the girl stood up and began to walk around (she was twelve years old). At this they were completely astonished. **43** He gave strict orders not to let anyone know about this, and told them to give her something to eat.

_____

c 36 Or *Ignoring*

Jesus and his disciples now crossed over (not through – see comments on Mark 4:35–41) the Sea of Galilee and returned to Jewish lands. As was now the normal pattern, a crowd gathered, and a synagogue leader named Jairus came near.[99] Clearly at this stage not all officials were opposed to Jesus, and Jairus's attitude would suggest that opposition at this stage was mainly clustered around Jerusalem and the Temple. Like Legion, Jairus fell at Jesus's feet and begged for help (the word translated 'pleaded earnestly' also punctuates the account of Legion at Mark 5:10, 12, 17, 18). His little daughter was dying, and he wanted Jesus to lay his hands on her and heal her.

As Jesus went in with Jairus, the crowd followed and pressed in. Within the throng was a woman who had suffered for twelve years with bleeding (literally a 'flow of blood'), a phrase that occurs in Leviticus 15:25 which would suggest her ailment also renders her ritually unclean, although this is not addressed in the passage.[100] All

_____

[99] Bauckham has argued, convincingly, that those named in the Gospels are the eyewitnesses who related the events. See Bauckham, *Eyewitnesses*.

[100] I coyly quote Hooker on this: 'Her complaint was presumably vaginal bleeding (a vital fact that male commentators assume, but which most coyly omit to state!)' Morna D. Hooker, *The Gospel According to Saint Mark* (London: Continuum, 1991), 148.

the help she has sought thus far has come to nothing.[101]

Unlike the synagogue ruler, the woman did not approach Jesus. Rather, she simply reached out to touch his cloak. It is not clear why she felt that power resided in his clothes, and some have speculated that this is indicative of some magical superstition. However, we do read of the waters of the Jordan separating when being struck by Elijah's cloak (2 Kings 2:13–15), and in the apostle Paul's ministry, 'even handkerchiefs and aprons that had touched him were taken to those who were ill, and their illnesses were cured and the evil spirits left them' (Acts 19:12). We should also acknowledge that in this instance the woman herself *was* healed, and when she touched his garment, 'Jesus realised that power had gone out from him' (verse 30). Is this an instance of a magical garment, or 'proof' that some items may have the power to heal or otherwise bless? After all, in recent years some have sought to sell items that contain God's power – handkerchiefs and the like – and have pointed to passages such as this one to legitimate their trade.

We might find an answer to that question in the exchange between Jesus and the woman. He was clearly keen to identify who had touched him, and when she fell at his feet he assured her that 'your faith has healed you'.[102] He was keen that there be no misunderstanding as to the source of the healing: it was faith, not magical clothing. The woman's faith was demonstrated in her reaching out to Christ, and it was that which had brought her to health. The clothes were incidental to all this. The point is that, like Jairus, she came to Jesus. Those who did so boldly, like Jairus, or hesitantly, like the unnamed woman, received the same response.

At this point, our attention snaps back to Jairus, as the news came that this daughter had died. In fact, we are told that the news came as Jesus was speaking with the woman, and the reader might assume that had this conversation not taken place, Jesus would have

---

[101] Witherington notes that 'Mark includes a comment derogatory toward physicians in v. 26, which Luke interestingly omits'. Witherington, *Mark*, 186.

[102] The word for 'fell' used here is different from that used of Jairus earlier in this passage. The action of the woman was more that of a suppliant. She came in fear and trembling, not doubt, as her conversation with Jesus would bring her unclean condition out into the open.

arrived at Jairus's house in time. However, this is not made clear in the passage (unlike in the account of the death of Lazarus in John 11), so one should be wary of drawing any conclusions from this.

Overhearing the message, Jesus echoed his message to the trembling woman: 'Don't be afraid; just believe.'[103] Here is the core of the gospel: faith dispelling fear. People seek peace in many ways, even travelling the globe to discover it, yet it is close at hand. The path to peace goes through faith. Prayer dispels fear.

Jesus then dismissed all but Peter, James and John – the inner core of his disciples – and went to Jairus's home, where a crowd of mourners had already assembled.[104] These might well be mourners paid for their work, something not unknown (see, for example, Jeremiah 9:17–18). On entering the house, Jesus declared that the girl was only sleeping and questioned why the mourners were present.

It is important to realise that Jesus was simply using a metaphor to describe the temporary nature of her condition, rather than literally suggesting she was simply asleep. The fact that the mourners had gathered indicates a certainty in the diagnosis, and it would seem unlikely that the Gospel would make the effort to record Jesus simply correcting a misdiagnosis.

Jesus cleared the room of all but the disciples and the girl's parents, took the girl by the hand and told her to get up. There are some remarkable things to note here: the lack of any prayer, the fact that touching a corpse would render Jesus unclean (Numbers 19:11), and the sheer ease of the healing. This speaks to more than a simple faith healer being at work. These are the acts of a divine person.

Such was its impact that Peter (Mark's source) can remember the very words used to the girl, and he himself repeated the command when Dorcas was raised from the dead (Acts 9:40). There is no magical process at play here, simply the command of Christ, and Peter was keen to ensure that healing was only done in that name (Acts 3:12–16). At Jesus's word, the twelve-year-old rose and walked

---

[103] The verb is in the present continuous tense, and so might be translated, 'Keep on believing.'

[104] Quite why Andrew – the fourth of the initial disciples – is omitted is not clear.

around. Jesus commanded secrecy and then, in a very practical manner, suggested they feed her.

Mark carefully put these two accounts together, using the 'sandwich' technique he employed at various stages in his Gospel. When this literary device is used, it alerts us that the two accounts sit together and interpret each other, and this is heightened by the fact that the woman had been suffering for twelve years and the girl was aged twelve. Normally, the 'filling' gives us the theme of the passage as a whole,[105] and in this case we can see the theme of faith at play. It was faith that healed the woman – not any power residing in the clothing – as it was faith that brought Jesus to the newly dead girl, not the act of the laying-on of hands which Jairus requested. We might also note that in this passage we see both ends of the Jewish social scale: the named synagogue ruler and the unnamed and ritually unclean woman. All may come to Christ. Faith is a gift to be found in all sorts of people.

This focus on faith might also account for the command of secrecy. Rather than simply seeing Jesus as a faith healer, he was to be understood as the one in whom life resides (a great theme of the Gospel of John). If news of Jairus's daughter were to spread, the focus might not be upon the faith that brought it about but rather on a quasi-magical understanding of Jesus's ministry. Christianity is deeper than mere magic.

We might also note that salvation encompasses the whole person (1 Thessalonians 5:23). The word translated as 'healed' in verse 34 may also be translated as 'saved'. Depending on the context, it might be translated as 'rescue', 'heal' or 'bring to salvation'. There is more than simply a ticket to heaven in mind, but rather an entire renewal of the person (Romans 12:1–2; 2 Corinthians 5:17). The faith of the woman brought about not only her healing, but also her salvation. She found peace. Michael Green brings this out well when he insists that this passage:

. . . makes a marvellous sermon illustration for evangelistic preaching. Here is a woman with a disease which makes her ceremonially impure and increasingly weak physically. She has

---

[105] See James R. Edwards, 'Markan Sandwiches. The Significance of Interpolations in Markan Narratives', *Novum Testamentum* 31, no. 3 (1989).

tried all the remedies that she knows, and was nothing bettered but rather grew worse. She hears of Jesus; she comes to Jesus in simple (if superstitious) faith that he can cure her or, as Matthew and Mark put it, that she could be 'saved' (Mark 5:28; Matt. 9:21). She was assured by Jesus that her faith had 'saved' her, and she went out into a new life of peace and wholeness. We have here a paradigm of Christian conversion in the apostolic church.[106]

4. Rejection • Mark 6:1–29

This first part of the Gospel (Mark 1:16–6:29), which deals with Jesus's initial ministry in Galilee, ends with his rejection in his homeland. He was first rejected by his home town and then he sent out the Twelve to preach, giving them instructions as to what to do should their ministry also be rejected. After they went, the events leading to the execution of Jesus's herald – John the Baptist – are recounted.

These accounts demonstrated that rejection of Jesus's followers was often the path of discipleship, either by those who knew them best or by those who did not want to lose face.

Jesus rejected at home (6:1–6a)

A prophet without honour

6 Jesus left there and went to his home town, accompanied by his disciples. **2** When the Sabbath came, he began to teach in the synagogue, and many who heard him were amazed.

'Where did this man get these things?' they asked. 'What's this wisdom that has been given him? What are these remarkable miracles he is performing? **3** Isn't this the carpenter? Isn't this Mary's son and the brother of James, Joseph,[a] Judas and Simon? Aren't his sisters here with us?' And they took offence at him.

4 Jesus said to them, 'A prophet is

---

[106] Michael Green, *The Meaning of Salvation* (London: Hodder & Stoughton, 1965), 113.

not without honour except in his own town, among his relatives and in his own home.' 5 He could not do any miracles there, except lay his hands on a few people who were ill and heal them. 6 He was amazed at their lack of faith.

_____

a 3 Greek *Joses*, a variant of *Joseph*

Jesus left the home of the synagogue leader and returned to his homeland (*patrida*). This would appear to be Capernaum (Mark 2:1; Matthew 4:13–17), where he settled after leaving Nazareth.[107] The synagogue would therefore be the same building as we encountered in Mark 1:21, and once more those who heard him were amazed.

This amazement stemmed from their familiarity with Jesus: to them, he was simply the local carpenter,[108] and so his wisdom and miracles were inexplicable. Rather than allowing these miracles to act as signs that would lead to a deeper understanding of who Jesus might be, they were blinded by their presuppositions. His family was also well known, and clearly there was nothing about them that might explain Jesus's words and deeds.

Tellingly, this familiarity with Jesus caused the locals to take 'offence' at him, a word echoing the rocky ground in the parable of the sower (Mark 4:17). A partial knowledge of Jesus is a dangerous thing and often leads to outright rejection. Within the West, the echoes of Christianity that still exist in the wider culture give a partial image of Christ as simply a good teacher who behaved well towards others. In this context, the real teachings of Jesus still cause offence as they did in his home town, a situation which, as Jesus pointed out, was a hallmark of the prophets. The Russian Orthodox theologian Metropolitan Anthony of Sourozh once counselled that we should be wary of only paying attention to the passages of Scripture with which we agree. Rather, we should pay special attention to those with which we disagree: 'We should note these passages carefully. They are a measure of the distance between God and us and also they are a measure of the distance between ourselves as we are now

_____

[107] Some argue that it was Nazareth – e.g., Larry W. Hurtado, *Mark* (Grand Rapids: Baker Books, 2011), 92.
[108] The word *tektōn* might also be translated as 'builder'.

and our potential definitive selves.'[109] We should beware following – or rejecting – the Jesus we create in our minds, rather than the Jesus revealed to us in Scripture.

The great gift of our day is that the church is both global in scope and, through improved communications, more accessible than ever before. There is great wisdom in engaging with Christian literature from both other parts of the world and previous ages. This protects us from simply projecting our own values onto Jesus or approaching Scripture with all the assumptions of wider society.

The fact that Jesus 'could not do any miracles' is, at first glance, surprising: was Jesus so easily confounded? Mark noted that he did, in fact, heal a few people so the issue is not that he was unable to perform such work in his home town. Given the stress on faith in the previous passage, it would seem that the lack of faith of those in the synagogue was the key issue. 'Something essential for cures was required on both sides – faith on the part of the patients, power on that of the healer.'[110]

We should note that the haemorrhaging woman was told, 'Your faith has healed you' (Mark 5:34), and Jairus was urged, 'Don't be afraid; just believe' (Mark 5:36). In contrast, at the end of the following passage, Mark remarked that Jesus 'was amazed at their lack of faith'. Rather than thinking that Jesus was foiled in his attempt to work miracles, we would be better off thinking that Jesus realised that this was not the context in which to work them: the lack of faith would only bring misunderstanding, confusion or more opposition.

We might also contrast this passage with the earlier incident in the synagogue at Capernaum, in the first chapter, where the crowd were also amazed at Jesus, but rather than taking offence they simply wondered at his teaching and the news was spread throughout Galilee.

---

[109] Metropolitan Anthony of Sourozh, *Courage to Pray*, trans. Dinah Livingstone (London: Darton, Longman and Todd, 1973), 19.

[110] Gregory of Nazianzus, *Oration 30*, 10, *On God and Christ: The Five Theological Orations and Two Letters to Cledonius*, trans. F. Williams and L. Wickham (Crestwood: St Vladimir's Seminary Press, 2002), 100.

NOTE: JESUS'S WIDER FAMILY

The listing of Jesus's family raises some questions. Joseph is not mentioned, which is unusual in a culture where children were normally known by reference to their father. There have been several explanations offered, the most common being:

a) children may be referred to by their mother's name if her lineage is more significant;[111]
b) this is a reference to the virginal conception of Jesus;
c) the son of a widow was known by his mother's name;
d) the brothers are from Joseph's earlier marriage, and Jesus was the product of Joseph's marriage to Mary;[112]
e) this is an informal address, given that Mary was better known than Joseph who had died many years before; or
f) this is a slur, suggesting Jesus is illegitimate.

We might dismiss option (a) given the Davidic significance of Joseph's heritage (see the genealogies in Matthew 1:1–17 and Luke 3:23–38), and the fact that Jesus is referred to as the Son of David by Bartimaeus demonstrates Mark was well aware of this (Mark 10:47). Option (b) also seems unlikely since nowhere else in the Gospels is the virgin birth seen as common knowledge, and as to option (c), this lacks support from wider Jewish literature.[113]

The argument that these are brothers from an earlier marriage of Joseph is an old one and can be found in Syrian writings of the second century. Richard Bauckham argued, pretty convincingly, that the use of Mary's name was to distinguish Jesus from other children within the family who were the product of an earlier marriage of Joseph.[114] This practice may be seen elsewhere in the Old Testament (Genesis 4:19–22; 22:20–24; 36:10–14; 46:10; Exodus 6:15;

---

[111] Tan Ilan, "'Man Born of Woman." (Job 14:1) the Phenomenon of Men Bearing Metronymes At the Time of Jesus,' *Novum Testamentum* 43, no. 1 (1992).

[112] Richard Bauckham, 'The Brothers and Sisters of Jesus: An Epiphanian Response to John P. Meier', *The Catholic Biblical Quarterly* 56, no. 4 (1994).

[113] Harvey K. McArthur, 'Son of Mary', *Novum Testamentum* 15, no. 1 (1973).

[114] See Bauckham, 'Brothers and Sisters'.

1 Chronicles 2:3–4, 18–19, 21, 24, 25–6, 46, 48–9; 3:1–9), as well as in rabbinic literature.[115]

The final two options are also likely. It could simply be an Informal way of referring to Jesus – 'Oh yes! that's Mary's boy from down the street'[116] – or it could be a slur: we don't know who his father is! This smear may also be present in John 8:19 and John 8:41,[117] and is made explicit in rabbinic writings and wider early anti-Christian literature.[118]

The Twelve sent out (6:6b–13)

Jesus sends out the Twelve

Then Jesus went around teaching from village to village. 7 Calling the Twelve to him, he began to send them out two by two and gave them authority over impure spirits.

8 These were his instructions: 'Take nothing for the journey except a staff – no bread, no bag, no money in your belts. 9 Wear sandals but not an extra shirt. 10 Whenever you enter a house, stay there until you leave that town. 11 And if any place will not welcome you or listen to you, leave that place and shake the dust off your feet as a testimony against them.'

12 They went out and preached that people should repent. 13 They drove out many demons and anointed with oil many people who were ill and healed them.

Rather than being discouraged by the response in the synagogue in the preceding passage, Jesus embarked on a teaching tour around the villages. Rejection in one place did not mean an end to his ministry; rather, it was a sign to move on. As we will see later in this passage, there is an assumption that not all preaching is successful. As with the parables dealing with the seeds, the sower's task is to sow. The results are in God's hands.

---

[115] If this were the case, however, one might expect the mother of the other children to be mentioned.

[116] McArthur, 'Son of Mary', 57.

[117] Raymond E. Brown, *The Gospel According to John I–XII* (New York: Doubleday, 1966), 357.

[118] For instance, the slur that Jesus was fathered by a soldier named Panthera is dealt with by Origen (*c.* 185–*c.* 253) in *Against Celsus*, from 1.32.

Once again, Mark highlights the fact that it was teaching, rather than healings, that was at the heart of Jesus's ministry, and we here witness his commission to his disciples to go out and replicate his ministry. As faith is put into practice, it grows.

The disciples were to go in pairs, which might have been for their protection or to provide the necessary two witnesses required in the Law for legal cases (see Deuteronomy 17:6; 19:15; Matthew 18:16; 2 Corinthians 13:1). While there is no suggestion that the Twelve would be required to testify at trial, they would be passing judgment if they were to shake the dust off their feet 'as a testimony against them' (Mark 6:11). They could also testify later as to what they had encountered when they went. There is still wisdom in this approach, since it allows for accountability and mutual support. Christianity is not a solitary affair but is carried out by the body of Christ as a whole. The history of the church is littered with pairs who encouraged each other in the ministry, as Francis Turretin (1623–87) was keen to point out: 'In the Reformation, he raised up John Hus and Jerome of Prague in Bohemia, Zwingli and Oecolampadius in Switzerland, Luther and Melanchthon in Germany, Calvin and Farel in France.'[119]

The Twelve were given authority over impure spirits, which does not imply that they were sent out to exorcise rather than preach. In the Gospel thus far Jesus had silenced the spirits so that he might preach and, echoing Mark 1:15, the Twelve went about preaching that 'people should repent'. That is the context in which they were to both drive out demons and heal. This was, of course, precisely the ministry for which they were chosen (Mark 3:14–15). As ever, the focus was on the teaching and not on the miracles. The content of the preaching was that people should repent. Once more there is the insistence that repentance lies at the heart of the proclamation of the gospel, and we see this at the heart of apostolic mission. God 'commands all people everywhere to repent' (Acts 17:30), and Jesus's warning was stark: 'unless you repent, you too will all perish' (Luke 13:3). Repentance implies more than just regret over the actions of the past and the present. It is a complete and entire change of mind,

---

[119] Francis Turretin, *Institutes of Elenctic Theology, Volume 1* (Phillipsburg: P&R Publishing, 1992), 589.

worldview and outlook. It issues in a change of behaviour and a desire to cast sin aside. It sets its compass by the light of Christ and seeks to live as a citizen of heaven. It is a change from the inside out.

The Twelve were instructed to travel light, having only a staff and sandals. They were to take no bag – the *pēra* was a traveller's bag, which might also be used for begging either money or bread. Rather, they were to rely upon the providence of hospitality and were not even permitted a second shirt (tunic) which might give warmth on a cold night. Their ministry was to be carried out in entire dependence upon God.

Rather than move from house to house, these pairs were told to stay in a single dwelling so long as their message was being received. If they were not made welcome, then they were to simply move on, shaking the dust from their feet as they did so. They were responsible for making sure that the Word was preached, but not for its reception. An improper focus on reception may give rise to a temptation to trim the gospel or to harass those who do not respond. While it is important to make links with people, it is more important to ensure that the whole message of the gospel is received. The whole truth is needed, not a small part.

It is notable that to hear the gospel is to be presented with a choice, and a deep decision must be made. As the Puritan preacher Thomas Manton (1620–77) said, 'The preaching of the word will be a witness that men had warning, enough, but that they unthankfully neglected their opportunity, and did cast away their own mercies.'[120]

As they preached, the apostles both drove out demons and anointed the sick. Jesus's teaching brought with it demonic opposition, and so it is not surprising that the same occurred as the apostles preached repentance. Similarly, Jesus's authority was demonstrated by his ability to heal the sick, and so it was for the apostles. It is not entirely clear why the sick were anointed, as this did not echo Jesus's practice. It may be symbolic, demonstrating that, unlike Jesus, the power to heal comes from outside themselves (see James 5:14).

---

[120] Thomas Manton, 'Sermons Upon 2 Corinthians 5, Sermon XV', in *The Complete Works of Thomas Manton, Volume 13* (London: James Nisbet & Co., 1873), 68.

The death of the herald (6:14–29)

John the Baptist beheaded

14 King Herod heard about this, for Jesus' name had become well known. Some were saying,[b] 'John the Baptist has been raised from the dead, and that is why miraculous powers are at work in him.'

15 Others said, 'He is Elijah.'

And still others claimed, 'He is a prophet, like one of the prophets of long ago.'

16 But when Herod heard this, he said, 'John, whom I beheaded, has been raised from the dead!'

17 For Herod himself had given orders to have John arrested, and he had him bound and put in prison. He did this because of Herodias, his brother Philip's wife, whom he had married. **18** For John had been saying to Herod, 'It is not lawful for you to have your brother's wife.' **19** So Herodias nursed a grudge against John and wanted to kill him. But she was not able to, **20** because Herod feared John and protected him, knowing him to be a righteous and holy man. When Herod heard John, he was greatly puzzled[c]; yet he liked to listen to him.

21 Finally the opportune time came. On his birthday Herod gave a banquet for his high officials and military commanders and the leading men of Galilee. **22** When the daughter of[d] Herodias came in and danced, she pleased Herod and his dinner guests.

The king said to the girl, 'Ask me for anything you want, and I'll give it to you.' **23** And he promised her with an oath, 'Whatever you ask I will give you, up to half my kingdom.'

24 She went out and said to her mother, 'What shall I ask for?'

'The head of John the Baptist,' she answered.

25 At once the girl hurried in to the king with the request: 'I want you to give me right now the head of John the Baptist on a dish.'

26 The king was greatly distressed, but because of his oaths and his dinner guests, he did not want to refuse her. **27** So he immediately sent an executioner with orders to bring John's head. The man went, beheaded John in the prison, **28** and brought back his head on a dish. He presented it to the girl, and she gave it to her mother. **29** On hearing of this, John's disciples came and took his body and laid it in a tomb.

---

b 14 Some early manuscripts *He was saying*

c 20 Some early manuscripts *he did many things*

d 22 Some early manuscripts *When his daughter*

The account of the Twelve is now interrupted and does not resume until verse 30. There were rumours, which had come to Herod's ears, that Jesus was in fact a raised John the Baptist (or Elijah).[121] Herod feared that Jesus was in fact John the Baptist returned from the dead, no doubt influenced by the guilt he felt over his execution. It is sobering that in the context of the great success of the disciples set out in the next passage, we are reminded that discipleship might cost everything.

Given the mention of Elijah, it is interesting to note the parallels between this passage and the dealings of that prophet with Ahab and Jezebel (1 Kings 16–21). Morna Hooker noted that Ahab had a problematic marriage and was a weak man. He listened to Elijah but was more influenced by his wife, who eventually plotted the downfall of the prophet. She failed, but Herodias succeeded.[122] We often see patterns of behaviour in the Bible, and here is one such example. John, 'the Elijah who was to come' (Matthew 11:14), shared the same opposition as his illustrious forebear yet suffered a fate more grim.

It is fair to say that Herod had a complicated family tree. He was the son of Herod the Great and was known as Herod Antipas. During a trip to Rome, he stayed with his brother Herod II (also known as Herod Philip) and decided to marry his brother's wife, Herodias. She in turn was the granddaughter of Herod the Great and daughter of Aristobulus IV, who was Herod Antipas's half-brother. She was therefore Herod Antipas's half-niece as well as ex-sister-in-law.[123]

Although such a marriage was allowable in Roman law, it fell foul of the injunction in Leviticus 20:21, and John the Baptist stated his opposition.[124] While Christians are urged to obey those who are in

---

[121] The Old Testament closes with a prophecy of Elijah's return: 'See, I will send the prophet Elijah to you before that great and dreadful day of the LORD comes. He will turn the hearts of the parents to their children, and the hearts of the children to their parents; or else I will come and strike the land with total destruction' (Malachi 4:5–6). Elijah had not died (2 Kings 2), so his return was anticipated.

[122] Hooker, *Mark*, 160–61.

[123] Josephus wrote: 'However, he fell in love with Herodias, this last Herod's wife, who was the daughter of Aristobulus their brother, and the sister of Agrippa the Great'. *Jewish Antiquities*, 18.5.1.

[124] If the brother had died and there were no children, then such a marriage was permitted and was known as a levirate marriage.

authority, (for example, Romans 13:1–7; 1 Peter 2:13–17), this does not imply a passive quietism or withdrawal from society. Criticism may be made, especially when a person in authority is acting in a manner contrary to God's commands or, more fundamentally, a state commands that which God forbids. John criticised Herod, and elsewhere Jesus called him a 'fox' (Luke 13:32).

The king, knowing John to be righteous and holy, would often go to hear him, and though puzzled by what John said, he still liked to listen. Holiness and truth remain attractive and prick the consciences of even the least likely people. Yet for all that, to listen to the truth is not to submit to it (see Ezekiel 33:30–33). Herod was glad to hear John but was unwilling to give up Herodias. His was a conscience troubled, but he had not the faith to act on it. He was the stony ground of the parable of the sower. To be close to the kingdom of God is still to lie outside its bounds (see also Mark 12:34).

Unsurprisingly, Herodias took against John the Baptist, and she sought to do him harm. Her chance came at Herod's birthday party, an event that would have been considered pagan by pious Jews.[125] At this stage it is important to put to one side the legends that have grown up around this account, especially the images conjured up by artists over the years. The daughter's name is not given (Salome is mentioned later by Mark, but as a witness to the resurrection, not as Herodias's daughter), and she was referred to by the diminutive form of the word 'girl'. She was likely a child dancing, and there is no hint of eroticism. When Herod makes his extravagant oath, he is joking with a little girl.

In making his oath, Herod handed Herodias her chance. Jesus's command is sound: 'Do not swear an oath at all . . . All you need to say is simply "Yes," or "No"; anything beyond this comes from the evil one' (Matthew 5:34,37). A Christian's character is marked by holiness, not oaths, a lesson starkly illustrated by the sorry affair of Jephthah's oath (Judges 11).

Herodias, though, saw her opportunity and suggested the young girl asked for John's head. The girl then went to the king and

---

125 Strauss, *Mark*, 265.

embellished her mother's request: she not only wanted John's head, but also wanted it served up on a dish.

It was here that Herod's folly was laid bare. He was trapped between losing face and executing an innocent man. He was clearly distressed by this request but wanted to save face. All through this passage we see a man who was intrigued by what is right, but in the end was weak in the face of his family and friends. He would not give up Herodias and so set in motion a chain of events leading to John's death. All this is a stark contrast with John the Baptist, who was willing to speak the truth, whatever the cost. Herod, seemingly without pause, sent the executioner to kill John and bring his head. This was placed on a dish and presented to the young girl.

This done, John's disciples came and laid his corpse in a tomb.

This tale is a reminder that holding fast to God's commands can be costly indeed, especially when the king – or state – promotes an alternative view. As some parts of the word secularise, the Christian will only find greater points of conflict in issues of morality, and those living under atheistic regimes will similarly find divergences. The Christian living in a non-Christian or post-Christian land will have to stand firm. Such fearlessness might cost one dearly, but it is the path set out for us by Christ himself.

3

From Jew to Gentile

MARK 6:30–8:21

1. Bread and water • Mark 6:30–56

The twin miracles of the feeding of the five thousand and the walking on the water are closely tied together and are best taken as a pair. After he had walked on the water, Jesus climbed into the boat, and the disciples were 'completely amazed, for they had not understood about the loaves' (Mark 6:51–2). These two miracles together demonstrated something deep about Jesus's true nature and pointed to his divinity.

Feeding of the five thousand (6:30–44)

Jesus feeds the five thousand

30 The apostles gathered round Jesus and reported to him all they had done and taught. **31** Then, because so many people were coming and going that they did not even have a chance to eat, he said to them, 'Come with me by yourselves to a quiet place and get some rest.'

32 So they went away by themselves in a boat to a solitary place. **33** But many who saw them leaving recognised them and ran on foot from all the towns and got there ahead of them. **34** When Jesus landed and saw a large crowd, he had compassion on them, because they were like sheep without a shepherd. So he began teaching them many things.

35 By this time it was late in the day, so his disciples came to him. 'This is a remote place,' they said, 'and it's already very late. **36** Send the people away so that they can go to the surrounding countryside and villages and buy themselves something to eat.'

37 But he answered, 'You give them something to eat.'

They said to him, 'That would take more than half a year's wages^e! Are we to go and spend that much on bread and give it to them to eat?'

38 'How many loaves do you have?' he asked. 'Go and see.'

When they found out, they said, 'Five – and two fish.'

39 Then Jesus told them to make all the people sit down in groups on the green grass. **40** So they sat down in groups of hundreds and fifties.

41 Taking the five loaves and the two fish and looking up to heaven, he gave thanks and broke the loaves. Then he gave them to his disciples to distribute to the people. He also divided the two fish among them all. **42** They all ate and were satisfied, **43** and the disciples picked up twelve basketfuls of broken pieces of bread and fish. **44** The number of the men who had eaten was five thousand.

_____
e 37 Greek *take two hundred denarii*

This passage begins by referring back to the sending out of the twelve (Mark 6:7–13), who are now called apostles. This preaching tour fulfilled the nature of their calling ('that they might be with him and that he might send them out to preach and to have authority to drive out demons' Mark 3:14–15) and underscored their particular ministry. The apostles were those sent by Christ to preach and to extend his work, and as they returned they were clearly keen to report back.

There is an irony here as they still had not fully grasped Jesus's mission. Later in this chapter we read that 'their hearts were hardened' (Mark 6:52), and a little later Jesus asked, 'Are you so dull?' (Mark 7:18). God is able to use imperfect ministers (2 Corinthians 4:7), and the task of deepening discipleship is lifelong. Success should not bring stagnation.

Once they had reported back, Jesus invited the apostles to go to a place of rest. The place where they were was bustling to such an extent that it was not even possible to eat. He was aware of their need for rest, and his concern was for them as people rather than their work. An important lesson for us to learn. From Matthew 14:13 we learn that Jesus had just been informed of John the Baptist's death, and this may also have given a reason to go aside. Thomas Aquinas (1225–74) identified three main benefits in this type of withdrawal:

rest for the body, an opportunity for prayer (see Luke 6:12) and to guard against seeking popularity.[1] Time spent aside with God is not time that is wasted, but rather should be the regular punctuation of the Christian life.

This coming aside was intended to take the disciples away from the bustle of the crowds so that they may have rest in a desolate place (literally 'wilderness').[2] Jesus, though, was to be with them. Here was a retreat to commune with Christ, rather than simply to escape busyness. This was a preparation for the miracles to come. We are not told where the group headed, but it would seem they were going to the far side of the Sea of Galilee (Mark 6:53). Wherever it was, the crowd were able to follow along the shore.

Rather than escaping the crowds, Jesus was now faced with a large crowd and he had compassion on them because 'they were like sheep without a shepherd'. This is a phrase with rich Old Testament overtones (see 1 Kings 22:17; Ezekiel 34:4–5) and is a judgment on the poor leadership of Israel which was all too evident in the previous passage. The use of the phrase in Ezekiel is essentially one of hope, since God himself 'will search for my sheep and look after them. As a shepherd looks after his scattered flock when he is with them, so will I look after my sheep. I will rescue them from all the places where they were scattered on a day of clouds and darkness' (Ezekiel 34:11–12). God himself will gather the lost sheep.

The imagery of shepherdless sheep and the wilderness come together in Numbers 27:17 when the Hebrews stood at the edge of the Promised Land. Having been informed that he himself would not enter, Moses asked God to appoint another leader so that 'the LORD's people will not be like sheep without a shepherd'. It then fell to Joshua to lead the people from the wilderness into the land flowing with milk and honey.[3] Jesus here stood as the true leader of the people, the one who would lead them to the promised rest in the Promised Land.

---

[1] *Summa Theologica*, 3 q.40 a.1 ad 3.
[2] This word is often translated as 'wilderness', and elsewhere in the Gospel can be found in Mark 1:3, 4, 12, 13, 35, 45.
[3] For more on this, see Ulrich Mauser, *Christ in the Wilderness: The Wilderness Theme in the Second Gospel and Its Basis in the Biblical Tradition* (London: SCM Press, 1963).

This shepherding role of Jesus lies at the heart of the unity of the church (see John 10:16). It is as the church follows its one leader that it becomes one flock. It is important to note that Jesus's shepherd-like compassion resulted in teaching, and not feeding (unlike in Mark 8:2). Once more the message was at the fore, and it was the disciples who, later in the day, were concerned about the hunger of the crowd. The gospel is to be preached as well as lived; words are needed as well as deeds. The whole gospel is to be preached to the whole person: mind, body and soul.

Jesus's actions in feeding the crowd are an example of his mercy, and all were fed without distinction and without coercion. This was no 'bait and switch' exercise where the crowds were given food in return for following Christ.[4] Rather this was an exercise of common grace, where God's mercy extended to believer and unbeliever alike.

The shepherd imagery also calls to mind Psalm 23, where there are a number of parallels to be found. The crowd are beside water and seated on green grass (see Psalm 23:2 and Mark 6:39). There is imagery of a banquet, implied by the crowd sitting in groups (*symposia symposia*), which describes 'a party of people eating together'. In fact, the literal meaning of *symposia* is 'drinking together', which would evoke the cup of Psalm 23:5, and there is abundant provision (Psalm 23:5, see Mark 6:43).

There are still other important Old Testament allusions. Feeding a multitude in the wilderness recalls the provision of manna in Exodus 16,[5] and at the time of Christ a tradition had developed that the Messiah would feed his people with manna (2 Baruch 29:8). This would account for the reaction of the crowd in John's account (John 6:14–15).[6] However, as Jesus made clear in John 6:32, it was not Moses who provided the manna but the LORD himself (in Exodus 16:10 we see the presence of the LORD in the cloud). The implication is clear:

---

[4] N. R. M. Fredes, 'The Kingdom of God: Latin American Biblical Reflections on Eschatology', in *Majority World Theology: Christian Doctrine in Global Context*, ed. G. L. Green, S. T. Pardue and K. K. Yeo (Downers Grove: IVP Academic, 2020), 660.
[5] Some might object that there are no fish provided with the manna, but Mark downplays the role of the fish in the passage and the real focus is on the loaves.
[6] The 'Prophet' refers to Moses (see Deuteronomy 18:14–22).

Jesus was no second Moses or Prophet (Deuteronomy 18:14–22). He was fulfilling the prophesied actions of the LORD.

This theme of God feeding his people in the wilderness can also be found in Isaiah 49:9–10, which prophesied a return from exile which echoed the Exodus. In that passage we have the LORD feeding his people on the way, leading them by the water and having mercy on them. As was the case with the provision of manna, it was the LORD who would feed and not a second Moses. In fact, within Isaiah 40–50, it was prophesied that the LORD himself would shepherd his people once more (Isaiah 40:11; see also Exodus 15:13; Psalm 77:20; 78:52), the wilderness would be transformed into a place of fertility and provision (Isaiah 43:19–20; 49:9ff; see also Exodus 17:2–7; Numbers 20:8) and the people would be fed and watered (Isaiah 49:9–10; see 48:21). This Exodus-like return would be preceded by a second period in the desert (see Hosea 2:14; Ezekiel 20:35–8; Isaiah 40:3; 48:20–22) where Israel would once more encounter God. A further echo of the Exodus in the feeding of the five thousand can be seen in the numbers of people in the groups (verse 40) which echoes the division of the men at that time (Exodus 18:21, 25).

For many years, especially at the beginning of the last century, this passage was held to have eucharistic overtones owing to the similarities of language and action to the events in the upper room. Recent years, however, have seen a reconsideration. The actions of Jesus in taking, breaking and blessing the bread are common to Jewish meals, with Jesus taking the role of the host as, for example, Paul did in Acts 27:35. There are also significant differences between this account and the Last Supper which undermine the parallels: there is no wine but there is fish, there is no body/blood reference and there is food left over.[7]

Given all this, it would appear that the three strongest Old Testament echoes in this passage are the manna of Exodus 16, the

---

[7] Some have also noted parallels to Elisha's multiplication of loaves (2 Kings 4:42–4): Elisha takes barley loaves and tells his servant to distribute the food; the servant objects that there is not enough to feed a hundred people; the distribution is commanded nonetheless, and some was left. However, it is best to see the feeding of the five thousand and the provision by Elisha as both alluding to the manna independently of each other.

shepherd of Psalm 23 and the hope for a return from exile in Isaiah. These are all actions carried out by God. It is the LORD who is the shepherd and the LORD who provided the manna and the LORD who will once more feed his people while they are on the way back from exile. Jesus is shown to be divine since he carries out the actions of the LORD.

Mark concludes by numbering the crowd: five thousand *men*. While it might be that he is simply not recording the women and children who were present, some have found military implications in that phrase. John the Baptist had just been killed, and might it be that a group of men had come out, ready for a revolution? If this is the case, might the division of men into various groups also have military overtones? The fact that, in John's Gospel, we read that the crowd were seeking to make Jesus king gives some credence to this idea (John 6:15). The men were seeking an armed rebellion, but Jesus was seeking something deeper.[8]

Walking on the water (6:45–56)

Jesus walks on the water

45 Immediately Jesus made his disciples get into the boat and go on ahead of him to Bethsaida, while he dismissed the crowd. 46 After leaving them, he went up on a mountainside to pray.

47 Later that night, the boat was in the middle of the lake, and he was alone on land. 48 He saw the disciples straining at the oars, because the wind was against them. Shortly before dawn he went out to them, walking on the lake. He was about to pass by them, 49 but when they saw him walking on the lake, they thought he was a ghost. They cried out, 50 because they all saw him and were terrified.

Immediately he spoke to them and said, 'Take courage! It is I. Don't be afraid.' 51 Then he climbed into the boat with them, and the wind died down. They were completely amazed, 52 for they had not understood about the loaves; their hearts were hardened.

53 When they had crossed over, they landed at Gennesaret and anchored there. 54 As soon as they got out of the

---

[8] For an influential article on this, see Hugh Montefiore, 'Revolt in the Desert', *New Testament Studies* 8, no. 2 (1962).

boat, people recognised Jesus. 55 They
ran throughout that whole region and
carried those who were ill on mats to
wherever they heard he was. 56 And
wherever he went - into villages,
towns or countryside - they placed
those who were ill in the market-
places. They begged him to let them
touch even the edge of his cloak, and
all who touched it were healed.

No sooner had the crowd been fed than the disciples were dismissed.
The word translated 'he made' (ēnagkasen) is a strong one and is
normally translated as 'compelled' or 'forced' (e.g., Luke 14:23; 2
Corinthians 12:11). This suggests that the disciples were unwilling
to be dismissed and leave Jesus behind. As we have seen, the crowd
were seeking to make Jesus king (John 6:15), and we might speculate
that this was in the minds of the disciples too. Jesus wanted them
out of the way, and once he had dealt with the crowd, he withdrew.

Only here in Mark's Gospel did Jesus depart from his disciples.[9]
This fact, coupled with Jesus' withdrawal up the mountain, gave a
pregnant pause before the walking on the water. Mountains are places
of great significance in the Old Testament: God came to Israel from
the mountain (Deuteronomy 33:2, Habakkuk 3:3), and at the great
theophany at Sinai, God moved down from the mountain to the
tabernacle (Exodus 40:34). More significant than all that is the purpose
for which Jesus ascended that height: to pray. Here is an enduring
lesson: even for Christ, prayer was an essential prelude to his activity.

Jesus remained on the mountain until the evening, and the text
emphasises that after coming down he was alone on the land (Mark
6:47). It was evening (opsias refers to the period between later afternoon and darkness), and he saw the disciples struggling because the
wind was against them.

This passage has often been interpreted as a rescue tale, rather
like the stilling of the storm in chapter 4. If this is correct, the point
of the miracle was to demonstrate Jesus's mastery over nature, but
the passage itself does not support this reading. The word translated
as 'straining' (basanizomenous) has overtones of torture and torment,
which would suggest that the disciples were in pain, but not in

---

[9] Bas M. Van Iersel, *Mark: A Reader-Response Commentary* (Sheffield: Sheffield
Academic Press, 1997), 231.

danger of death.[10] There is no mention of a storm, simply that the wind was in the wrong direction, and some note that crossing the Sea of Galilee, even in bad conditions, would take between six and eight hours.[11] The most significant thing, though, was Jesus's own reaction. If the disciples were in danger of death, would he have taken so long in coming to them? He saw them in the evening, and then went to them shortly before dawn.

There is also the question of quite why Jesus, when he got to them, wanted to pass by them. This is all rather strange, since it suggests that the point of Jesus's actions was not to help the disciples but rather to go on by to some other location. The Greek is clear: he *intended* to pass them by. There have been many answers given to this, but it is best understood against the context of the Old Testament.

In Exodus 33:18–34:6 we find the verb for passing by used in several places:

Then Moses said, 'Now show me your glory.'

And the LORD said, 'I will cause all my goodness to *pass* in front of you, and I will proclaim my name, the LORD, in your presence . . .'

Then the LORD said, 'There is a place near me where you may stand on a rock. When my glory *passes by*, I will put you in a cleft in the rock and cover you with my hand until I have *passed by* . . .'

Then the LORD came down in the cloud and stood there with him and proclaimed his name, the LORD. And he *passed* in front of Moses, proclaiming, 'The LORD, the LORD . . .'[12]

---

[10] The other occurrences of the verb in the New Testament do not have any hint of mortal danger (Matthew 8:6, 29; 14:24; Mark 5:7; Luke 8:28; 2 Peter 2:8; Revelation 9:5; 11:10; 12:2; 14:10; 20:10).
[11] Eduard Schweizer, *Good News According to Mark*, trans. Donald A. Madvig (London: SPCK, 1971), 142. See also James R. Edwards, *The Gospel According to Mark* (Leicester: Apollos, 2002), 197.
[12] My emphasis.

There is similar language used in I Kings 19:11, where God appeared to Elijah after he had fled to Horeb:

> The LORD said, 'Go out and stand on the mountain in the presence of the LORD, for the LORD is about to *pass by*.'[13]

A further evocative passage (involving walking on water) is Job 9:8–11, where Job speaks of God:

> He alone stretches out the heavens
>   and treads on the waves of the sea.
> He is the Maker of the Bear and Orion,
>   the Pleiades and the constellations of the south.
> He performs wonders that cannot be fathomed,
>   miracles that cannot be counted.
> When he *passes me*, I cannot see him;
>   when he goes by, I cannot perceive him.[14]

The best understanding of 'passing by' is not that Jesus wished to walk on beyond the disciples, or even that he went to them to rescue them, but rather that Jesus intended to manifest his glory in the manner of the theophanies to Moses and Elijah.[15] To 'pass by' is a term closely associated with theophany (an appearing of God) within the Old Testament.[16]

This link to the appearances of the LORD in the Old Testament is further strengthened by the words Jesus used when he spoke to the disciples. First he told them not to be afraid, a phrase that can be found in the appearances of God to Abraham (Genesis 15:1, 26:24). Moses also told the people not to be afraid when they saw the great cloud on top of Mount Sinai at the giving of the Law

---

[13] My emphasis.

[14] My emphasis.

[15] These two figures reappear at the transfiguration.

[16] Joel Marcus comments that it is 'almost a technical term for divine epiphany in the Septuagint'. Joel Marcus, *Mark 1–8: A New Translation with Introduction and Commentary* (New York: Doubleday, 2000), 426.

(Exodus 20:18–20), and when a mighty angel appeared to Daniel, Daniel is told, 'Do not be afraid' (Daniel 10:12).

In passing, we might note that this divine command not to be afraid is grounded upon God himself. The disciple is not to be afraid since he or she may rest upon the mighty power and love of God (1 John 4:18). Freedom from fear, even in the midst of persecution or trouble, is the birthright of the Christian who has been adopted by God (Romans 8:15). Better to gaze upon God than upon the trouble that confronts.

Second, and even more telling, is the phrase, 'It is I,' which is more literally translated as, 'I am.' Here is the divine name (Exodus 3:14), which is normally rendered 'the LORD' in Bible translations. The combination of the very name of God with Jesus's desire to 'pass by' strongly evokes Exodus 34:6: 'And he passed in front of Moses, proclaiming, "The LORD, the LORD . . ."' Jesus's desire was fulfilled: he had passed by the disciples and proclaimed his name to them. He is the LORD.

After this, he climbed into the boat with the disciples and the wind was stilled. The disciples 'were completely amazed, for they had not understood about the loaves; their hearts were hardened' (Mark 6:52). This raises the question: what had they failed to understand? To answer this, we must identify the link between this passage and the feeding of the five thousand. What was misunderstood cannot be the fact that Jesus was the Messiah. As has been seen, there was a strong hope for a messiah who would provide manna, and it would seem a sound conclusion that the disciples were summarily dismissed because they had understood Jesus to be simply a human messiah, a religious and political leader.

Yet messiahs do not walk on water, nor do they describe themselves in terms so reminiscent of the divine name. Nor, it should be repeated, did Moses feed the Israelites with manna. That was the work of the LORD, who appeared in a cloud at the time.

It would seem that the only satisfactory way to interpret both passages together is by means of theophany. It is what links the feeding of the multitude (see Exodus 16:15) with the walking on the sea (see Job 9:8–11), the passing by of the disciples (see Exodus 34:6), the command not to be afraid (see Genesis 26:24) and the self-identification as 'I am' (see Exodus 3:14; 34:6).

Yet, for all this, the disciples failed to grasp the importance of what they had witnessed (verses 51–2). This was not because such an event was obscure or difficult to interpret, but simply because their hearts were hardened (and, it would appear, were still hardened in Mark 8:17). It is not entirely clear why their hearts were so hardened, but there may be parallels to the hardening of Pharaoh's heart so that God's power might be more fully displayed (see Romans 9:17–18).

Thomas Manton drew a helpful distinction between what he termed a total (permanent) or partial (temporary) hardness of heart. The Christian still retains some of the stony heart of old and, for a season, may experience a distance or coldness to things spiritual (see Psalm 119:36). This is a matter of lament, which in itself proves that this is not a total hardening of the heart. He described the condition:

A Christian is a compound creature; he hath hardness as well as softness. When their hardness prevaileth, for the present they mourn less for sin, and do not tremble at the word, and are not affected with providences, slight the warnings and motions of the Holy Spirit, are more dead in duty, find not alike savour in the promises, and duties seem more irksome to them. An hard heart maketh their work seem hard and tedious.[17]

This partial hardness is a matter for prayer.

Rather than land at Bethsaida (Mark 6:45), the disciples landed at Gennesaret, which is some five miles or so to the west of Bethsaida and a couple of miles to the west of Capernaum. The boat was brought into the harbour and anchored. As soon as he came ashore, Jesus was recognised and the sick were gathered so that he might heal them. It would appear that the rejection he had suffered in his home town did not extend this far around the shore, although it would seem he was more in demand as a healer than as a teacher. Christ the shepherd tended his flock.

---

[17] Thomas Manton, 'Sermons Upon Mark 3:5, Sermon I', in *The Complete Works of Thomas Manton, Volume 17* (London: James Nisbet & Co., 1974), 198.

2. The Gentiles • Mark 7:1–8:21

After the revelation of the true nature of Christ in the previous section, there now follows a series of incidents that mark the inclusion of the Gentiles into the purposes of God. There is an argument about the traditions surrounding the Law, which leads Jesus to declare, 'Nothing outside a person can defile them by going into them. Rather, it is what comes out of a person that defiles them' (Mark 7:15). As if to underscore that point, Jesus then ministers among the Gentiles, where he finds in a Syrophoenician woman an understanding missing from the Pharisees and the teachers of the law. As she debated with Jesus, she noted that 'even the dogs under the table eat the children's crumbs'. At the feeding of the four thousand, we see that enacted as the Gentiles receive that which had earlier been given to five thousand Jews.

Traditions, commandments and that which defiles (7:1–23)

That which defiles

7 The Pharisees and some of the teachers of the law who had come from Jerusalem gathered round Jesus ²and saw some of his disciples eating food with hands that were defiled, that is, unwashed. ³(The Pharisees and all the Jews do not eat unless they give their hands a ceremonial washing, holding to the tradition of the elders. ⁴When they come from the market-place they do not eat unless they wash. And they observe many other traditions, such as the washing of cups, pitchers and kettles.[a])

⁵So the Pharisees and teachers of the law asked Jesus, 'Why don't your disciples live according to the tradition of the elders instead of eating their food with defiled hands?'

⁶He replied, 'Isaiah was right when he prophesied about you hypocrites; as it is written:

' "These people honour me
    with their lips,
  but their hearts are far from
    me.
7 They worship me in vain;
    their teachings are merely
    human rules."[b]

⁸You have let go of the commands of God and are holding on to human traditions.'

9 And he continued, 'You have a fine way of setting aside the commands of God in order to observe[c] your own traditions! 10 For Moses said, "Honour your father and mother,"[d] and, "Anyone who curses their father or mother is to be put to death."[e] 11 But you say that if anyone declares that what might have been used to help their father or mother is Corban (that is, devoted to God) – 12 then you no longer let them do anything for their father or mother. 13 Thus you nullify the word of God by your tradition that you have handed down. And you do many things like that.'

14 Again Jesus called the crowd to him and said, 'Listen to me, everyone, and understand this. 15 Nothing outside a person can defile them by going into them. Rather, it is what comes out of a person that defiles them.' [16][f]

17 After he had left the crowd and entered the house, his disciples asked him about this parable. 18 'Are you so dull?' he asked. 'Don't you see that nothing that enters a person from the outside can defile them? 19 For it doesn't go into their heart but into their stomach, and then out of the body.' (In saying this, Jesus declared all foods clean.)

20 He went on: 'What comes out of a person is what defiles them. 21 For it is from within, out of a person's heart, that evil thoughts come – sexual immorality, theft, murder, 22 adultery, greed, malice, deceit, lewdness, envy, slander, arrogance and folly. 23 All these evils come from inside and defile a person.'

---

a 4 Some early manuscripts *pitchers, kettles and dining couches*
b 6,7 Isaiah 29:13
c 9 Some manuscripts *set up*
d 10 Exodus 20:12; Deut. 5:16
e 10 Exodus 21:17; Lev. 20:9
f 16 Some manuscripts include here the words of 4:23.

Once more we find the religious leaders seeking out Jesus, and here they enter into a debate with him about the 'tradition of the elders'. The Pharisees were concerned not only with the keeping of the Old Testament Law but also with the traditions that had grown up around it. This set them apart from other groupings in ancient Israel, as the first-century historian Josephus noted:

What I would now explain is this, that the Pharisees have delivered to the people a great many observances by succession from their fathers, which are not written in the law of Moses; and for that reason it is that the Sadducees reject them and say that we are to esteem those observances to be obligatory which are in the written word, but are not to observe what are derived from the tradition of our forefathers; and concerning these things it is that great disputes and differences have arisen among them, while the Sadducees are able to persuade none but the rich, and have not the populace obsequious to them, but the Pharisees have the multitude on their side.[18]

This observance of tradition brought the Pharisees into dispute with Jesus over a number of issues: eating with sinners (Mark 2:16), fasting (Mark 2:18), Sabbath (Mark 2:24; 3:2), handwashing (Mark 7:5) and divorce (Mark 10:2). Intertwined with this was a desire to see Old Testament priestly purity laws applied to the population as a whole. As Jacob Neusner noted, 'Pharisaism compared the table to the altar, the home to the Temple, and the private person to the priest.'[19] So, for example, the ceremonial washing in this passage might be seen as the population following the laws given to the priesthood in Exodus 30:20–21. The fact that 'all the Jews' did this points to the popularity of the Pharisees and their teaching.

Jesus countered by quoting Isaiah 29:13, a passage that drew a contrast between actions and motivations. To say the right things does not imply your heart is right, and human-made rules of worship are vain. There is a dangerous tendency for human rules to trump the rules of God, or for interpretations of Scripture to become more important than the Scripture itself. We should beware separating the commands of God from God himself: this simply leaves us with bare rituals and traditions.

Jesus passed sentence on the Pharisees: 'You have let go of the commands of God and are holding on to human traditions.' He illustrated the problem by giving the example of Corban, the practice of declaring something as a sacrificial offering before the sacrifice itself was actually carried out. If such a declaration was made, then the thing offered could not be used by any others even if the offering

---

[18] *Jewish Antiquities*, 13.297–8. Translation from Whiston, *Works of Josephus*, 355.
[19] Jacob Neusner, *The Idea of Purity in Ancient Judaism: The Haskell Lectures, 1972–1973* (Eugene: Wipf and Stock, 2006), 3.

was never made. This was seen as a way of denying other people the use of an object. You could designate something as Corban with no intention of sacrificing it, and so stop it being used by others.

Here is an example of something that might be seen as a good intention (making an offering to God) being used for malevolent ends. Honouring parents is one of the Ten Commandments, Proverbs 28:24 addresses robbing parents and Exodus 21:17 stipulates that those who curse their father or mother should be put to death. All this had been trumped by the human tradition of Corban.

Practices introduced with good intentions can soon become twisted, or be followed by those whose hearts are far from God. It is easy to point the finger at traditions in other forms of Christianity without ever considering our own. So, for example, it is important to separate evangelical culture from evangelical theology. The latter is crucial; the former is simply a flavour. All too often it is said that 'proper' churches must have a particular style of worship or pattern of meetings, yet these are issues of culture. There is a danger in attempting to impose one culture onto another. Rather, a church's 'flavour' should be the product of the seed of the gospel taking root in local soil. All worship is to be held up to the standard of the Scriptures, but that does not mean it should all look the same.

Before we move on to the next section of this passage, Jesus's words regarding Scripture are worthy of some attention. He was happy to introduce the words of Moses as the 'commands of God' (verse 9). This illustrates his view of both the inspiration of the Old Testament and its authorship. The words are those of both Moses and God. There is a 'double agency' in their authorship.[20]

Jesus called the crowd to him so that he could teach on this matter, and he gave a weighty introduction: 'Listen to me, everyone, and understand this.' Being defiled, he taught, is an inside-out matter, and someone cannot be defiled by what they consume. It is what comes from within that defiles: it is a matter of the heart (for more see the comments on Mark 1:12–13). Jesus 'breaks the bond between

---

[20] Henri A. G. Blocher, 'God and the Scripture Writers: The Question of Double Authorship', in *The Enduring Authority of the Christian Scriptures*, ed. D. A. Carson (Grand Rapids: Eerdmans, 2016), 499.

the ethical and the physical'.[21] It is the heart where obedience is to be found, not simply in actions. Christianity is to do with the renovation of the soul, not mere moralism. Physical acts are not the basis of ethics, but rather the attitude of the heart. Ritualism will not do. Physical acts will not make up for an unchanged heart.

Once back in the privacy of a house, the disciples quizzed Jesus, as they had not understood the teaching. At this stage the disciples often failed to understand Jesus since the resurrection had yet to fully reveal him to them. To divorce Jesus from the resurrection, to have Jesus as simply a good teacher, will lead to a radical misunderstanding of what he taught. He explained that it is the condition of the heart that defiles, and by saying this echoed the prophetic tradition seen in Isaiah 1:11–16, Jeremiah 7:22–3, Hosea 6:6 and Amos 5:21–7. More than that, as Mark noted, he declared all food clean (Mark 7:19; see also Peter's vision in Acts 10:9–16).

This raises questions: what about food laws in Leviticus 11? Might we also set aside other Old Testament laws? There are a few answers that might be given here. First of all, Jesus here only speaks about food laws, and there is no discussion of other areas of the Law. To see this as setting aside all laws is not warranted by the text. Second, we should note that when Jesus is speaking about what *does* defile, he includes many attitudes that are subjects of Old Testament Law. If his intention was to release everyone from the need for obedience to the entirety of Law, why would he then immediately rebind them?[22]

External things do not cause defilement, he explained; rather, 'evil thoughts'. Jesus then listed twelve sins that arise from these thoughts, before restating that all these come from inside a person.[23] This insistence on the internal nature of sin is vital to a proper understanding of it. The human is one who is fallen, where the likeness to God (Genesis 1:26–7) has become blurred. Jesus left no place for the notion of a sinless person, nor for a denial of the fallen nature of humanity.

Elsewhere, Jesus contrasted the prayers of the Pharisee and the

---

[21] Herman Bavinck, *Reformed Dogmatics Volume 3: Sin and Salvation in Christ* (Grand Rapids: Baker Books, 2006), 135.

[22] See also the discussion on the Law in the comments on Mark 1:40–45.

[23] See also Matthew 5:27–30 where this teaching is reinforced.

tax collector (Luke 18:9–14), and we see in that parable the contrast between pride and humility. The fall still dogs the Christian. 'The fallen Christian understands that the sin is of his own making, and he sorrows and beats his breast,' said Cyprian of Carthage (c. 210–58). 'The schismatic swells with pride in his fallen condition, and taking his pleasure in his own sins . . . he entices the sheep from their shepherd, he upsets solemn obligations to God.'[24]

All of this means that proper attention should be given to thoughts, and not simply to actions. Evil thoughts are not simply sinful when they are acted out, but are sinful in and of themselves. The battle against sin begins in the mind. 'Desiring must be right as well as doings, and Pharisaic externality is not enough,' as J. I. Packer put it.[25]

The list of the twelve thoughts is instructive, and may be used as a checklist for the soul. The first six are plural and generally denote acts. The second six, all in the singular, refer to attitudes or states of mind. The two sets are, obviously, linked: our attitudes drive our actions, and our actions inform and harden our attitudes. The ongoing work of sanctification – the 'renewing of your mind' (Romans 12:2) – affects both thoughts and deeds. Whereas lists of external sins were not uncommon among the rabbis, Jesus looked also to the heart.[26]

In an age where sexual liberation is normalised, it is sobering to see that Jesus places sexual immorality (*porneia*) at the top of the list. The Judeo-Christian view of sexual relations as belonging solely within marriage (understood as between one man and one woman) stood in contrast to the nations around them, and served to protect *all* women, regardless of their social standing. A woman was no longer a chattel 'but a partner of equal dignity before both man and God'.[27] Harper notes that 'Jewish and Christian πορνεία [*porneia*] could evoke the whole array of extramarital sex acts of

---

[24] *On The Unity of the Catholic Church*, 19. Translation taken from Cyprian of Carthage, *On the Church: Select Treatises*, trans. Allen Brent (Crestwood: St Vladimir's Seminary Press, 2006), 172–3.

[25] J. I. Packer, *Concise Theology: A Guide to Historic Christian Beliefs* (Wheaton: Tyndale House, 1993), 93.

[26] Edwards, *Mark*, 213.

[27] Friedrich Hauck and Seigfried Schulz, 'Pornē Ktl', in *Theological Dictionary of the New Testament*, ed. Gerhard Kittel, Geoffrey W. Bromiley and Gerhard Friedrich (Grand Rapids: Eerdmans, 1964), 6.590.

which Greek and Roman culture approved',[28] and we might see such an array listed in the section of the Law dealing with sexual immorality (Leviticus 18), as well as Romans 1:24–7. The importance given to the avoidance of sexual immorality can be seen in its inclusion in the apostolic prohibitions of Acts 15:20, 29 and 21:25 as well as the repeated warnings of 1 Corinthians 5:1–13, 6:9–20, 7:1–5; 2 Corinthians 12:19–21; Ephesians 5:3–12; Colossians 3:5–11; 1 Thessalonians 4:3–8; 1 Timothy 1:8–11; Hebrews 12:15–17; 13:4; Revelation 21:8, 22:15. This is no slight matter.

The remaining items of the list are clearer in their meaning, but are no less important for all that. Theft might be major, but it might as easily be some small 'borrowing' unnoticed by others. Murder is a clear evil, but Jesus warned that to be angry is to be liable to judgment (Matthew 5:21–2). Adultery might be committed in the heart (Matthew 5:28), and in a world where pornography is widely accepted this should give us pause for thought. Greed is stirred up when advertisers place desires in our heads, and malice stalks the pages of social media. Deceit might be the omission of the truth, and lewdness is all too often a sin caused by trying to fit in with peers. Envy denies the hand of God in providence, and slander is another common feature of social media. Arrogance can happen in the smallest of groups, and folly denies that we are the Lord's and accountable to him.

Who can find themselves absent from such a list as this? What comfort it is that 'Christ Jesus came into the world to save sinners' (1 Timothy 1:15)! Each and every one of us falls into that category, and so we can throw ourselves on Christ's abundant grace.

The Syrophoenician woman (7:24–30)

Jesus honours a Syro-Phoenician woman's faith

24 Jesus left that place and went to the vicinity of Tyre.g He entered a house and did not want anyone to know it; yet he could not keep his presence secret. 25 In fact, as soon as she heard about him, a woman

---

[28] Kyle Harper, 'Porneia: The Making of a Christian Sexual Norm', *Journal of Biblical Literature* 131, no. 2 (2012), 383.

whose little daughter was possessed by an impure spirit came and fell at his feet. **26** The woman was a Greek, born in Syrian Phoenicia. She begged Jesus to drive the demon out of her daughter.

27 'First let the children eat all they want,' he told her, 'for it is not right to take the children's bread and toss it to the dogs.'

28 'Lord,' she replied, 'even the dogs under the table eat the children's crumbs.'

29 Then he told her, 'For such a reply, you may go; the demon has left your daughter.'

30 She went home and found her child lying on the bed, and the demon gone.

_____

g 24 Many early manuscripts _Tyre and Sidon_

Jesus travelled out of Galilee, about thirty-five miles to the north into the coastal region of Tyre, which Josephus described as 'notoriously our bitterest enemies'.[29] It would appear that Jesus was seeking to withdraw from the crowds, and there is no hint in the passage that he was seeking to engage in a mission to this area. That he knew a house in which he might stay suggests that Jesus had some connections in that area. However, his desire for secrecy was frustrated. A Greek woman sought him out as her daughter had been possessed by an impure spirit. Like Legion and Jairus, she fell at his knees in an attitude of prayer and begged him for help.

The woman is identified as coming from Syrian Phoenicia, which would most likely place her as coming from the southern part of Syria. There has been plenty of discussion as to quite where the term 'Syrophoenician' originates. Some suggest it was to distinguish the Phoenicians who came from Libya from those who came from Syria. Others suggest it was to distinguish northern Syrians from southern Syrians. Some argue that Mark's use of the term points to the Gospel being written in Rome, where we see the earliest use of the word. Yet others take it as being evidence that the Gospel came from Syria itself. All in all, it is better to simply concentrate on the text rather than attempting to mine it for extraneous material.[30]

_____

[29] Josephus, _Against Apion_ 1.13 1.13.70. Translation from Flavius Josephus, _The Life, Against Apion_, trans. H. St J. Thackery (London: William Heinemann, 1926), 191.

[30] See the discussions in Hengel, _Studies_, 29, and Theissen, _Context_, 244–7.

To modern ears, Jesus's answer to her was shocking: was he equating her to a dog? Was he being racist, as some suggest? It is true that his words would not have been shocking to a fellow Jew. It was not uncommon to refer to the Jews as children of God,[31] and Gentiles were often nicknamed 'dog' since, like that animal, they were considered unclean.[32] Yet even given all this, one would not expect to find this sort of language on the lips of Jesus. We are left with three options: Jesus sinned (he was just a man of his times), racism is not a sin or Jesus was not being racist. The author of the Letter to the Hebrews is quick to point out that Jesus did not sin (Hebrews 4:15, see also 1 Peter 2:22), and the logic of salvation requires a sinless saviour (2 Corinthians 5:21; 1 John 3:5). Racism *is* a sin: it is to curse one made in the image of God (James 3:9), and it is a lack of love for neighbour (Mark 12:31, 33). But is it possible for Jesus's use of 'dogs' to not be racist? Fortunately, it is.

In the Greek text it is clear that Jesus is subverting stereotypes.[33] The word translated 'dog' is, in fact, a diminutive. It does not indicate the wild dogs with which the Gentiles were identified, but rather a domestic dog. Also, he was not denying that this type of dog should receive any food, but rather that the children should eat first.[34] He was guiding her in this debate. He was teasing her towards a particular response. These were, in a happy phrase of Samuel Rutherford (1600–61), 'tempting reproaches'.[35]

The woman clearly understood Jesus's intention and was quick to join him in this verbal joust. Referring to him as 'Lord', she agreed that the food of the children should not be fed to the dogs (and she also used the diminutive form). Once again there is a subtlety in the Greek text which is not picked up in most modern translations. When Jesus referred to 'children', he used the word *teknon*, which refers to biological children. However, when the woman replied she

---

[31] Exodus 4:22–3; Deuteronomy 14:1; 32:20; Isaiah 1:1–2; 63:8; Jeremiah 3:19; Hosea 11:1.

[32] France, *Mark*, 298.

[33] See Edwards, *Mark*, from page 219.

[34] See also Romans 1:16–17 and Romans 9–11.

[35] Samuel Rutherford and Andrew Alexander Bonar, *Letters of Samuel Rutherford: With a Sketch of His Life* (Edinburgh: Banner of Truth, 1984), 306.

used a different word – *paidion* – which refers to all the children in a household, whether they are the biological children of the owner or not. The children of servants would also be covered by the term. The woman had, in turn, subverted Jesus's words.

Jesus was clearly impressed by her answer. She understood that the blessings of God would extend beyond the people of Israel (Genesis 12:3), even if they were to begin with those 'children'. She demonstrated understanding where the disciples often did not. In fact, she was the first to demonstrate a proper understanding of one of Jesus's parables.[36] 'For such a reply' the woman's request was granted, and her daughter freed from the demon.

In all of this we see Jesus demonstrating that his mission was global in scale and encompassed the Gentiles. Yes, the children were to eat the bread (the feeding of the five thousand), but the 'dogs' might also eat the crumbs (the feeding of the four thousand).

We might also note the patience of Jesus as he spoke with the woman. Evangelism is often a slow affair, a long wooing. As essential as preaching is, there is also a place for it to be accompanied by patient dialogue.

Ears opened and the tongue loosed (7:31–7)

Jesus heals a deaf and mute man

31 Then Jesus left the vicinity of Tyre and went through Sidon, down to the Sea of Galilee and into the region of the Decapolis.[h] 32 There some people brought to him a man who was deaf and could hardly talk, and they begged Jesus to place his hand on him.

33 After he took him aside, away from the crowd, Jesus put his fingers into the man's ears. Then he spat and touched the man's tongue. 34 He looked up to heaven and with a deep sigh said to him, *'Ephphatha!'* (which means 'Be opened!'). 35 At this, the man's ears were opened, his tongue was loosed and he began to speak plainly.

36 Jesus commanded them not to tell anyone. But the more he did so, the more they kept talking about it. 37 People were overwhelmed with amazement. 'He has done everything well,' they said. 'He even makes the deaf hear and the mute speak.'

---

h 31 That is, the Ten Cities

---

36 Edwards, *Mark*, 221–2.

Jesus travelled to the far side of the sea of Galilee into the Gentile region of Decapolis.[37] His route carefully avoided Jewish areas and totalled more than a hundred miles. This would suggest that he was keeping away from the growing opposition in Israel as he continued to minister among the Gentiles. This was a dramatic extension of the understanding of the scope of the Messiah: the whole world, and not just Israel, was in view.

Jesus returned to the area of his encounter with Legion and once again the sick were brought to him, this time a man who was deaf and had some kind of speech impediment. The Greek word used (*mogilalos*) is unique in the New Testament and was used only once in the Greek translation of the Old Testament (known as the Septuagint) made a couple of centuries earlier:[38]

Rejoice, O thirsty wilderness!
   Let the wilderness be glad,
   and let it blossom like a lily!
And the deserted places of the Jordan
   shall blossom and be glad.
And the glory of Lebanon has been given to it,
   as well as the honor of Carmel,
and my people shall see the glory of the Lord
   and the loftiness of God.

Be strong, you weak hands
   and feeble knees!
Give comfort,
   you who are faint of heart and mind!
   Be strong; do not fear!
Look, our God is repaying judgment;
   yes, he will repay;
   he himself will come and save us.

---

[37] A grouping of towns that shared the same Greek culture. In the Old Testament this region is known as Gilead.

[38] Edwards is particularly insightful here. Edwards, *Mark*, 224–5.

Then the eyes of the blind shall be opened,
   and the ears of the deaf shall hear;
then the lame shall leap like a deer,
   and the tongue of stammerers shall be clear,
because water has broken forth in the wilderness
   and a gully in a thirsty land;
the dry place shall turn into marshlands,
   and in the thirsty land there shall be a spring of water;
the joy of birds shall be there –
   a bed of reed and marshlands.
(Isaiah 35:1–6, NETS)

There are interesting parallels here. The reference to the wilderness brings to mind the feeding of the five thousand, and the region of Tyre and Sidon, visited in the previous passage, was also known as Lebanon. God 'himself will come and save us', and the 'blind', 'lame' and 'stammerers' will be healed. Here we have a prophetic fore-shadowing of Jesus's ministry among these Gentile regions.

No doubt the crowd surrounding Jesus was noisy and bustling, so he took the man aside. There was a very practical reason for this: when the deaf man's hearing was restored, the shock of the noise would have been overwhelming. Jesus's healings were acts of compassion, and not for the benefit of the watching crowds. Since the man was deaf, Jesus used touch to communicate his actions: first he touched his ears, and then he spat and touched the man's tongue.

The use of spittle here, and in Mark 8:23, is a striking part of the account. The use of saliva in healing was well known in the ancient world, and Pliny the Elder (AD 23–79) suggested that the saliva of a fasting woman was 'generally considered highly efficacious for bloodshot eyes'.[39] However, we should not understand this as an instance of Jesus using magic, or an example for us to follow.[40] It is

---

[39] Pliny the Elder, *The Natural History*, 28.22, trans. John Bostock (Medford: Taylor & Francis, 1855), 5304. See also Gundry, *Mark*, 389.
[40] 'The skin difference is that Jesus did not employ saliva as a rigid method of healing rather it was an occasional application. In Jesus ministry saliva symbolizes cleansing and recreation by divine virtue. The healing potency lays in Jesus the healer while in African the healing potent is believed to be in saliva itself which

more likely that Jesus was simply using touch to communicate to a man who could not hear him.

Jesus then looked to heaven, to indicate to the man the true source of his power, and sighed. Here we witness his deep compassion for the man and understand that Jesus experienced human emotion. He then uttered what is in Greek a single word, 'Be opened!' and the man was healed: he began to speak 'correctly', (*orthōs*) and his ears were opened. The healing moment was not the use of the spittle, but the single word of Christ.

Jesus commanded secrecy, but as was the case elsewhere the people did precisely the opposite. The response was overwhelming amazement, and this incident, coupled with the healing of Legion, eloquently demonstrated Jesus's concern for the Gentiles and their appreciation of him. The crowd exclaimed, 'He has done everything well.' The Jewish Messiah was winning the favour of the Gentile masses.

The Gentiles fed (8:1–10)

Jesus feeds the four thousand

8 During those days another large crowd gathered. Since they had nothing to eat, Jesus called his disciples to him and said, **2** 'I have compassion for these people; they have already been with me three days and have nothing to eat. **3** If I send them home hungry, they will collapse on the way, because some of them have come a long distance.'

4 His disciples answered, 'But where in this remote place can anyone get enough bread to feed them?'

5 'How many loaves do you have?' Jesus asked.

'Seven,' they replied.

6 He told the crowd to sit down on the ground. When he had taken the seven loaves and given thanks, he broke them and gave them to his disciples to distribute to the people, and they did so. **7** They had a few small fish as well; he gave thanks for them also and told the disciples to distribute them. **8** The people ate

---

can be used by an herbal man or by an individual as the occasion calls for.' T. O. Ebhomienlen and C. A. Ogah. 'Saliva: A Healing Technique of Jesus in African Context', *ISOR: Journal of Humanities and Social Science.* 16, no. 2 (2013): 1–7, 7. See also Michael Young Nabofa, 'Saliva Symbolism in African Belief', *Orita: Ibadan Journal of Religious Studies* 28, no. 1–2 (1996): 11–35.

and were satisfied. Afterwards the disciples picked up seven basketfuls of broken pieces that were left over. **9** About four thousand were present. After he had sent them away, **10** he got into the boat with his disciples and went to the region of Dalmanutha.

This passage sits as a pair with the feeding of the five thousand, and with it bookends a section of Mark's Gospel dealing with the inclusion of the Gentiles within Jesus's ministry and the purposes of God. As the apostle Paul commented, the gospel came 'first to the Jew, then to the Gentile' (Romans 1:16).

Presumably Jesus was still in the Decapolis, and as was the case with the five thousand, he had compassion on the crowd. This time the compassion was not because they were sheep without a shepherd, but rather because of their hunger. They had been with Jesus for three days.

Mark used an unusual word for 'with me'. *Prosmenein* does not simply mean that they were present, but rather that they were 'steadfast in association'.[41] These Gentiles were showing a loyalty that was absent from other crowds, and they had gathered from 'a long distance' to hear him. Jesus, the servant of the LORD, is 'a light for the Gentiles, that my salvation may reach to the ends of the earth' (Isaiah 49:6).

As with the five thousand, the fact that they were once again in a wilderness caused the disciples to wonder where food might be found. Jesus replied, 'How many loaves do you have?' It is tempting to think that Jesus was prompting their memory, since the disciples appeared to have so quickly forgotten the five thousand. The disciples had provisions with them – seven loaves – and this time they didn't have to go and look for bread. As with the five thousand, Jesus told the crowd to sit down (the imagery of Psalm 23 is missing here), and rather than look up and give a blessing he simply gave thanks. The bread was distributed, along with some small fish that had been similarly blessed. Afterwards, seven baskets of leftovers were collected.

There are clear parallels to the feeding of the five thousand, but to simply dismiss the feeding of the four thousand as some sort of confusion in the tradition – a kind of double reporting – is to miss

---

[41] BDAG, 883.

the point. Mark often used the literary technique of sandwiching, and this is what we have here. The Jews were fed, Jesus ministered in Gentile areas, and then the Gentiles were fed. In fact, this event might be seen as an outworking of the discussion Jesus had with the Syrophoenician woman: 'even the dogs under the table eat the children's crumbs'. We might also see parallels with the opening of the ears of the deaf man: the Gentiles now remain with Jesus to hear him teach. It is no mistake that this passage occurs after a series of encounters in Gentile areas that follow his increasing rejection in Israel (Mark 6:1–6a).

There are also some key differences between the passages. The most obvious difference is between Jews and Gentiles, but afterwards seven baskets full of scraps remained, rather than the twelve baskets left when the Jews were fed. Seeking imagery in biblical numbers is a rather hazardous occupation, but one is tempted to contrast the twelve tribes of Israel with the seven nations of Deuteronomy 7:1. It is also worth noting that the word used for basket is different in both events. When the five thousand were fed, there were twelve 'large carrying baskets' (*kophinōn*) left, whereas here there were seven 'baskets' or 'hampers' *(spuridas)*.

The final difference is the number fed: five thousand men were fed in Israel whereas four thousand people were fed here.[42] At one level we might simply say that the numbers were simply a reflection of what happened and we should not read anything into them. At another, we might see this as a reflection of Jew first and then Gentile (see Romans 1:16), the fact that the gospel of Christ spread from Jew to Gentile. Whatever is the case, once fed, the crowd were sent away, having been satisfied (Mark 8:8). Rather than having to force his disciples away, Jesus this time travelled with them to Dalmanutha.[43]

---

[42] Unlike in Mark 6:44, the Greek here is not gender specific.

[43] The whereabouts of this place is unknown, and it is not known outside the New Testament. In Matthew 15:39 the place is identified as Magadan, which would appear to be an Aramaic word, and it is likely that Dalmanutha is nearby. Archaeological work has identified a possible anchorage in that area (see James F. Strange, 'Dalmanutha', in *The Anchor Bible*, ed. David Noel Freedman (New Haven: Yale University Press, 1992).

Signs refused (8:11–13)

11 The Pharisees came and began to question Jesus. To test him, they asked him for a sign from heaven. 12 He sighed deeply and said, 'Why does this generation ask for a sign? Truly I tell you, no sign will be given to it.' 13 Then he left them, got back into the boat and crossed to the other side.

In contrast to his welcome among the Gentiles, Jesus now faced questioning from the Pharisees. He had their attention, but they did not welcome him. They were suspicious and sought to test him. The word used for 'test' (*peirazein*) carries negative overtones and is used elsewhere of the attempts of the Pharisees to entrap Jesus (Mark 10:2; 12:15), as well as in the testing in the wilderness (Mark 1:13). They asked for 'a sign from heaven'.

This curious phrase may well imply that the Pharisees thought that there was a demonic source for Jesus's miracles (see Matthew 9:34; 12:24). To ask for a sign 'from heaven' is to ask for something beyond demonic reach. This, we see in 1 Corinthians 1:22, was a typical marker of authority for the Jews of the time, and Jesus himself pointed to his miracles as signs of his identity (John 5:36). However, the Pharisees were seeking to test and catch Jesus out rather than understand who he was.

In response Jesus 'sighed deeply', a word not used elsewhere in the New Testament and which has overtones of distress. Stephen Charnock (1628–80) observed that since Jesus had the highest honour for the Father, he also had the greatest grief at his dishonour.[44] To confuse the works of God for works of demons is a grave blasphemy (Mark 3:28–9). Here was a man who had fed multitudes and had restored sight, hearing and physical wholeness. A man whose ministry, like that of Moses, was pivotal in redemptive history and was underscored by signs (Hebrews 2:3–4). What more could he do?

In response, Jesus stated that no signs would be given to 'this generation', a phrase with negative overtones in the Old Testament.[45]

---

[44] Stephen Charnock, 'A Discourse of Mourning for Other Men's Sins', in *The Complete Works of Stephen Charnock, Volume 5* (London: James Nisbet and Co., 1866), 385.
[45] See Genesis 7:1; Deuteronomy 1:35; Jeremiah 2:31; 7:29.

His primary ministry was one of teaching, and his words caused the amazement of crowds. That Jesus worked miracles was not the substance of his ministry, and in any case miracles were not necessarily a marker of authenticity (Deuteronomy 13:1–5). No sign would be given to satisfy the testing of the Pharisees.

We should be very wary of placing emphasis on signs in mission. The gospel is about a change of heart, not simply a healing of the body. Again and again in his ministry, Jesus responded to physical needs by teaching: he was not simply a healer or wonder-worker. The miracles he worked were signs of his identity and pointed towards his message. There is a danger in seeking to separate Christ from his benefits, to downplay his teaching in favour of his miracles.

This is not to say that we should not seek the miraculous acts of God. Every prayer is a plea for God to act within his creation, and a prayer answered is a sign in itself. However, these signs are not for personal benefit or gain (Acts 8:21–2), nor may they be demanded as if they were our right. Much of the Christian life is the ordinary business of prayer, discipleship, the reading of Scripture and the living out of what we read.

In response to this testing, Jesus simply left the Pharisees, got into a boat and went away. A stark judgment in itself.

The yeastlike opposition of Pharisees and Herod (8:14–21)

The yeast of the Pharisees and Herod

14 The disciples had forgotten to bring bread, except for one loaf they had with them in the boat. 15 'Be careful,' Jesus warned them. 'Watch out for the yeast of the Pharisees and that of Herod.'

16 They discussed this with one another and said, 'It is because we have no bread.'

17 Aware of their discussion, Jesus asked them: 'Why are you talking about having no bread? Do you still not see or understand? Are your hearts hardened? 18 Do you have eyes but fail to see, and ears but fail to hear? And don't you remember? 19 When I broke the five loaves for the five thousand, how many basketfuls of pieces did you pick up?'

'Twelve,' they replied.

20 'And when I broke the seven

loaves for the four thousand, how many basketfuls of pieces did you pick up?'

They answered, 'Seven.'

21 He said to them, 'Do you still not understand?'

This section of Mark's Gospel concludes with a final episode of a lack of bread. Two multitudes had been fed from a small quantity of bread, and yet the disciples were still concerned when they realised that they had only a single loaf between them. They had forgotten to bring any more bread, had forgotten the miracles of the two feedings of the multitudes and had also forgotten who it was who was with them. John Flavel (c. 1627–91) put it well: 'A bad heart and a slippery memory deprive men of the comfort of many mercies, and defraud God of the glory due for them.'[46]

Jesus was emphatic in his order: 'Be careful . . . Watch out . . .' The Pharisees and Herod represented the two sources of Jesus's opposition, and between them composed the religious authorities and the state. As is so often the case, danger comes from two directions, but on this occasion these two disparate groupings had come together to plot against Jesus (Mark 3:6). Both these groupings were described as yeast, a living organism that spreads, and so they were not to be seen as a static danger.

We might see also Herod and the Pharisees as representing two attitudes that are particularly harmful for the believer. Herod was intrigued by John the Baptist but eventually had him killed because he did not want to lose face. The Pharisees had become more enamoured by the 'traditions of the elders' than with the heart-changing intent of the Scriptures. Both had witnessed Christ, and both had rejected him.

The Pharisees were to be given no signs (Mark 8:11–13), but the disciples had received many. Yet for all this they still failed to understand. Patience is often required in discipleship, and we should not expect too much from the young believer. The disciples clearly did not understand what Jesus was saying, and this parable remained

---

[46] John Flavel, 'Divine Conduct: Or, the Mystery of Providence, Opened in a Treatise Upon Psal. 57:2', in *The Whole Works of the Reverend John Flavel, Volume 4* (London: W. Baynes and Son, 1820), 336.

opaque to them. Jesus rebuked them in language reminiscent of Mark 4:12, with its reference to Isaiah 6:9–10. These insiders were now in no better place than the outsiders. They were blind as to who Jesus truly was, which nicely set up the miracle in the next passage.

Their lack of understanding had its root in their inability to understand the sign of the two feedings, so Jesus went on to ask seven questions in order to prompt the disciples to think their way to a true understanding, ending with two questions concerning the baskets of food left over. The disciples had collected up the surplus food and so had witnessed the super-abundance of Jesus's provision.

Jesus then asked the question, 'Do you still not understand?' The question is left hanging in the air and should remain in the mind of the reader as we move on to the startling revelation of Christ contained in the next section of the Gospel. The disciples were still thinking of Jesus as a teacher, and as a Messiah who would act politically in driving out the Romans and restoring Jewish rule. This was the yeast of the Pharisees and Herod. What they should have understood is that Jesus is far greater than that. He is the Son of God.

4

The Christ and His Followers

MARK 8:22–10:52

1. The revelation of Christ • Mark 8:22–9:13

In the previous section of the Gospel, Jesus had worked wonders, revealed his identity and demonstrated the global nature of his mission. Yet both the Pharisees and his disciples misunderstood, along with the Herodians. Here Jesus once more revealed his true nature, and the section begins with a man gaining his sight, first imperfectly and then perfectly. This event serves as a model for the section as a whole as Peter imperfectly identifies the Christ before the full revelation is given at the transfiguration.

The two-stage healing of a blind man (8:22–6)

Jesus heals a blind man at Bethsaida

22 They came to Bethsaida, and some people brought a blind man and begged Jesus to touch him. **23** He took the blind man by the hand and led him outside the village. When he had spat on the man's eyes and put his hands on him, Jesus asked, 'Do you see anything?'

24 He looked up and said, 'I see people; they look like trees walking around.'

25 Once more Jesus put his hands on the man's eyes. Then his eyes were opened, his sight was restored, and he saw everything clearly. **26** Jesus sent him home, saying, 'Don't even go into^a the village.'

---

a 26 Some manuscripts *go and tell anyone in*

169

Although its precise location is a matter for some debate, Bethsaida sat on the northern shore of the Sea of Galilee, somewhere near where the river Jordan flows into the sea. Its name translates as 'house of fishing'.

The healing of the blind was associated with the age of the Messiah (e.g., Isaiah 29:18; 35:5; 42:7), but in this case it was also a highly symbolic act. Restoration of sight may be spiritual as well as physical, and this passage follows directly on from the disciples failing to understand Jesus's identity. His question, 'Do you still not understand?' continues to echo.

A blind man was brought to Jesus and, as in Mark 7:31–5, Jesus took the man away from the crowd. Here is an act of compassion, since it allowed the blind man to hear Jesus clearly without the hubbub of the crowd. Jesus deals with us individually, and we are to listen to his words carefully. As in 7:31–5, Jesus used saliva in his healing, presumably so that the man could feel his actions, and then laid his hands on the man. Once this was done, he asked the man what he could see.[1]

This type of questioning was not present in the other miracles, and the answer given – 'trees walking around' – suggests only a partial success, which would be odd. Are we to suggest that Jesus was having an off day? This is highly unlikely, since Jesus achieved tasks that one would assume were more difficult in a single move (such as the raising of Lazarus, Jairus' daughter and so on). For the Son of God (Mark 1:1), healing the blind was no challenge, and the Servant of the LORD was to bring sight to the blind (Isaiah 42:1–9). What is more likely is that this healing took the form of an enacted parable on the 'process of revelation', introducing a cluster of passages concerning the nature of Christ.[2] The disciples then progressed through levels of understanding before being able to see clearly.[3]

This miracle, therefore, was also a lesson for the disciples, and Jesus's questioning was designed to bring this out. The man had faulty vision

---

[1] For comments on the use of saliva, see the section dealing with Mark 7:31–7.
[2] Edwards, *Mark*, 244. See also Joel Marcus, *Mark 8–16: A New Translation with Introduction and Commentary* (New York: Doubleday, 2009), from page 597.
[3] One might find similar ideas in Philo (*On the Life of Abraham*, 70–71 and *On the Prayers and Curses Uttered by Noah When He Became Sober*, 3).

at first, and then perfect vision. The enlightening of the disciples who still did not understand (Mark 8:21) would similarly be a two-stage affair. Peter would first have a faulty, incomplete understanding of Jesus as the Messiah (Mark 8:27–30) before gaining a full revelation at the transfiguration (Mark 9:2–13). Jesus the Good Shepherd gently led his flock to a proper understanding.

It is possible to come to a partial understanding as to who Christ is, to see a glimmer of light without seeing clearly. This imperfect understanding is not wrong, but rather it is not complete. It is skewed in some manner, and in need of a further 'application of virtue'.[4] The ongoing work of discipleship, and the study of the things of God, are the means by which this clearer vision breaks.

After the healing was completed, Jesus once more sought to maintain his secrecy and sent the man directly to his house.

The partial revelation: Peter confesses Christ (8:27–30)

Peter declares that Jesus is the Messiah

27 Jesus and his disciples went on to the villages around Caesarea Philippi. On the way he asked them, 'Who do people say I am?'

28 They replied, 'Some say John the Baptist; others say Elijah; and still others, one of the prophets.'

29 'But what about you?' he asked. 'Who do you say I am?'

Peter answered, 'You are the Messiah.'

30 Jesus warned them not to tell anyone about him.

Jesus and his disciples made a twenty-five-mile journey north, into the area surrounding the notoriously pagan centre of Caesarea Philippi. The city itself was not ancient – it had been built by Herod the Great's son (Philip II) some thirty years earlier and named for himself and Caesar – but there had long been pagan activity on the site. It had been

---

4 John Owen, 'The Grace and Duty of Being Spiritually Minded Declared and Practically Improved', in *The Works of John Owen, Volume 7*, ed. William H. Goold (Edinburgh: T&T Clark, no date), 339–40. He commented, 'Nor will our perfect vision of things above be a grace absolutely of another kind from the light of faith which we here enjoy; only what is imperfect in it will be done away, and it will be made meet for the present enjoyment of things here at a distance and invisible.'

known as Paneas or Panion, named after the Greek god Pan, and as part of the development Philip had built a temple to Pan on the site.

It is tempting to suggest, as some have done, that Jesus was purposely revealed as the Messiah in this deeply pagan city, but the text makes it clear that they were heading to the villages surrounding Caesarea Philippi rather than to the city itself. That said, this was an area dominated by its pagan connections, and to have Jesus proclaimed as Messiah in that region spoke loudly of his mission to the Gentiles as well as to the Jews.

Mark stated that the group were 'on the way' (Mark 8:27), a phrase which we have seen is significant,[5] and which is found at the beginning of Mark's Gospel: 'Prepare the way for the Lord, make straight paths for him' (Mark 1:3). The LORD was leading his people, but it would seem that they did not understand who he was. Like the blind man of the previous passage, they were in need of light. So it was that Jesus asked his disciples who people thought he was. Here was the beginning of the first phase of their enlightenment (see the comment on Mark 8:22–6).

We have already seen that the question of who Jesus was had troubled Herod, who had thought Jesus was John the Baptist back from the dead. We have also seen Jesus called 'Son of God' by the impure spirits (Mark 3:11; 5:7), and others had simply identified him as 'Mary's son' (Mark 6:3). Jesus had discouraged people from speaking of the miracles he had worked (Mark 1:43–4; 5:43; 7:36), silenced the impure spirits (Mark 1:24–5, 34; 3:11–12) and referred to himself as the 'Son of Man' (Mark 2:10, 28). This question of Jesus's identity was a live one at the time.

The answer given by the disciples demonstrated both the confusion over Jesus's identity and the hopes that the people had. Some, like Herod, thought him John the Baptist. Others, looking to Malachi 4:5, thought him to be a returning Elijah who would come 'before that great and dreadful day of the LORD comes'. Still others thought him another of the prophets returned.[6]

---

[5] See the section on Mark and the Old Testament in the Introduction.

[6] A late first-century Jewish apocalypse foresaw the return of Isaiah and Jeremiah (2 Esdras 2:18–19).

So much for the crowds. Jesus asked a second question: 'Who do you say I am?' This was a key question, given the disciples' previous misunderstandings. In the end, it is our own understanding of who Jesus is that is all important. Faith cannot be inherited, nor is it caught by simply being present in a church or being part of a church community. It is a personal affair: we must all decide who we think Jesus is. The crowds may say one thing, but you might say another. Peter came to the fore and stated that Jesus was the Messiah.

As we will see in the next passage, Peter had a faulty understanding of who the Messiah truly was to be. Rather like the blind man in the previous passage, he saw but he saw imperfectly. At the time of Christ, any understanding that the Messiah would suffer or any connection between the Suffering Servant of Isaiah with the Messiah was rare.[7] Rather, the Messiah was understood to be a descendent of David (as Jesus was) who would rule once more. David was a warrior king, and so naturally the hopes were for a leader who would drive out the Roman overlords and 'purge Jerusalem from Gentiles'.[8] Jesus told them to keep this identity secret, no doubt as Peter's faulty understanding of Messiahship was shared by the wider crowds. Jesus's true identity would be revealed at the transfiguration: his identity was to be defined by that event and not by the theories of anyone else.

The fate of the Messiah (8:31–3)

Jesus predicts his death

31 He then began to teach them that the Son of Man must suffer many things and be rejected by the elders, the chief priests and the teachers of the law, and that he must be killed and after three days rise again. **32** He spoke plainly about this, and Peter took him aside and began to rebuke him.

---

[7] Markus Bockmuehl, *This Jesus: Martyr, Lord, Messiah* (London: T&T Clark, 2004), chapter 2.

[8] *Psalms of Solomon* 17:22. This dates from the fifty years preceding the birth of Jesus. Translation from James H. Charlesworth, *The Old Testament Pseudepigrapha and the New Testament: Expansions of the 'Old Testament' and Legends, Wisdom, and Philosophical Literature, Prayers, Psalms and Odes, Fragments of Lost Judeo–Hellenistic Works* (New Haven; London: Yale University Press, 1985), 2:667.

33 But when Jesus turned and looked at his disciples, he rebuked Peter. 'Get behind me, Satan!' he said. 'You do not have in mind the concerns of God, but merely human concerns.'

Jesus now began to teach his disciples about his future. Rather than referring to himself as the Messiah, he used the title 'Son of Man' (see introduction) and began to speak of his fate, starting with the first of his three predictions of his betrayal, death and resurrection (see also Mark 9:31 and 10:33–4). While he had taught in the past by means of parables, he now spoke 'plainly'.

Peter did not like what he heard, no doubt because it did not correspond to his view of Messiahship, so he took Jesus to one side to rebuke him. This is a strong word, indicating strong disapproval, yet it is not the role of a disciple to rebuke the leader. The follower does not define the one leading.

We might be tempted to see Peter's actions as the height of arrogance, yet there is a strong urge to conform Jesus to our own way of thinking. The Jesus Seminar, a grouping of scholars who gathered from the mid 1980s to debate which sayings and deeds of Jesus were authentic, is often criticised for presenting us with a Jesus who looks rather more like the members of the seminar than a figure from first-century Judea. As one critic put it, 'Their Jesus is not very Jewish . . . and suspiciously resembles the values of the scholars who depict him.'[9] Better to follow the advice of another scholar and 'let Jesus be a stranger to us and not to cast an image of him in our own cultural likeness and theological preference'.[10] This tendency, though, runs deep. How often do we say, 'I'm sure God wouldn't mind,' or, 'The God I believe in wouldn't object,' or, 'I can't believe in a God who would do that'? It is not for us to define God, but rather to glory in what is revealed to us. God is not to be remade in our image. That is idolatry of the self.

Jesus responded to Peter's rebuke by telling him to 'get behind' him. The proper place for a disciple is to follow, not to seek to lead.

[9] Craig S. Keener, *The Historical Jesus of the Gospels* (Grand Rapids: Eerdmans, 2009), 15.

[10] Adela Yarbro Collins, 'The Origin of the Designation of Jesus as "son of Man"', *The Harvard Theological Review* 80, no. 4 (1987), 407.

He then called him Satan, which surely brought Peter up short. It is true that the word might simply mean 'adversary', but this is very unlikely to be the meaning here, given the use of the word elsewhere in the New Testament. It is more likely that Peter was tempting Jesus with the same kind of worldly temptation seen in Satan's temptation in Mark 1:12–13 (see Matthew 4:1–11; Luke 4:1–13). In following the wisdom of the world, he was following the ruler of this world (John 12:31; 14:30; 16:11).

Ironically, by his unwise counsel, Peter was placing obstacles in the way of his own salvation, since Jesus's death was necessary for Peter's eternal life.[11] There is a great lesson here. Christianity can transcend culture, time and geography precisely because it is deeper than any one culture. When we try to remake the faith in the image of the wider society, it becomes bound to a particular time and place and quickly becomes irrelevant. The task of the Christian is to be shaped by the faith, and not to try to shape it. The essence of faith is to trust to the path of Christ.

The fate of the disciple (8:34–9:1)

The way of the cross

34 Then he called the crowd to him along with his disciples and said: 'Whoever wants to be my disciple must deny themselves and take up their cross and follow me. **35** For whoever wants to save their life[b] will lose it, but whoever loses their life for me and for the gospel will save it. **36** What good is it for someone to gain the whole world, yet forfeit their soul? **37** Or what can anyone give in exchange for their soul? **38** If anyone is ashamed of me and my words in this adulterous and sinful generation, the Son of Man will be ashamed of them when he comes in his Father's glory with the holy angels.'

9 And he said to them, 'Truly I tell you, some who are standing here will not taste death before they see that the kingdom of God has come with power.'

---

b 35 The Greek word means either *life* or *soul*; also in verses 36 and 37.

---

[11] Bernard of Clairvaux, *Sermons on Song of Songs*, 20. Translation from Bernard of Clairvaux, *St. Bernard's Sermons on the Canticle of Canticles*, trans. A Priest of Mount Melleray (Dublin; Belfast; Cork; Waterford: Browne and Nolan, 1920), 200.

This passage is closely tied to the previous one, but this is obscured in the NIV translation. A more literal translation of Jesus's words in verse 34 would be, 'If anyone wishes to follow behind me . . .' The word 'disciple' is not present in the Greek, and Jesus used the same phrase for 'behind me' (*opisō mou*) as he did in Mark 8:33 when he told Peter to get 'behind me'. Peter was to get behind Jesus, and Jesus called together the whole crowd as well as his disciples to describe what this getting behind looks like. This is the calling of all Christians, not simply the apostles.

The description was, frankly, shocking. To his hearers, the cross signified shame, torture, death and criminality. This certainly is not aligning yourself with 'human concerns' (Mark 8:33) but is embracing the prospect of death. Ironically, it is in losing your life that you gain it. To do the opposite, to gain the whole world, is to lose your soul. Here is the Messianic Secret laid bare.

It is worth paying careful attention to the words Jesus used: 'whoever loses their life for me and for the gospel will save it'. What is in mind is not simply a self-sacrificial lifestyle but a radical identification with both Jesus *and* the gospel. Jesus came not simply to set an example, but also to deliver a message. The gospel cannot be separated from Christ, since the two come as one. To reject Jesus's words is to reject Jesus himself: a doctrineless Christianity is no faith at all.

It is also important to note that there is no neutral ground in sight here. To be ashamed of Jesus and his words – was this a reference to Peter? – was to be part of a sinful and adulterous generation. As Cyprian said, 'How can he be with Christ who blushes and fears to be associated with Christ?'[12] This is a challenging thought, especially in those parts of the world where persecution is a daily reality, yet we remain called to stand beside the Son of Man and his 'words'. It is the teaching as well as the person of Christ in view here. To deny the one is to deny the other, and to face the shame of the returning Christ.

Adultery was commonly used by the prophets as an image of Israel's pursuit of other gods and, as we have seen when looking at Mark

---

[12] Cyprian, *The Fallen.*, 28. Translation from Brent, *On the Church*, 135.

8:12, 'this generation' has negative overtones in the Old Testament. It may well be that many modern societies believe they have rejected the idea of other gods, but they have simply transformed them into values and rights. We still need to be watchful. Paul writes of the Christian's 'citizenship' being 'in heaven' (Philippians 3:20–21). The disciple is one who lives with an eye to heaven and a heart orientated towards things eternal. The Christian is an expatriate, a stranger in a strange land. 'We must obey God rather than human beings' (Acts 5:29).

At the end of this passage we look towards the transfiguration as Jesus proclaimed, 'Truly I tell you, some who are standing here will not taste death before they see that the kingdom of God has come with power.' While some see this 'coming with power' as either Pentecost, the crucifixion or even the destruction of the Temple in AD 70, it is best understood as referring to the transfiguration. The 'some who are standing here' referred to the three who accompanied Jesus up the mountain, and this passage is closely linked to the transfiguration account that follows. It is on the mount of transfiguration that we see Jesus glorified and 'no longer in that somewhat shabby appearance that belongs to us', as Cyril of Alexandria (c. 376–444) put it.[13]

The full revelation: the transfigured Christ (9:2–13)

The transfiguration

2 After six days Jesus took Peter, James and John with him and led them up a high mountain, where they were all alone. There he was transfigured before them. **3** His clothes became dazzling white, whiter than anyone in the world could bleach them. **4** And there appeared before them Elijah and Moses, who were talking with Jesus.

5 Peter said to Jesus, 'Rabbi, it is good for us to be here. Let us put up three shelters – one for you, one for Moses and one for Elijah.' **6** (He did not know what to say, they were so frightened.)

7 Then a cloud appeared and covered them, and a voice came from the cloud: 'This is my Son,

---

[13] *Homilies on Luke*, 51. Translation from Cyril of Alexandria, 'Homily 51 on Luke', in *Light on the Mountain: Greek Patristic and Byzantine Homilies on the Transfiguration of the Lord* (Yonkers: St Vladimir's Seminary Press, 2013), 100.

whom I love. Listen to him!'

8 Suddenly, when they looked around, they no longer saw anyone with them except Jesus.

9 As they were coming down the mountain, Jesus gave them orders not to tell anyone what they had seen until the Son of Man had risen from the dead. 10 They kept the matter to themselves, discussing what 'rising from the dead' meant.

11 And they asked him, 'Why do the teachers of the law say that Elijah must come first?'

12 Jesus replied, 'To be sure, Elijah does come first, and restores all things. Why then is it written that the Son of Man must suffer much and be rejected? 13 But I tell you, Elijah has come, and they have done to him everything they wished, just as it is written about him.'

Mark rarely used time references, and so we would do well to pay attention to the 'six days' with which he introduced the account of the transfiguration. The phrase serves to tie the account of the transfiguration closely to the previous verses, which spoke of the kingdom of God coming with power. That becomes the interpretative context to the glory upon the top of the mountain.

Moreover, there are several Old Testament references to 'six days' – the creation account, the Sabbath, the collection of manna, the taking of Jericho – but it is in the giving of the Law on Sinai that we might find the closest parallel. In that event we have a mountain, a cloud, a voice and the shining transformation of Moses, and all this was preceded by six days of waiting (Exodus 24:16).

Jesus took with him Peter, James and John, who between them provided the two or three witnesses required in Deuteronomy 17:6 and 19:15. These three go on to form the core of the early church, referred to by the apostle Paul as 'those esteemed as pillars' (Galatians 2:9). It is likely that part of their prominence derived from their witnessing of this pivotal event.[14]

No location is given for this 'high mountain'. If we are still in the region of Caesarea Philippi then this might well be Mount Hermon, which stands 9,230 feet (2,800 metres) tall and is a place

---

[14] D. Wenham and A. D. A. Moses, '"There Are Some Standing Here": Did They Become the "Reputed Pillars" of the Jerusalem Church? Some Reflections on Mark 9:1, Galatians 2:9 and the Transfiguration', *Novum Testamentum* 32, no. 2 (1994), 147.

of great pagan significance, upon which more than twenty temples have been identified.[15] If this is the case, then there is an appropriateness that the revelation of the true nature of Christ should take place among so many temples to false gods. However, since Mark did not identify the site, it is unwise to speculate too much precisely where this all took place.

Within Isaiah, a 'high mountain' is the place where the longed-for return of God to his people is to be announced:

You who bring good news to Zion,
   go up on a high mountain.
You who bring good news to Jerusalem,
   lift up your voice with a shout,
lift it up, do not be afraid;
   say to the towns of Judah,
'Here is your God!'
(Isaiah 40:9)

As Edward Young (1907–68) put it, 'After the long night of sin and warfare, the time of darkness brought on by the sins of the people, at last God Himself is coming again to His own.'[16]

It is not uncommon for commentators to see in the transfiguration something of the experience of Moses in Exodus 34, but this comparison does not really stand up to scrutiny. There is no mention of any change to Jesus's face, only his clothes, and the radiance is not apparent to the disciples who remained at the foot of the mountain and showed no fear. It is true that the three companions themselves were terrified, but that is on the mountain rather than at the base (see Exodus 19:16). Moses does not seem to be the target of the allusion.

Having said that, a supernatural effect of some kind is in view. Jesus's clothing 'became dazzling white', and in Daniel's vision, the Ancient of Days was one whose 'clothing was as white as snow' (Daniel 7:9).

---

[15] Rami Arav, 'Hermon', in *The Anchor Bible*, ed. David Noel Freedman (New Haven: Yale University Press, 1992). He comments that this is 'an unprecedented number in comparison with other regions of the Phoenician coast', 159.

[16] Edward J. Young, *The Book of Isaiah: Chapters 40–66* (Grand Rapids: Eerdmans, 1972), 38.

Ezekiel's vision of 'the likeness of the glory of the LORD' was of a bright, shining figure (Ezekiel 1:26–8), and other Jewish literature of the time associated white shining clothes with God:

> And the Great Glory was sitting upon it – as for his gown, which was shining more brightly than the sun, it was whiter than any snow. None of the angels was able to come in and see the face of the Excellent and the Glorious One; and no one of the flesh can see him. (1 Enoch 14:20–21)[17]

All of this is to say that what Mark was describing was not a temporary transformation such as was Moses's experience, but rather an unveiling of Jesus's true identity. As Morna Hooker put it, 'The true nature of Jesus is a hidden mystery which breaks out from time to time.'[18] Peter's confession of Christ was akin to the imperfect sight which the healed man experienced at first. Here was the true sight.

Alongside Jesus stood Moses and Elijah, and their presence has given rise to many interpretations. It is commonly held that between them these two demonstrate that the Law and the prophets bear witness to Jesus, but it should be remembered that the disciples heard nothing of the conversation between the three, and so such witness would be limited. If the rationale is that Jesus superseded the Law and the prophets and is thereby an authority greater than the books of Moses and the prophets, one wonders why a prophet who did not write (Elijah) appeared? Also, Moses was, above all, seen as the greatest of the prophets rather than simply a lawgiver (Deuteronomy 18:14–22).

The best way to explain the presence of Moses and Elijah is to understand that God had 'passed by' them both. As we saw in the account of the walking on the water, where Jesus had intended to 'pass by' his disciples, this term denoted an appearance of God: a theophany. Moses had been passed by on Mount Sinai at the giving of the Law (Exodus 33:19–23), and when he later recalled these events he told the Hebrews, 'Then the LORD spoke to you out of the fire. You heard the sound of words but saw no form; there was

---

[17] Translation from Charlesworth, *Pseudepigrapha*, 1:21.
[18] Hooker, *Mark*, 214.

only a voice' (Deuteronomy 4:12). He himself had, of course, seen the back of the form (Exodus 33:23), and as Paul wrote, Jesus 'was in the form of God' (Philippians 2:6, see NIV footnote). Moses had asked, 'Now show me your glory' (Exodus 33:18), and he had seen Christ, 'the radiance of God's glory and the exact representation of his being' (Hebrews 1:3). No wonder Jonathan Edwards wrote of this: 'What he saw was doubtless the back parts of a glorious human form in which Christ appeared to him, and in all likelihood the form of his glorified human nature in which he should afterwards appear.'[19]

Elijah had fled to Mount Horeb after battling the prophets of Baal. There he was told by the LORD: 'Go out and stand on the mountain in the presence of the LORD, for the LORD is about to pass by' (1 Kings 19:11). In the following verses we read of wind, earthquake, fire and whisper.

The reappearance of these two on a mountain would no doubt have evoked memories of the events of both these theophanies in the minds of the three disciples,[20] and in turn provides us with the key to understanding the passage.

We should remember that Jesus said of himself, 'Before Abraham was born, I am' (John 8:58). His ministry should not be thought of as beginning at the incarnation at Bethlehem, since he was 'with God in the beginning' (John 1:2). Moreover, John's Prologue stated, 'No one has ever seen God, but the one and only Son, who is himself God and is in the closest relationship with the Father, has made him known' (John 1:18). It is Jesus who makes God known since no one can see God. As Paul wrote of Jesus, 'The Son is the image of the invisible God' (Colossians 1:15).

Both Moses and Elijah had encountered God, and in so doing had encountered the preincarnate Christ. As Cornelius Van Til (1895–1987) noted:

After the entrance of sin God could no longer walk and talk with man in the familiar way in which he had walked and

---

[19] Jonathan Edwards, 'Sermon Six', in *A History of the Work of Redemption*, ed. J. F. Wilson and J. E. Smith (New Haven, London: Yale University Press, 1989), 197.
[20] Marcus, *Mark 8–16*, 632.

talked with him before the fall. But through the 'special principle' of which Christ is the center, this became possible and
actual again. Christ is the Immanuel.[21]

When God is with us (Immanuel), we encounter Christ. Christ is, to
use the appropriate phrase of Oskar Skarsaune, 'the appearing God'.[22]
This principle lies behind several New Testament passages. For
example, the apostle John wrote, after quoting from Isaiah, 'Isaiah
said this because he saw Jesus' glory and spoke about him' (John
12:41). This is best explained as a reference to the vision in Isaiah 6,
wherein Isaiah exclaimed, 'I am ruined! For I am a man of unclean
lips, and I live among a people of unclean lips, and my eyes have
seen the King, the LORD Almighty' (Isaiah 6:5). Paul wrote of the
'spiritual rock' that accompanied the Hebrews at the Exodus and
stated, 'that rock was Christ' (1 Corinthians 10:3-4).[23] Both these
authors assume Christ's preincarnate ministry.

It is Jesus who makes God known (John 1:18). He did so to both
Moses and Elijah, and here made God known to the three apostles.

Peter's confusion is evident from the passage. Quite why he wanted
to build booths is not clear, maybe even to Peter himself, and given
Mark's comment in verse 6 it is probably not wise to read too
much into Peter's words or attempt to discern his intentions. Best
to simply accept Mark's explanation that Peter did not know what
to say. He had received, Richard Sibbes (1577-1635) says, 'a glimpse
of the glory of heaven, and he was spiritually drunk as it were, he
knew not what he said'.[24]

Within the Old Testament, a cloud is often symbolic of the presence
of the LORD, not least at Sinai. Elsewhere in the Old Testament, the

---

[21] Cornelius Van Til, *An Introduction to Systematic Theology* (Phillipsburg: The
Presbyterian and Reformed Publishing Company, 1979), 122.

[22] Oskar Skarsaune, *The Proof from Prophecy. A Study in Justin Martyr's Proof-Text
Tradition: Text-Type, Provenance, Theological Profile* (Leiden: Brill, 1987), 208.

[23] For a fuller discussion of all this, see Larry W. Hurtado, *Lord Jesus Christ: Devotion
to Jesus in Earliest Christianity* (Grand Rapids: Eerdmans, 2005), 564-78.

[24] Richard Sibbes, 'The Excellency of the Gospel Above the Law', in *The Complete
Works of Richard Sibbes, Volume 4*, ed. Alexander Balloch Grosart (London: James
Nisbet, 1863), 286.

cloud is a visible sign of the presence of God, most overpower-
ingly at the Tent of Meeting in Exodus 40:35, the dedication of the
Temple in 1 Kings 8:10–11, and most significantly at the Exodus.
The coupling of the cloud and the voice at the transfiguration is
highly suggestive of Exodus 24:16.

From the cloud came a voice, saying, 'This is my Son, whom
I love. Listen to him!' Here, as at his baptism (Mark 1:11), Jesus is
affirmed by God as his Son, whom he loves. As Jesus went on to
face rejection, beatings and crucifixion, those with him were to
remember that Jesus is loved by God. This dark path of redemption
should not be seen as the act of an unloving God. In fact, as he
died, Jesus was once more proclaimed as God's Son, but this time
by a Roman centurion (Mark 15:39).

The disciples are then urged to 'listen to him'. Once more the
point is made that Jesus's teaching is to the fore – he is not simply
an example to be followed. Yet the phrase has a very significant Old
Testament echo, something Peter drew on when he later preached
at Solomon's Colonnade (Acts 3:22–3). In Deuteronomy 18:15–19,
as Moses addressed the Israelites, we read:

> The LORD your God will raise up for you a prophet like me
> from among you, from your fellow Israelites. You must listen
> to him. For this is what you asked of the LORD your God at
> Horeb on the day of the assembly when you said, 'Let us not
> hear the voice of the LORD our God nor see this great fire
> any more, or we will die.'

> The LORD said to me: 'What they say is good. I will raise up for
> them a prophet like you from among their fellow Israelites, and
> I will put my words in his mouth. He will tell them everything
> I command him. I myself will call to account anyone who does
> not listen to my words that the prophet speaks in my name.

Jesus, then, is the long-hoped-for prophet. The Israelites could not
bear the unmediated voice of God, nor the great fire, so he now
came in human flesh. The words of Jesus are the words of God, and
those who ignore them will be held to account.

The transfiguration then ends with a sudden return to normality. Returning to the two-stage healing of the blind man (Mark 8:22–6), this is the full sight. The immediate context of the 'two-stage' healing of blindness suggests that a two-stage unveiling of Christ was to follow. The events of the transfiguration acted as a high point of revelation prior to the journey to Jerusalem and ultimately Jesus's death. The Caesarea Philippi/transfiguration event operates as the central hinge in Mark's Gospel with its focus on the two titles operating within it: the Son of God and Jesus Christ. The Gospel opens with, 'The beginning of the good news about Jesus the Messiah, the Son of God,' and this pairing is set forth in this section of Mark. Jesus is heralded by Peter as the Christ in Mark 8:29 and revealed as the Son of God in the transfiguration. At the crucifixion, the theme will return again as the centurion acknowledges Jesus to be the Son of God while he was crucified for being a messianic figure (the 'King of the Jews'). It is crucial to hold these two together.

As they descended the mountain, Jesus told Peter, James and John not to tell anyone what they had witnessed until the 'Son of Man' had risen from the dead'. That event would provide the key to understanding Jesus, and a Christianity without the resurrection of Christ is no Christianity at all. That Jesus urged secrecy is not a surprise in this Gospel, but it did create a hierarchy among the apostles. Not all were treated equally within Jesus's ministry, and some were given particular experiences. Quite why these three were chosen is not clear. It is true they were among the first to be called, but then so was Andrew. In the end, calling is a matter for God, and it is best left to him. We may discern those called by God – for example, by considering gifts – but we cannot demand nor impose a calling. It is not a right.

Jesus's use of the title 'Son of Man' in the context of the transfiguration is a strong allusion to Daniel 7:13–14 where the prophet saw:

. . . one like a son of man, coming with the clouds of heaven. He approached the Ancient of Days and was led into his presence. He was given authority, glory and sovereign power; all nations and peoples of every language worshipped him. His dominion is an everlasting dominion that will not pass away, and his kingdom is one that will never be destroyed.

Jesus then went on to give a reason why this kingdom will never be destroyed: the King will rise from the dead. Here is an eternal kingdom under the rule of an eternal king, one whom death cannot hold.

The three disciples discussed among themselves what this might mean. While some Jews of the time held to a generalised hope of some sort of relating to God after death, the coming back to life of an individual was not anticipated.[25] It is one thing to have a hope of heaven, another to expect the resuscitation of a corpse. It is clear the disciples were struggling to understand what Jesus was teaching, and their minds turn to Elijah, who was taken into heaven in a whirlwind (2 Kings 2:11).

Malachi had predicted the return of Elijah before the 'day of the LORD' (Malachi 4:5), and the three had just witnessed that prophet speaking with Jesus on the mountain. He had raised the son of the widow of Zarephath (1 Kings 17), and it may well be that Jesus's comment about being raised had brought this to mind. This coupled with Jesus's reference to the Son of Man would have raised all sorts of questions, and so they asked Jesus about Elijah.[26]

Jesus affirmed that Elijah does come first to restore all things, a reference to Malachi 4:6, but that does not negate the suffering of the Son of Man which is foreseen in the Old Testament writings (e.g., Psalm 118:22, Isaiah 53). In fact, Jesus asserted that Elijah *had* come, and had shared the same fate as the Son of Man would suffer. In Matthew 17:13 the identification of this returning Elijah with John the Baptist is made clear, but in Mark it is implied. As was noted above when dealing with Mark 6:14–29, there are parallels between the dealings of John and Herod/Herodias and of Elijah's dealings with Ahab/Jezebel.

2. The nature of discipleship • Mark 9:14–10:52

The Messiah had been revealed in all his transfigured glory, and we now come to a section in which his followers learned what it is to

---

[25] See, for example, Daniel 12:2.
[26] A number of traditions had arisen around the return of Elijah in the previous centuries.

follow. They failed to drive out an impure spirit because of their lack of prayer and argued about which of them was the greatest. They sought to police who might, or might not, be followers of Jesus, only to be rebuked by Christ. They were warned not to make others stumble, and a debate over divorce demonstrated how petty interpretations may lead others to stumble.

A rich man came to Jesus, only to find his wealth too much of a burden. Two of his followers privately sought preferment from Jesus, and amid this Jesus again predicted his death. The theme is this: to follow Jesus is not a path to glory, but rather a path of service. Christ calls whom he will to follow him, and it is not up to the disciples to decide who is worthy.

At the end of the section Jesus healed the blind Bartimaeus, and his healing was also symbolic. Jesus had reached Jerusalem and his true mission was now to be seen.

The vital nature of prayer (9:14–29)

Jesus heals a boy possessed by an impure spirit

14 When they came to the other disciples, they saw a large crowd around them and the teachers of the law arguing with them. 15 As soon as all the people saw Jesus, they were overwhelmed with wonder and ran to greet him.

16 'What are you arguing with them about?' he asked.

17 A man in the crowd answered, 'Teacher, I brought you my son, who is possessed by a spirit that has robbed him of speech. 18 Whenever it seizes him, it throws him to the ground. He foams at the mouth, gnashes his teeth and becomes rigid. I asked your disciples to drive out the spirit, but they could not.'

19 'You unbelieving generation,' Jesus replied, 'how long shall I stay with you? How long shall I put up with you? Bring the boy to me.'

20 So they brought him. When the spirit saw Jesus, it immediately threw the boy into a convulsion. He fell to the ground and rolled around, foaming at the mouth.

21 Jesus asked the boy's father, 'How long has he been like this?'

'From childhood,' he answered. 22 'It has often thrown him into fire or water to kill him. But if you can do anything, take pity on us and help us.'

23 ' "If you can"?' said Jesus. 'Everything is possible for one who believes.'

24 Immediately the boy's father exclaimed, 'I do believe; help me overcome my unbelief!'

25 When Jesus saw that a crowd was running to the scene, he rebuked the impure spirit. 'You deaf and mute spirit,' he said, 'I command you, come out of him and never enter him again.'

26 The spirit shrieked, convulsed him violently and came out. The boy looked so much like a corpse that many said, 'He's dead.' **27** But Jesus took him by the hand and lifted him to his feet, and he stood up.

28 After Jesus had gone indoors, his disciples asked him privately, 'Why couldn't we drive it out?'

29 He replied, 'This kind can come out only by prayer.ᵃ'

_____

a 29 Some manuscripts *prayer and fasting*

As Jesus, Peter, James and John descended the mount of transfiguration they found a large crowd disputing with the teachers of the law. If we are still in the region around Caesarea Philippi, and the text gives us no reason to believe that we are not, the teachers of the law had travelled a great distance north. Their presence would surely have brought Jesus's teaching in Mark 8:31 to mind: 'He then began to teach them that the Son of Man must suffer many things and be rejected by the elders, the chief priests and the teachers of the law, and that he must be killed and after three days rise again.' Here was a group who would reject Jesus.

When the crowd saw Jesus, their attitude quickly changed from argument to wonder. They stopped their dispute with the teachers of the law and ran to Jesus, a symbolic act which would not have pleased the teachers of the law. The crowd were 'overwhelmed with wonder', with the Greek indicating an intense emotional state.

As they gathered around him, Jesus asked them about the argument, and a man came forward whose son was possessed by a spirit that had robbed him of speech and induced seizures.[27] The disciples had failed to cast out the spirit, something Jesus ascribed to unbelief: 'You unbelieving generation.' It would seem that this was the cause of the heightened emotion of the crowd. No one could help this child: neither the teachers of the law nor Jesus's disciples.

_____

[27] While it has been common to refer to the boy as epileptic, this is without any real warrant in the text.

When the boy was brought to Jesus, the spirit reacted, a pattern we have seen earlier in the Gospel. The child immediately convulsed and was thrown to the ground, described in vivid language. Rather than immediately healing the child, Jesus asked the father how long the boy had suffered in this way. This might be seen as Jesus reaching a diagnosis, or simply calming the father. In any case, the father replied that he had been afflicted since his childhood, and then pleaded for Jesus's help: 'If you can do anything, take pity on us and help us.' As with the Syrophoenician woman, Jesus was guiding the conversation to a key moment of exchange.

The subject of belief was raised once again, and the father (and no doubt the nearby disciples) were told, 'Everything is possible for one who believes.' The response of the father serves to demonstrate something of the nature of faith: 'I do believe; help me overcome my unbelief!' When our experience of faith is weak, we might rest assured on the promises of God.

Here, then, is an image of faith. It is active – the boy was brought to Jesus – but does not make demands of God. The man asked for pity and threw himself upon the mercy of Jesus rather than ordering him to heal the boy. He then asserted his faith, but also his desire for greater faith. Our faith is all too often fringed with unbelief, but faith as small as a mustard seed is sufficient. What an encouragement this is: our faith might be small, but our God is great.

It would appear that, as in the other healings, Jesus had taken the boy to one side, as the crowd was now running to join them. Before they could reach him, he commanded the impure spirit to leave. With a shriek it did so, convulsed the boy and left him as if dead. Yet as is so often the case, first impressions were false. Jesus took the boy by the hand, something he had done with Peter's mother-in-law (Mark 1:31), Jairus's daughter (Mark 5:41) and the blind man (Mark 8:23). Here was a compassionate touch, a gentleness to assist the child to his feet.

The disciples understandably wanted to know why they could not do as Jesus did. After all, they had already been given authority over impure spirits when they were sent out in pairs (Mark 6:7). The answer was a salutary one for the Christian and the church: 'This kind can come out only by prayer.'[28] The man had demonstrated faithful prayer by bringing his son to Jesus, asking for mercy and placing what faith he had in Jesus. Here lies the distinction between prayer and what often passes for exorcism. The disciples had no authority over spirits themselves, even though Jesus had earlier given them the power to cast out spirits. True exorcism relies upon God and not the believer: it is not in their control. Within Judaism, certain portions of Scripture were sometimes held to have power over demons,[29] but in fact it is God alone who can deal with them. We can simply ask for mercy. We cannot direct God.

Death and glory (9:30–37)

Jesus predicts his death a second time

30 They left that place and passed through Galilee. Jesus did not want anyone to know where they were, **31** because he was teaching his disciples. He said to them, 'The Son of Man is going to be delivered into the hands of men. They will kill him, and after three days he will rise.' **32** But they did not understand what he meant and were afraid to ask him about it.

33 They came to Capernaum. When he was in the house, he asked them, 'What were you arguing about on the road?' **34** But they kept quiet because on the way they had argued about who was the greatest.

35 Sitting down, Jesus called the Twelve and said, 'Anyone who wants to be first must be the very last, and the servant of all.'

36 He took a little child whom he placed among them. Taking the child in his arms, he said to them, **37** 'Whoever welcomes one of these little children in my name welcomes me; and whoever welcomes me does not welcome me but the one who sent me.'

Jesus and his disciples now headed south from the region around Caesarea Philippi and re-entered the Jewish region of Galilee. Jesus was beginning his long journey towards Jerusalem, and death, and so engaged in a period of teaching aimed only at his disciples.

---

[28] Some manuscripts add 'and fasting', but this would appear to be a later addition.
[29] Such as the *Shema* (Deuteronomy 6), Psalm 3 or Psalm 91. Witherington, *Mark*, 226.

Here he gave the core of his mission: he was the Son of Man (see introduction) who was to be delivered into human hands so that he might be killed, and then he would rise after three days. There was irony here: the one given authority over all in Daniel 7 was to be handed over to human authorities.

All of this was clearly taught, so as to give the disciples the knowledge they would need to understand what was about to occur. They did not understand at that stage – and were fearful to ask – but once the resurrection had taken place they would gain a full understanding.

Their confusion and failure to ask for clarity had given way to arguments. Perhaps their pride was bruised when they failed to understand Jesus's teachings, but it was foolish not to seek more understanding. 'Where there is strife, there is pride, but wisdom is found in those who take advice' (Proverbs 13:10). When they reached Capernaum, Jesus asked them what had caused the dispute. Embarrassed, they kept silent, but we are told that they had been arguing over which of them was greatest. Their focus had quickly switched from the fate of the Messiah to their own sense of self-importance. What danger there is when churches turn their gaze inward instead of keeping it fixed on Jesus, from whom they derive their purpose and meaning. What danger there is when Christians seek power rather than 'get behind' Jesus as followers. Power intoxicates and may bring self-delusion.

Assuming the position of a rabbi, Jesus sat to teach his disciples. To be first is not something to be grasped. Rather it comes through service to others. James Edwards noted that the word for servant (*diakonos*) 'refers to personal devotion in service as opposed to service as a slave or for hire or as a priest, for example'.[30] This was not to be a begrudging service.

To make the point, Jesus placed a small child before them and then took him or her into his arms. Given that we are in 'the house', which suggests this is Peter's house, this child may well have been part of Peter's family. In ancient societies, children were not highly valued and were seen as the very last. They needed to be fed and cared for but could not yet make any economic contribution. There was also the harsh reality of high infant mortality rates, and a child's

---

[30] Edwards, *Mark*, 287.

very presence in society was somewhat frail. Yet these were precisely the kinds of people who were to be served and welcomed 'in my name'. To welcome them is to welcome Jesus, and to welcome Jesus is to welcome the Father.

Humble service is an antidote to the corruption of power. To serve and not seek acclaim is the path of the Christian (see Galatians 2:20).

For Christ (9:38–41)

Whoever is not against us is for us

38 'Teacher,' said John, 'we saw someone driving out demons in your name and we told him to stop, because he was not one of us.'

39 'Do not stop him,' Jesus said. 'For no one who does a miracle in my name can in the next moment say anything bad about me, 40 for whoever is not against us is for us. 41 Truly I tell you, anyone who gives you a cup of water in my name because you belong to the Messiah will certainly not lose their reward.

Jesus's statement about welcoming 'in my name' (Mark 9:37) provoked a question from John about another person who was working in Jesus's name. The issue was that he was 'not following us' (ESV),[31] which is a rather telling phrase. Was John, who was one of those who witnessed the transfiguration, now equating himself with Jesus? Or might it be that the disciples now thought of themselves as the 'official' band of Jesus's followers who might act on his behalf? Whatever might be the case, the issue was that it was not for the followers to decide who else might follow. The question is not, 'Are they following us?' but rather, 'Are they following Jesus?' and Jesus alone. Both the disciples and the person driving out demons were servants of the same master.[32] There are clear echoes here of Peter's rebuke of Jesus in Mark 8:32, and Jesus's retort that Peter must get behind him. Those who follow Jesus are not to have their own followers.

There is a lamentable tendency for theological ghettos to form, often strongly influenced by a particular time and culture, and those

---

[31] The NIV translation here, 'not one of us', is rather loose.
[32] There are interesting parallels here to Numbers 11:26–30.

outside the carefully constructed boundaries are then seen as barely Christian at best. It is not for us to draw up the bounds of the church: they are Christ's to set.

The disciples (Jesus switched to the plural) were told not to stop the exorcist. To work a miracle in Jesus's name, a phrase that implies his authority, demonstrated that the worker was 'for' Jesus, at least for that moment, and sought to give glory to Christ.[33] This working in Jesus's name is not simply restricted to miraculous acts. Even giving a cup of water to someone because they 'belong to the Messiah' earns its reward. The crucial element is that all these acts are Christ-focused, not simply general acts of kindness. They are to be done in the name of the Messiah, a rare use of this title by Jesus. They are the fruit of faith.

Do not cause others to stumble (9:42–50)

Causing to stumble

42 'If anyone causes one of these little ones – those who believe in me – to stumble, it would be better for them if a large millstone were hung round their neck and they were thrown into the sea. 43 If your hand causes you to stumble, cut it off. It is better for you to enter life maimed than with two hands to go into hell, where the fire never goes out. [44] b 45 And if your foot causes you to stumble, cut it off. It is better for you to enter life crippled than to have two feet and be thrown into hell. [46] b 47 And if your eye causes you to stumble, pluck it out. It is better for you to enter the kingdom of God with one eye than to have two eyes and be thrown into hell, 48 where

'"the worms that eat them do not die,
and the fire is not quenched."c

49 Everyone will be salted with fire. 50 'Salt is good, but if it loses its saltiness, how can you make it salty again? Have salt among yourselves, and be at peace with each other.'

b 44,46 Some manuscripts include here the words of verse 48.
c 48 Isaiah 66:24

---

[33] In Matthew 7:21–3 we see that some who work in Jesus's name will not enter the kingdom of heaven, since they are not carrying out the will of the Father. They are simply invoking Jesus's name as some sort of token. To properly work in Jesus name is to also work according to the Father's will.

Key to the interpretation of this passage is the identification of the people Jesus referred to as 'little ones'. Commonly it is assumed that this refers to children: after all, did not Jesus recently talk about receiving children (Mark 9:36–7)? This, however, does not seem likely since the immediate context is those who were working in Jesus's name but were not among the twelve disciples. These are those 'who believe in me', and the following passages would also support this interpretation. Even to cause these other disciples to stumble (not, it should be noted, fall) is a terrible thing, as can be seen by the starkness of the imagery Jesus gives.

A large millstone (*mulos onikos*) refers to a great stone which had to be turned by a donkey, and so Jesus made his point strongly. There is no way to the surface if you are cast into the sea with such a stone around your neck. No less blunt was his warning about hands, feet and eyes leading a person to 'stumble': be ruthless about what you do with your hands, where you go and what you look at. Better to cut it off. We should take heed of the seriousness of the warning. Jesus clearly believed in hell and was more than willing to teach his disciples on the topic.

It is worth emphasising that the starkness of Jesus's warnings was a product of his view of hell. Echoing Isaiah 66:22–4, he described it as a place of perpetual ongoing destruction.[34] The term used for hell, Gehenna, was used for a valley to the south of Jerusalem which was also referred to as the Valley of Ben Hinnom (see 2 Chronicles 28:1–5; 33:1–6; Jeremiah 7:31–4; 19:1–6; 32:30–35). It was a place of sacrifice – often of children – to the Canaanite gods and so was associated with a certain evil horror. King Hezekiah brought the practice to an end by desecrating it (2 Kings 23:10), but from the second century before Christ it became associated with the hell of final judgment.[35] In a world jettisoning the notions of sin and judgment, we need to stand firm: Jesus's warnings are dire and need to be heard. In much of the modern church there is a disbelief in hell, or an apathy towards the concept at best. This is at odds with

---

[34] Some manuscripts repeat this description in verses 44 and 46, as can be seen in the King James Version.

[35] For example, 1 Enoch 26–7; 2 Esdras 7:26–36; 2 Baruch 59:5–11; Sibylline Oracles 1:103; 2:291; 4:186. The latter describes the 'the repulsive recesses of Gehenna'.

Jesus's own teaching, and that alone should give some pause. It is a short step from a denial of hell to a denial of the sinfulness of sin. In such situations one would wonder why a saviour was needed at all.

Jesus then continued with a pair of sayings connected to salt, the first of which has given rise to a number of interpretations: what does it mean to be 'salted with fire'? It is here that some of the early manuscripts of Mark might be helpful, since some scribes sought to make this clear by adding 'and every sacrifice will be salted with salt'.[36] This was a reference to Leviticus 2:13 where salt was to be added to the grain offerings to make them acceptable to God. Elsewhere in the New Testament, fire was used to describe the temptations or testing Christians face (1 Corinthians 3:12–15; 1 Peter 4:12), and so it may well be that Jesus was suggesting that these trials are the salt that makes the 'living sacrifice' (Romans 12:1) of the Christian life pleasing to God. Note that trials will come. Our task is to endure.

Less contentious is Jesus's teaching about the value of salt. Salt had many uses in the ancient world – preservation, cleaning, fertilising or flavouring – but salt that has no saltiness is useless; it cannot be made salty again.[37] It has lost its fruitfulness and is no longer fit for purpose. The Christian is to guard against temptation and to keep a close guard on eyes, feet and hands (verses 43–7).

The passage concludes with a command that the disciples were not to cause division with those who were not part of the inner core ('not following us', verse 38, ESV), but rather must seek peace between the followers of Christ.

Marriage, divorce and hardness of heart (10:1–12)

Divorce

10 Jesus then left that place and went into the region of Judea and across the Jordan. Again crowds of people came to him, and as was his custom, he taught them.

---

[36] See Comfort, *Textual Commentary*, 133.

[37] France explained that 'the "salt" used in Palestine, derived either from the deposits around the Dead Sea or from salt pans in which its water was evaporated, was not pure sodium chloride, and the salt could leach out leaving other minerals like gypsum. Once that has happened, it is ludicrous to think of trying to season (ἀρτύω) that which should itself have been seasoning.' France, *Mark*, 384–5.

2 Some Pharisees came and tested him by asking, 'Is it lawful for a man to divorce his wife?'

3 'What did Moses command you?' he replied.

4 They said, 'Moses permitted a man to write a certificate of divorce and send her away.'

5 'It was because your hearts were hard that Moses wrote you this law,' Jesus replied. **6** 'But at the beginning of creation God "made them male and female".ᵃ **7** "For this reason a man will leave his father and mother and be united to his wife,ᵇ **8** and the two will become one flesh."ᶜ So they are no longer two, but one flesh. **9** Therefore what God has joined together, let no one separate.'

10 When they were in the house again, the disciples asked Jesus about this. **11** He answered, 'Anyone who divorces his wife and marries another woman commits adultery against her. **12** And if she divorces her husband and marries another man, she commits adultery.'

—————

a 6 Gen. 1:27

b 7 Some early manuscripts do not have *and be united to his wife.*

c 8 Gen. 2:24

Continuing on his journey to Jerusalem, Jesus entered into the Roman province of Judea, to the south of Galilee. Rather than travel through the rather hostile Samaritan regions, he crossed the Jordan so that he might travel down the east bank. Here he was recognised, and crowds flocked, prompting Jesus to teach them, 'as was his custom'. Once more we see that the emphasis of Jesus's ministry was on teaching, rather than wonder-working.

This drew the attention of the Pharisees who had come to test him, a word that may carry a flavour of entrapment. This time the trap is baited with divorce, the rules for which are set out in Deuteronomy 24:1–4 (adultery) and Exodus 21:10–11 (abandonment).

At the time, the debates surrounding divorce centred on the interpretation of Deuteronomy 24:1–4,[38] which reads:

> If a man marries a woman who becomes displeasing to him because he finds something indecent about her, and he writes

—————

[38] For a helpful discussion of this, see David Instone-Brewer, 'Mishnah Gittin and Mark 10:1–12: Marriage and Divorce', in *Reading Mark in Context*, ed. Ben C. Blackwell, John K. Goodrich and Jason Maston (Grand Rapids: Zondervan, 2018).

her a certificate of divorce, gives it to her and sends her from his house, and if after she leaves his house she becomes the wife of another man, and her second husband dislikes her and writes her a certificate of divorce, gives it to her and sends her from his house, or if he dies, then her first husband, who divorced her, is not allowed to marry her again after she has been defiled. That would be detestable in the eyes of the LORD. Do not bring sin upon the land the LORD your God is giving you as an inheritance.

At issue was what was meant by 'indecent' in Deuteronomy 24:1. Traditionally, it was interpreted to mean adultery, but the rabbinic school of Hillel had broadened the meaning to include anything that might displease a woman's husband. The Hebrew can be more literally translated as 'indecency of a thing', and the Hillelites understood that to mean 'indecency *or* a thing'.[39] The problem is that 'thing' can mean pretty much anything. So it was that in the first century both Josephus and Philo (*c.* 20 BC–*c.* AD 50) wrote about divorce for any cause.[40] Opposing this view was the school of Shammai, who held to the more traditional interpretation that this verse dealt with sexual immorality. This was the argument in which the Pharisees wished to trap Jesus,[41] and at its heart were more 'little ones' (Mark 9:42): the wives who got rather lost in this debate.

Jesus took his questioners back to the text and asked them what Moses said. Rather dodging the issue, they replied that Moses

---

[39] 'The Shammaites interpreted this verse in the same way that most English translations do, as if it said "a thing of indecency," which they understood as a reference to adultery. The Hillelites agreed that it referred to adultery, but argued that the word "thing" was superfluous, and if one takes the order of the words seriously one could conclude that "thing" referred to a separate, unspecified ground for divorce. The word "thing" (Hebrew davar) has a wide range of meanings, including "word," and in legal contexts it could mean "a cause." Therefore, the Hillelites said that this phrase in Deuteronomy 24:1 implied two reasons for divorce: "adultery" and "any cause."' Instone-Brewer, 'Divorce', 152.

[40] Josephus, *Jewish Antiquities*, 4.253; Philo, *The Special Laws*, 3.30.

[41] Matthew makes explicit what is in implied in Mark: 'Some Pharisees came to him to test him. They asked, "Is it lawful for a man to divorce his wife for any and every reason?"' (Matthew 19:3).

permitted a certificate of divorce (Deuteronomy 24:1, 3) but failed to give any grounds for that divorce. Jesus's answer was rather unexpected: this was permitted 'because your hearts were hard', a phrase that normally describes rebellion against God. Divorce was not the intention at creation, and Jesus quoted both Genesis 1:27 and Genesis 2:24 to make his point: humans were created male and female so that man and wife might be united as one. Jesus's use of Genesis to make his point indicates that this is not a simply a cultural norm, something temporary and ever-changing, but rather it is an eternal principle grounded in creation itself. This pattern of marriage was both intended and created by God and so is not to be broken by man.[42] It is a part of the created order, and anything outside this pattern is contrary to both the design and will of God.

Marriage is not some temporary affair, to be easily broken by the writing of a certificate, but rather a design of creation. It is a spiritual matter, wherein man and wife become one flesh. Jesus here criticised those who took marriage lightly, like the Hillelites, and were content to divorce at will. Divorce was dealt with in the Law, but that was for cases where hearts had been hardened against the will of God. Some in Jesus's day had taken an exception and made it a rule.

We can see this problem in those societies that reflect a more 'modern' approach to marriage. Rather than being seen as a life-long relationship, marriage becomes a consumer item, a means for convenience and pleasure. One historian has written that in the modern view, marriage is understood as being:

> . . . for the mutual pleasure and satisfaction of the consenting parties, and that is all. It is, one might say, a sentimental union, and once the pleasurable sentiments that it stimulates have dissipated, it should be dissolved at the will of the contracting parties. This is the essential rationale of our modern thinking on marriage, defined as it is by the logic of no-fault divorce.[43]

---

[42] This also argues against the practice of polygamy, which was at that time still practised by some Jews who lived in Israel. See Adiel Schremer, 'How Much Jewish Polygyny in Roman Palestine', *Proceedings of the American Academy for Jewish Research* 63 (1997); Instone-Brewer, 'Divorce', 155–7.

[43] Carl R. Trueman, *The Rise and Triumph of the Modern Self: Cultural Amnesia,*

When they were apart from the crowd, back in the house, the disciples quizzed Jesus further. He then went on to restate his position: to divorce and to remarry is to commit adultery.

This, of course, raises questions, particularly in countries where divorce is widespread. It is not uncommon to find in a church congregation those who are divorced or remarried, either before or after conversion, and so passages such as this one can induce guilt and shame. We will return to this pastoral point a little later, but before we do it would be well to consider Jesus's teaching on divorce as a whole, as well as what may be found elsewhere in the Bible.

In Matthew's account of this incident, Jesus added the words 'except for sexual immorality' (Matthew 19:9), which reflects the more traditional interpretation of Deuteronomy 24:1 found in the school of Shammai. Since this passage was dealing with a well-known argument at the time, it may well be that Mark omitted the phrase 'except for sexual immorality' as it would have been understood to have been implied. When Jesus was asked about divorce, the exception for sexual immorality would have been understood. David Instone-Brewer illustrates this point well.

> As it stands, this question is as misleading as, 'Is it lawful for a sixteen-year-old to drink?' — because all humans need to drink. It would be pedantic to add the words 'alcoholic beverages' to this modern expression, because everyone knows that this is the subject of the question. Equally, in the early first century it would have been pedantic to specify that the question 'Is it lawful for a man to divorce his wife?' concerned divorce 'for any cause,' because this was the big divorce debate of the day. Therefore, everyone knew that this much was implied.[44]

Mark and Matthew are not in conflict. One is simply fuller than the other.

Alongside Jesus's exception for sexual immorality, the Old

Expressive Individualism, and the Road to Sexual Revolution (Wheaton: Crossway, 2020), 154.

[44] Instone-Brewer, 'Divorce', 154.

Testament permitted divorce for wives who were not provided with 'food, clothing and marital rights' (Exodus 21:10). These were women who had been abandoned, and whose husbands had simply walked away from the marriage. There are echoes of this teaching in 1 Corinthians 7:10–16, where Paul stated that should a believer be married to an unbeliever then they should remain married as long as the other party was willing. However, 'if the unbeliever leaves, let it be so. The brother or the sister is not bound in such circumstances' (1 Corinthians 7:15). Here is an example of Paul applying the regulations of Exodus 21:10 to a local situation. The phrase that the abandoned believer 'is not bound' would suggest that remarriage is a possibility. Marriage was viewed as lifelong, but there is an acknowledgment that our fallen nature (our hardness of heart (Mark 10:5) can lead to marital breakdown.

So, to return to the pastoral question, how does all of this play out in modern church life in societies where divorce is widespread? First of all, we should reject any notion of marriage simply being for the benefit of the two parties involved, a temporary arrangement which might be broken at will. The Christian understanding of marriage has at its core a mutual service and an orientation towards God. It is a deeply theological arrangement and is part of God's creation ordinance. It reflects Christ himself (Ephesians 5:22–33) and his self-sacrifice is its model. The Russian émigré Alexander Schmemann (1921–83) was perceptive:

> A marriage which does not constantly crucify its own selfishness and self-sufficiency, which does not 'die to itself' that it may point beyond itself, is not a Christian marriage. The real sin of marriage today is not adultery or lack of 'adjustment' or 'mental cruelty.' It is the idolization of the family itself, the refusal to understand marriage as directed toward the Kingdom of God . . . In a Christian marriage, in fact, three are married; and the united loyalty of the two toward the third, who is God, keeps the two in an active unity with each other as well as with God.[45]

---

[45] Alexander Schmemann, *For the Life of the World: Sacraments and Orthodoxy* (Yonkers:

Second, humans are fallen people with hard hearts, and so marriages fail. This is a matter for lament and penitence, and in cases of sexual immorality (adultery) or abandonment, divorce is permitted. This is no divorce of convenience, but rather one of the last resort. Paul's writings would suggest that in these circumstances the abandoned party is free to remarry since he or she is no longer 'bound' (1 Corinthians 7:15). Remarriage of widows is envisaged by Paul at the end of that chapter (1 Corinthians 7:39–40), and one abandoned, being no longer 'bound', would seem to fall into the same category. The only advice Paul gives is that the remarriage should be to a believer (1 Corinthians 7:39) and that the Christian should not initiate the divorce (1 Corinthians 7:10–16).

Third, there has been some debate as to whether domestic abuse might fall under the category of abandonment. It would seem to me that it would, since the abuser has abandoned his or her marriage vow and the pattern of Ephesians 5:21–33. I would suggest that the teaching of Jesus in Matthew 19 and Paul in 1 Corinthians 7 are intended to protect a spouse from an intolerable situation, and abuse would fall into that category. It is an abandonment, even if the couple remain under the same roof.

Finally, there will be Christians who – either before or after their conversion – have divorced and remarried for reasons other than those permitted in the Scriptures. Should they now abandon their second marriages and, possibly, return to their former spouses? In those cases, I would follow John Murray (1898–1975) by suggesting that, even if they are counter to scriptural teaching, these second marriages are still marriages and so are subject to the same standards of any marriage. They should not be dissolved but be places of Christian love and service.[46]

There will be much guilt and shame surrounding this passage, and it is important to remember that it is only blasphemy of the Holy Spirit that is unforgivable. If one feels that they have sinned in their marital dealings, then he or she might take the words of 1

St Vladimir's Seminary Press, 2018), 109–10.

[46] John Murray, *Divorce* (Phillipsburg: Presbyterian & Reformed Publishing Company, 1961), 110–12.

John 1:9 to heart: 'If we confess our sins, he is faithful and just and will forgive us our sins and purify us from all unrighteousness.' There may be times when our hearts are hard, but these are prompts to confession and reconciliation. There are no sins beyond the reach of the cross for those who confess them to the God who sent his Son to save them.

Children and the kingdom (10:13–16)

The little children and Jesus

13 People were bringing little children to Jesus for him to place his hands on them, but the disciples rebuked them. 14 When Jesus saw this, he was indignant. He said to them, 'Let the little children come to me, and do not hinder them, for the kingdom of God belongs to such as these. 15 Truly I tell you, anyone who will not receive the kingdom of God like a little child will never enter it.' 16 And he took the children in his arms, placed his hands on them and blessed them.

We return once more to children. People were coming to Jesus in order to seek his blessing upon their children, and the disciples once more sought to determine who might or might not be allowed into Jesus's circle (see Mark 9:38). They rebuked the parents, no doubt so that the children would be kept away. Jesus was indignant: he insisted they should not be hindered, and then used them as an example of faith. The kingdom of God belongs to those who are like children.

Jesus was not here claiming that the Christian faith is childish, but rather that there is a quality of faith among children that can disappear in older age. Children are more willing to receive a gift and place their trust in a parent. This is not a call to childishness, nor is Jesus suggesting that faith is infantile. Rather, we are to have a quiet and entire trust in the God we call Father. We come, like a child, with empty hands and receive everything by grace. Power, caste or status in society is not important.

This passage is often to be found in the debates surrounding infant baptism and is read in the Baptism service in the *Book of Common Prayer* (1662). There is no link, however, with baptism in the passage, and so it is unwise to place too much weight upon it for this purpose. However, it should be noted that children were clearly intended to be part of the worshipping community. They may not entirely understand Christ's meaning, but they may receive his blessing. Children are to be part of the household of faith and fully participate in its life. We should not be concerned that those who die young are denied their place in heaven, since the kingdom of God 'belongs to such as these', and they may be recipients of grace from a young age. In fact, it was the common view of the Reformers that those who die in infancy are saved.[47]

The rich and the kingdom (10:17–31)

The rich and the kingdom of God

17 As Jesus started on his way, a man ran up to him and fell on his knees before him. 'Good teacher,' he asked, 'what must I do to inherit eternal life?'

18 'Why do you call me good?' Jesus answered. 'No one is good – except God alone. **19** You know the commandments: "You shall not murder, you shall not commit adultery, you shall not steal, you shall not give false testimony, you shall not defraud, honour your father and mother."[d]'

20 'Teacher,' he declared, 'all these I have kept since I was a boy.'

21 Jesus looked at him and loved him. 'One thing you lack,' he said. 'Go, sell everything you have and give to the poor, and you will have treasure in heaven. Then come, follow me.'

22 At this the man's face fell. He went away sad, because he had great wealth.

23 Jesus looked round and said to his disciples, 'How hard it is for the rich to enter the kingdom of God!'

24 The disciples were amazed at his words. But Jesus said again, 'Children, how hard it is[e] to enter the kingdom of God! **25** It is easier for a camel to go through the eye of a needle than for someone who is rich to enter the kingdom of God.'

26 The disciples were even more amazed, and said to each other, 'Who then can be saved?'

27 Jesus looked at them and said, 'With man this is impossible, but not with God; all things are possible with God.'

28 Then Peter spoke up, 'We have left everything to follow you!'

---

[47] See Charles Hodge, *Systematic Theology* (New York; London and Edinburgh: Charles Scribner and Company; T. Nelson and Sons, 1872), 1.27.

29 'Truly I tell you,' Jesus replied, 'no one who has left home or brothers or sisters or mother or father or children or fields for me and the gospel **30** will fail to receive a hundred times as much in this present age: homes, brothers, sisters, mothers, children and fields – along with persecutions – and in the age to come eternal life. **31** But many who are first will be last, and the last first.'

---

d 19 Exodus 20:12-16; Deut. 5:16-20
e 24 Some manuscripts *is for those who trust in riches*

Having dealt with children, we now move to a wealthy man. We shift from the powerless to the powerful, and once more consider the effect this has on faith. It is important to note that the rich man's wealth had not caused him to lose his focus on things eternal and, like the leper (Mark 1:40) and Legion (Mark 5:6), he fell on his knees before Christ in a position of humility. Here was a true seeker.

From his knees he asked Jesus how he might inherit eternal life, and the reply he received might be seen as pedantic. Jesus asked, 'Why do you call me good? . . . No-one is good – except God alone.' There is no denial here of Jesus's goodness, but rather a desire to ascribe goodness only to God. However good we might think ourselves – or others – to be, it is only in God that true, perfect goodness is found. God is the definition of goodness, the absolute from whom all other notions of goodness derive their meaning. 'Goodness is not a mere attribute that must be attached to God as a subject, but God is goodness. In him, ideas and being are one,' as Van Til asserts.[48]

We are only as good as the likeness of God we possess. We can only reflect God's goodness, not create our own. The absolute goodness of God is the standard by which all other goodness is to be measured, and to live a 'good life' is to live in accordance with that goodness. To love God is to seek his standards of goodness and, in return, 'in all things God works for the good of those who love him' (Romans 8:28).

Having established that God alone is good, Jesus went on to list six commandments that serve as a pattern of holiness. Five of the six are found in the Ten Commandments – murder, adultery, theft,

---

[48] Van Til, *Systematic Theology*, 238.

false witness and dishonouring parents – but the commandment against coveting is missing, having been replaced with a command against defrauding. Some suggest that the addition of defrauding indicates that the man was defrauding others. This might be the case, but we should note that the man insisted he had kept all these commandments since he was a child, and Jesus's response was one of warmth: he 'looked at him and loved him'. This should prevent us too quickly assuming that the man was untruthful in his claim.[49] Jesus issued no challenge to the man's statement. He simply looked at him and loved him. More likely is France's conclusion that the substitution is 'better seen simply as an attempt to draw out in more behavioural terms the implications of the tenth commandment: appropriating someone else's possessions is likely to be a practical result of coveting'.[50]

Later in the Gospel, Jesus summarised the Law as acknowledging that God is one, loving God with all your heart, soul, mind and strength and loving your neighbour as yourself (Mark 12:29–31). The list of commandments Jesus gave the man were moral acts, but the Law itself spoke more deeply of the love of God and neighbour. Here Jesus applied this summary of the Law to the man in front of him, and suggested he gave up his wealth in order to follow him. To give to the poor is to build up treasure in heaven; it is to transfer your wealth from earth to eternity.

'At this the man's face fell.' He was wealthy, and his possessions had possessed him. He walked away, and Jesus, looking around at his disciples, proclaimed, 'How hard it is for the rich to enter the kingdom of God!' A stark contrast with the children of the previous passage. Rather than coming as an empty-handed child, this man's hands were too full to receive grace.

Within Judaism, wealth was often seen as a blessing (e.g., Abraham, Job, David and Solomon), and so the disciples were amazed that Jesus should suggest that it is easier for a camel to pass through the eye of a needle than for a rich man to enter heaven. Some have sought

---

[49] See, for example, France, *Mark*, 403; Robert H. Stein, *Mark* (Grand Rapids: Baker Academic, 2008), 469; Edwards, *Mark*, 311. See also Philippians 3:6.
[50] France, *Mark*, 402.

to make Jesus's statement less a cause for amazement by suggesting that the word translated 'camel' should be translated as 'rope', or that the 'eye of a needle' is in fact a small gate. There is no evidence that either theory is true; rather, we should share in the disciples' amazement at Jesus's words. Those with possessions should grasp tightly the hope offered in Jesus's next words: 'With man this is impossible, but not with God; all things are possible with God.' Christianity can change the deepest attitudes such that we stop seeing possessions as having any intrinsic value, and instead see God alone as good.

Before drawing the conclusion that all rich people are to be viewed negatively, we would do well to remember that later in this Gospel both the unnamed woman with the expensive ointment (Mark 14:3–9) and Joseph of Arimathea (Mark 15:43, see Isaiah 53:9; Matthew 27:57) were viewed positively. Abraham was described as 'very wealthy' (Genesis 13:2), yet he 'believed the LORD, and he credited it to him as righteousness' (Genesis 15:6). Job owned vast numbers of livestock and was 'the greatest man among all the people of the East' (Job 1:3).

So what was the issue here? It was to do with the *attitude* to wealth (which, of course, is not only measured in monetary terms). It is the *love* of money that is the 'root of all kinds of evil' (1 Timothy 6:10), and it can become an alternative master to God ('You cannot serve both God and Money', Matthew 6:24). Money can be used for great good, but it can also become a source of security and comfort. It can become an idol taking the place of God. The rich man was not willing to give this up and to come to Jesus as simply as the children of the previous passage. It may be difficult to break the chains of wealth, but 'all things are possible with God' (Mark 10:27). The wealthy need to find their security in the goodness of God, not in their possessions.

Peter reminded Jesus that they had left everything for him – an expression of childlike faith – and Jesus promised that those who do so will be repaid a hundredfold. Echoes here of the parable of the sower. However, Jesus made one change to Peter's statement: all this comes to those who leave everything for 'me and the gospel'. Once again, Jesus brought attention to his teaching and placed it at the centre. To detach Jesus from his teaching is to miss the point of his ministry (see also Mark 8:35 where Jesus spoke of people losing their life 'for me and for the gospel'). We can also see something of the suffering of Mark 8:35 in this passage, as the disciples were promised not only repayment, but also 'persecutions'. This is no easy life, but it is the path to the eternal life which the rich man sought.

So it is that this passage, along with the previous incident with the children, demonstrate that 'many who are first will be last, and the last first' (Mark 10:31).

The third prediction of Jesus's death (10:32–4)

Jesus predicts his death a third time

32 They were on their way up to Jerusalem, with Jesus leading the way, and the disciples were astonished, while those who followed were afraid. Again he took the Twelve aside and told them what was going to happen to him. **33** 'We are going up to Jerusalem,' he said, 'and the Son of Man will be delivered over to the chief priests and the teachers of the law. They will condemn him to death and will hand him over to the Gentiles, **34** who will mock him and spit on him, flog him and kill him. Three days later he will rise.'

Jesus continued on to Jerusalem, ahead and leading his group into a place of danger. We have seen already in this Gospel that groups would come north from Jerusalem to challenge or entrap Jesus (Mark 3:22, 7:1); now he was walking south to face them on their own territory. This is the first time we see Jerusalem as the goal of Jesus's ministry, and it is clear that he was well aware of the fate that awaited him.

There would appear to be two groups with Jesus: the disciples (who were 'astonished', probably at the dangerous choice Jesus had made, even after Peter's attempts to dissuade him); and 'those who followed' who were afraid. Their fear did not prevent them from following Jesus, but neither did it evaporate as they followed. Discipleship requires courage. Even as Jesus's teaching had become bleaker, they followed. This was no gentle religion, all spirituality and no challenge. In many parts of the world, death stalks the path of the believer, and as Christendom crumbles in the West the comfort of Christians is challenged.

To prepare the Twelve for what would come, Jesus took them to one side and told them what was to occur. His use of the title 'Son of Man' gave what followed an apocalyptic flavour (see introduction), and it is notable that what came next was a series of acts that would be inflicted upon Jesus. He was not speaking of what he intended to do, but rather of what would happen to him: he would be delivered over to condemnation and death. These passives are reminiscent of the account of the Suffering Servant in Isaiah 53 and find their fulfilment in the crucifixion. There is no Docetic Christ here, one who only appeared to be human and did not suffer.[51] Jesus is as fully man as he is God. He actively obeyed the commands of the Father, whatever the cost.

It is easy to simply focus on the details of the prophecy, or its fulfilment in later passages, but that should not detract from the courage being shown by Jesus in facing this future. Resurrection may be a vindication of Jesus's ministry, but the crucifixion speaks of his great bravery and the loving purpose he had. Christ has walked the path of suffering ahead of you.

Two seek glory (10:35–45)

The request of James and John

35 Then James and John, the sons of Zebedee, came to him. 'Teacher,' they said, 'we want you to do for us whatever we ask.'

36 'What do you want me to do for you?' he asked.

37 They replied, 'Let one of us sit at your right and the other at your left in your glory.'

38 'You don't know what you are asking,' Jesus said. 'Can you drink the cup I drink or be baptised with the baptism I am baptised with?'

39 'We can,' they answered.

Jesus said to them, 'You will drink the cup I drink and be baptised with the baptism I am baptised with, **40** but to sit at my right or left is not for me to grant. These places belong to those for whom they have been prepared.'

41 When the ten heard about this, they became indignant with James and John. **42** Jesus called them together and said, 'You know that those who are regarded as rulers

---

[51] Docetism was an early heresy which taught that neither Jesus's humanity nor his suffering was real. Instead, they simply *appeared* to be real.

of the Gentiles lord it over them, and their high officials exercise authority over them. **43** Not so with you. Instead, whoever wants to become great among you must be your servant, **44** and whoever wants to be first must be slave of all. **45** For even the Son of Man did not come to be served, but to serve, and to give his life as a ransom for many.'

After a string of passages dealing with the humility of a disciple and the need for a childlike acceptance of grace, James and John, sons of Zebedee, were still pursuing an agenda of ambition. What it is to be human! They sought to sit alongside Jesus, a request they made without the knowledge of the other ten. Even Peter was to be sidelined since they envisaged no third place available adjacent to Jesus.

The question they asked is one that is all too often seen in our approach to prayer: 'We want you to do for us whatever we ask.' Here was Jesus as simply a dispenser of favours. What a contrast with his own prayer at Gethsemane: 'Yet not what I will, but what you will' (Mark 14:36). As was often the case, Jesus did not make a direct reply but rather encouraged his questioners to make themselves clearer. They wished to share in Jesus's glory, sitting one at each side of him.

It is not clear what was in the minds of the brothers. It might be that they had fully grasped Jesus's predictions of his death and resurrection, but that would seem unlikely. More probably these 'sons of thunder' (Mark 3:17) were assuming that Jesus would be welcomed into Jerusalem and take the throne. That, after all, is what many at the time expected the Messiah to do, and the language of sitting, rather than reclining as would be the case at a banquet, suggests a throne room.[52]

Yet the path of Jesus was one of suffering. 'You don't know what you are asking,' said Jesus, before asking, 'Can you drink the cup I drink or be baptised with the baptism I am baptised with?' The cup can be a symbol of blessing (e.g., Psalm 16:5 and 23:5), but more often it is indicative of God's judgment (e.g., Psalm 75:8; Job 21:20; Isaiah 51:17, 22; Jeremiah 25:15–28). Jesus goes to receive wrath, not blessing. The imagery of baptism is less clear. The verb denotes plunging, and so it might speak of overwhelming suffering

---

[52] France, *Mark*, 415.

or being plunged into the cup of suffering. Taken together, the two images are far from the glorious setting the brothers had in mind.

Their answer to this question was bold – 'We can' – and so Jesus replied that they would indeed drink the cup. This was no punishment from Jesus for their brashness, but rather a simple statement of what was to follow. A decade or so later James was killed by Herod (Acts 12:2), and was one of the martyrs seen by his brother in Revelation 6:9. However, the places beside Jesus had already been prepared for their occupants and so he could not grant their request to sit at his side. In fact, as Jesus was glorified at the crucifixion, he had criminals at either side of him.

The remaining disciples were indignant when they heard of the antics of the brothers. No doubt they wanted those two places for themselves. In recent chapters, Peter had sought to dissuade Jesus from his path of suffering (Mark 8:32), and the Twelve had argued over who was the greatest (Mark 9:34). They had wanted to prevent others from acting in Jesus's name (Mark 9:38) and tried to keep the children away (Mark 10:13). In response to all this, Jesus called them together and made it plain that the path of discipleship is not one of self-promotion. Theirs was not to be a highly stratified society, with strict hierarchies of authority (although note that Jesus referred to those *regarded* as rulers). All authority ultimately comes from God (John 19:11), and those who set themselves up in positions of authority without his calling are no rulers at all.

The path to greatness in the kingdom of God lies in service, which is to follow the example of Jesus. 'Even the Son of Man,' the one to whom authority is given in Daniel 7, was to serve and eventually give up his life as a ransom for many so that they may be free. Here we find echoes of Isaiah 53, and the servant who suffers for many.[53]

We serve the Jesus who came to serve, and in so doing he frees us from a death like his. The deadly seriousness of sin is evident in the high price of the ransom: Jesus's own life.

Before leaving this passage, there are two matters that deserve our attention. First, in Matthew's Gospel, it was James and John's

---

[53] For a discussion on the controversy around this verse, and a defence of the more traditional view expressed in this commentary, see Strauss, *Mark*, 459–62.

mother who approached Jesus (Matthew 20:20). However, when he replied to her request, Jesus did so in the plural, thereby addressing James and John, who in turn answered him. The request was theirs, and their mother was their mouthpiece. Mark simply omitted the mother since the issue lay with the brothers.[54]

Second, we would do well to spend some time considering the summary Jesus gave of his mission and ministry: 'the Son of Man did not come to be served, but to serve, and to give his life as a ransom for many'. The idea of Christian service is widespread and accepted throughout the church, but we should be careful not to read that back into this particular verse. Rather, we should take the verse as a whole and be careful not to ignore the second part of the saying. As part of this path of service, Jesus came to give up his life. His death was a core part of his service, not simply a consequence of his challenges to the authorities of his day. He was not simply a teacher of eternal truths, but a Messiah who had come to die a vicarious death. No understanding of Christ can be complete without this element of his purpose.

As our ransom, Christ has taken our place. There is an objective property to the Christian's salvation: the ransom paid by Christ. This past event resonates to our present salvation, and is the act upon which we may stand. Our place before God depends not upon our subjective feelings, nor upon our own sinlessness, but upon the ransom of Christ. The cross is no mere symbol, but a reminder of the work completed upon its harsh timbers. Here is the atonement, presented to us in contrast to the self-serving ambition of the brothers.

While the word 'ransom' is often associated with kidnapping, this is not the meaning it carried in the first century. It is vital to understand the word against its Old Testament context where it refers to a payment being made to escape death (e.g., Exodus 30:12; Numbers 35:31–2). The Hebrew word (kōper) is part of the word group that carries the meaning of atonement (kippūr), and is best defined as:

---

[54] One commentator writes, 'They have probably reasoned, "We have been messing up a lot lately, and Jesus has been exasperated with us, so we shouldn't ask directly. How can Jesus say no to Mom?"' Grant R. Osborne, *Matthew* (Grand Rapids: Zondervan, 2010), 739.

The material gift that establishes an amicable settlement between an injured party and the offending party . . . The injured family may insist that the owner be put to death, but may also accept the payment of *kōper* as an agreed settlement.[55]

This is the service Jesus carried out: to be the payment that secures our life. A payment made upon the cross.

The more the Christian looks to Jesus as a ransom, now paid, the more assurance of faith will develop. Thomas Brooks (1608–80) captured this well: 'How would such a daily eyeing of Christ scatter a Christian's fears, arm him against temptations, support him under afflictions, weaken his sins, strengthen his graces, cheer his soul, and mend his life!'[56]

The sight-giving faith of Bartimaeus (10:46–52)

Blind Bartimaeus receives his sight

46 Then they came to Jericho. As Jesus and his disciples, together with a large crowd, were leaving the city, a blind man, Bartimaeus (which means 'son of Timaeus'), was sitting by the roadside begging. **47** When he heard that it was Jesus of Nazareth, he began to shout, 'Jesus, Son of David, have mercy on me!'

48 Many rebuked him and told him to be quiet, but he shouted all the more, 'Son of David, have mercy on me!'

49 Jesus stopped and said, 'Call him.' So they called to the blind man, 'Cheer up! On your feet! He's calling you.' **50** Throwing his cloak aside, he jumped to his feet and came to Jesus.

51 'What do you want me to do for you?' Jesus asked him.

The blind man said, 'Rabbi, I want to see.'

52 'Go,' said Jesus, 'your faith has healed you.' Immediately he received his sight and followed Jesus along the road.

---

55 B. Lang, 'כֹּפֶר', in *Theological Dictionary of the Old Testament*, ed. G. Johannes Botterweck, Helmer Ringgren and Heinz-Josef Fabry (Grand Rapids; Eerdmans, 1995), 7.301.

56 Thomas Brooks, 'The Golden Key to Open Hidden Treasures', in *The Complete Works of Thomas Brooks, Volume 5*, ed. Alexander Balloch Grosart (London; James Nisbet, 1867), 253.

Jericho lies some eight hundred feet below sea level and is a city of great antiquity, having been first settled thousands of years before Christ. It lies beneath Jerusalem, some fifteen miles distant, and is an oasis in the Jordan Valley. As Jesus arrived with his disciples and a large crowd, making his way onwards to Jerusalem, the sense of momentum built as the city of David drew near. As the large group proceeded along the way, they came near to a blind man named Bartimaeus,[57] who was sitting by 'the way' (the word translated 'roadside' in fact means 'way').[58] This blind man was begging because his affliction had robbed him of the ability to work. He had purposely placed himself beside a busy route, most probably by a gate (Jesus and his followers were 'leaving the city' when they passed Bartimaeus). Hearing that Jesus was near, he cried out to him. Since Jesus was far from his native Galilee, he was now referred to as Jesus of Nazareth, but Bartimaeus called out to him using his Davidic title. The beggar was rebuked for his efforts (we don't know by whom) but he persisted and continued to cry out. Here was a persevering disciple, one who would not be put off by the disdain of others.

Once more Jesus overruled those who sought to restrict access to him (see Mark 10:13–16 which sits at the beginning of this section). He stopped and asked the rebukers to instead call the blind beggar to him. The call of Christ overcomes those who would keep others from him.

When Bartimaeus heard Jesus was summoning him, he jumped up and threw his cloak aside. This in itself was a great expression of faith since that cloak may have been all this beggar had, and it would not be easy for a blind man to find a cloak he has flung aside. Unlike the rich man, he was able to give up all that he had to come to Christ. This is a model for us of persevering prayer, and of a disciple who is willing to put Jesus above everything else, even his cloak. What a contrast he is to the disciples who wanted glory, to tell Jesus what he should do and define who could be his followers.

---

[57] The fact that he is named would suggest that he was still known to the church and was an eyewitness source. For a full discussion of this, see Bauckham, *Eyewitnesses*, especially 598–603.

[58] See the introductory section 'Mark and the Old Testament' for the significance of the phrase 'the way'.

Jesus echoed the request of James and John as he asked, 'What do you want me to do for you?' (see Mark 10:35–45). The beggar, unlike the disciples, did not seek glory but mercy. He referred to Jesus as 'Rabbi', as would be proper for a disciple, and asked for sight. This faith – calling Jesus Son of David, persisting in his calls for mercy, casting aside his cloak and requesting his sight – had brought about his healing. Regaining his sight, he got behind Jesus as one of his followers.

Jerusalem beckoned.

5

The Messiah and the Temple

MARK 11:1–13:37

1. The triumph • Mark 11:1–25

Jesus finally came to the end of his journey along 'the way' and entered Jerusalem. He was greeted as a king, but in fact he was the long-awaited returning LORD. As he entered the Temple, he found it to be barren, like a fruitless fig tree, and so it was cursed.

The triumph of the King (11:1–11)

Jesus comes to Jerusalem as king

11 As they approached Jerusalem and came to Bethphage and Bethany at the Mount of Olives, Jesus sent two of his disciples, **2** saying to them, 'Go to the village ahead of you, and just as you enter it, you will find a colt tied there, which no one has ever ridden. Untie it and bring it here. **3** If anyone asks you, "Why are you doing this?" say, "The Lord needs it and will send it back here shortly."'

4 They went and found a colt outside in the street, tied at a doorway. As they untied it, **5** some people standing there asked, 'What are you doing, untying that colt?' **6** They answered as Jesus had told them to, and the people let them go. **7** When they brought the colt to Jesus and threw their cloaks over it, he sat on it. **8** Many people spread their cloaks on the road, while others spread branches they had cut in the fields. **9** Those who went ahead and those who followed shouted,

'Hosanna!**a**'

'Blessed is he who comes in
the name of the Lord!'**b**

10 'Blessed is the coming kingdom
of our father David!'

'Hosanna in the highest
heaven!'

11 Jesus entered Jerusalem
and went into the temple

courts. He looked around at everything, but since it was already late, he went out to Bethany with the Twelve.

a 9 A Hebrew expression meaning 'Save!' which became an exclamation of praise; also in verse 10
b 9 Psalm 118:25,26

As Jesus reached Jerusalem, we encounter the Temple for the first time. It is hard to overestimate the importance of the Temple for the Jewish people, since it operated as both a religious and a national centre. Some two hundred years before, the Temple had been desecrated by Antiochus Epiphanes (164 BC) and its restoration was a national triumph, marked by the Feast of Dedication (Hanukkah). It had been greatly expanded by Herod the Great, and was an awe-inspiring structure:

> The exterior of the building wanted nothing that could astound either mind or eye. For, being covered on all sides with massive plates of gold, the sun was no sooner up than it radiated so fiery a flash that persons straining to look at it were compelled to avert their eyes, as from the solar rays. To approaching strangers it appeared from a distance like a snow-clad mountain; for all that was not overlaid with gold was of purest white. From its summit protruded sharp golden spikes to prevent birds from settling upon and polluting the roof. Some of the stones in the building were forty-five cubits in length, five in height and six in breadth.[1]

However, all was not well for this glorious edifice, and its magnificence masked a sense of lack. The Exile, which had been accompanied by the destruction of Solomon's Temple, was understood to have been a judgment upon Israel. Their activities had driven God from his sanctuary (Ezekiel 8:6). Later, that same prophet described how the glory of the LORD departed from Jerusalem and 'stopped above the mountain east of it', which is the Mount of Olives (Ezekiel 11:23). Later still, Ezekiel had a vision of a restoration of Israel's fortunes, with God stating, 'My servant David will be king over them' (Ezekiel 37:24)

---

[1] Josephus, *Jewish War*, 5.5.6. Translation taken from Flavius Josephus, *The Jewish War: Books 1–7*, trans. H. St. J. Thackeray (Cambridge; London; New York: Harvard University Press, 1927), 4:269.

and, 'I will put my sanctuary among them for ever. My dwelling-place will be with them; I will be their God, and they will be my people' (Ezekiel 37:26–7). In Ezekiel 43, there is a vision of the glory of the LORD returning to the Temple from the East. This had yet to occur.

This return of God to the Temple was also foreseen by Malachi in a passage already quoted by Mark at the beginning of the Gospel: 'I will send my messenger, who will prepare the way before me. Then suddenly the Lord you are seeking will come to his temple' (Malachi 3:1). Zechariah also looked forward to the return of the LORD (Zechariah 2:10; 8:3), as did Isaiah, who prophesied:

Listen! Your watchmen lift up their voices;
   together they shout for joy.
When the LORD returns to Zion,
   they will see it with their own eyes.
(Isaiah 52:8)

Yet for all its external glory, there was an emptiness at the heart of the Temple, and the people hoped and looked for the return of the LORD to his sanctuary.[2] There is always a risk of oversimplifying Jewish thought in the Second Temple period, but the literature points to a dissatisfaction with the Temple and a sense that it was not quite what it ought to be.[3] This is not to suggest an outright rejection by all, but there was certainly a sense of longing which even the Maccabean triumph with its subsequent cleansing of the Temple did not dispel.

Coming up from Jericho, which lies 850 feet below sea level, Jesus and the crowd come to the Mount of Olives which rises to 2,600 feet above sea level, 300 feet higher than Jerusalem itself. Bethphage is towards the summit, near Bethany, and from here Jesus sent an unnamed pair of disciples into the nearby village to get a colt. If they

---

[2] See 1 Enoch 25:3 and Jubilees 1:26–8 for similar hopes in the intertestamental period. There was also a growing trend of individuals carrying out cleansing rituals which normally would be associated with the Temple (e.g., Tobit 2), which meant that Judaism was well placed to continue once the Temple was destroyed in AD 70.

[3] Christopher Rowland, 'The Temple in the New Testament', in *Temple and Worship in Biblical Israel. Proceedings of the Oxford Old Testament Seminar*, ed. John Day (London: T&T Clark, 2007), 469.

were challenged, they were to say, 'The Lord needs it and will send it back here shortly.' There is no indication as to how Jesus knew about the colt, and conjecture is therefore unnecessary. The point is that Jesus needed a colt, and he described himself as 'the Lord', a suggestive title.

Within the wider ancient world there is evidence of kings using donkeys to make entrances into conquered cities, and of course this theme may also be seen in Zechariah 9:9. Mark stressed the fact that this colt had not been ridden before, and this might be seen as giving honour to the one who rode it first.[4]

As Jesus entered, he was greeted as an entering king, and the imagery of the shouting crowd would have been well known at the time. This kind of triumphant entry was experienced across the Roman Empire, and Alexander the Great had himself staged such an entry into Jerusalem some centuries before.[5] This entry would follow a normal pattern: the ruler or conqueror was met at the gates of the city by its leading inhabitants who then escorted him into the city to an accompaniment of hymns; the escorts would carry flowers, olive or palm branches, lights and incense; and the conqueror was accompanied by his army or retinue.[6] The goal of this procession was the city's temple, where the entering figure would offer a sacrifice and thereby take possession of the city.

The parallels with the entry into Jerusalem are clear enough: Jesus entered Jerusalem with his 'army' and was accompanied by messianic hymns of acclamation from those who were around him. His status was recognised by the laying of cloaks or palm branches on the road, and

---

[4] Gundry, *Mark*, 628. In support of this view he cites Numbers 19:2; Deuteronomy 21:3; 1 Samuel 6:7; 2 Samuel 6:3; Zechariah 9:9 (LXX). Derrett has noted that the Mishnah contains a prohibition on anyone riding an animal once ridden by a king. J. Duncan M. Derrett, 'Law in the New Testament: The Palm Sunday Colt', *Novum Testamentum* (1971), 238f.

[5] Josephus, *Jewish Antiquities*, 11.8.5.

[6] Sabine MacCormack, 'Change and Continuity in Late Antiquity: The Ceremony of "Adventus"', *Historia: Zeitschrift für Alte Geschichte* H. 4 (1972); D. R. Catchpole, 'The "Triumphal Entry"', in *Jesus and the Politics of His Day*, ed. Ernst Bammel and Charles Francis Digby Moule (Cambridge: Cambridge University Press, 1985); Paul Brooks Duff, 'The March of the Divine Warrior and the Advent of the Greco–Roman King: Mark's Account of Jesus' Entry Into Jerusalem', *Journal of Biblical Literature* 3, no. 1 (1992); Adela Yarbro Collins, *Mark: A Commentary* (Philadelphia: Fortress Press, 2007).

he visited the Temple. It was at this point, however, that the pattern had a significant variation: the Temple was rejected. More on this below.

Given all of this, it is not fanciful to see the entry into Jerusalem as welcoming the LORD as King back to Zion, and the theme of the LORD as King is one that gains prominence in the Psalms and prophetic books as well as the literature written in the time between the Old and New Testaments.[7]

Mark's Gospel opened with the call: 'Prepare the way for the Lord, make straight paths for him' (Mark 1:3). Throughout the first ten chapters of the Gospel, Jesus had been on 'the way' (Mark 2:23; 8:27; 9:33–4; 10:52) and now they had arrived. The 'way' had seen Jesus walk on the sea (Isaiah 43:16) and gather many in the wilderness (Isaiah 43:19). Now he was at the gates of Jerusalem, and the words of Isaiah 62:10–12 are particularly pertinent:

Pass through, pass through the gates!
　　Prepare the way for the people.
Build up, build up the highway!
　　Remove the stones.
Raise a banner for the nations.

The LORD has made proclamation
　　to the ends of the earth:
'Say to Daughter Zion,
　　"See, your Saviour comes!
See, his reward is with him,
　　and his recompense accompanies him."'
They will be called the Holy People,
　　the Redeemed of the LORD;
and you will be called Sought After,
　　the City No Longer Deserted.

---

[7] Numbers 23:21; 1 Samuel 12:12; 1 Chronicles 16:31; Esther (LXX) 13:9, 15, 14:3, 12; Psalms 10:16; 24:8, 10; 29:10; 47:2; 84:3; 89:18; 93:1, 2; 96:10; 97:1; 98:6; 99:1; Isaiah 6:5; 33:22; 43:15; 44:6; Jeremiah 8:19; 10:10; 48:15; 51:57; Zephaniah 3:15; Zechariah 14:9, 16; Malachi 1:14; Tobit 13:6, 10, 15; Judith 9:12; Sirach 51:1; 2 Maccabees 1:24; 3 Maccabees 2:2; 3 Maccabees 5:35; 1 Timothy 6:15; Revelation 17:14; Revelation 19:16; Enoch 9:4, 12:3, 25:3, 27:3.

The LORD had returned to Zion, and the king had returned. The glory of the LORD (glimpsed at the transfiguration) was now returning to the Temple, coming in from the Mount of Olives to the east, as foreseen by Ezekiel:

> Then the man brought me to the gate facing east, and I saw the glory of the God of Israel coming from the east. His voice was like the roar of rushing waters, and the land was radiant with his glory. The vision I saw was like the vision I had seen when he came to destroy the city and like the visions I had seen by the River Kebar, and I fell face down. The glory of the LORD entered the temple through the gate facing east. (Ezekiel 43:1–4)

Here was the fulfilment of so much hope.

When he arrived at the Temple, Jesus 'looked around at everything' and then left. Here is a deep irony: the LORD returned to Zion, those in the Temple failed to recognise his return, and he left unheralded. The populace greeted Jesus with a triumphant entry, but the king in their imagination was not the same as the King who was the returning LORD. There was a failure by both parties – the people and the Temple – to grasp the significance of the events that unfolded.

That Jesus left the Temple demonstrates both that his cleansing of the Temple was no spontaneous act and that he intended it to be carried out at a time when it would make the greatest impact. It was already late, and it is reasonable to assume the crowds at the Temple would have dwindled.

This 'triumphal entry' is best understood against the contexts of its day: the well-established pattern for kings or emperors entering a city; the hope for the return of God to Jerusalem. When these are acknowledged, along with the ironic portrayal of the entry of Jesus into the Temple, it can be seen that Mark is illustrating the return of the LORD to Zion. The LORD who had been seen feeding the five thousand and walking on water. The LORD who was revealed to the inner core of the disciples at the transfiguration, when the glorified Christ spoke with those who had also experienced mountaintop revelations. Here is the one who is both the

Son of God and the Son of Man. The descendant of David and the fulfilment of Scripture.

The fig tree and the Temple (11:12–26)

Jesus curses a fig-tree and clears the temple courts

12 The next day as they were leaving Bethany, Jesus was hungry. **13** Seeing in the distance a fig-tree in leaf, he went to find out if it had any fruit. When he reached it, he found nothing but leaves, because it was not the season for figs. **14** Then he said to the tree, 'May no one ever eat fruit from you again.' And his disciples heard him say it.

15 On reaching Jerusalem, Jesus entered the temple courts and began driving out those who were buying and selling there. He overturned the tables of the money-changers and the benches of those selling doves, **16** and would not allow anyone to carry merchandise through the temple courts. **17** And as he taught them, he said, 'Is it not written: "My house will be called a house of prayer for all nations"[c]? But you have made it "a den of robbers".[d]'

18 The chief priests and the teachers of the law heard this and began looking for a way to kill him, for they feared him, because the whole crowd was amazed at his teaching.

19 When evening came, Jesus and his disciples[e] went out of the city.

20 In the morning, as they went along, they saw the fig-tree withered from the roots. **21** Peter remembered and said to Jesus, 'Rabbi, look! The fig-tree you cursed has withered!'

22 'Have faith in God,' Jesus answered. **23** 'Truly[f] I tell you, if anyone says to this mountain, "Go, throw yourself into the sea," and does not doubt in their heart but believes that what they say will happen, it will be done for them. **24** Therefore I tell you, whatever you ask for in prayer, believe that you have received it, and it will be yours. **25** And when you stand praying, if you hold anything against anyone, forgive them, so that your Father in heaven may forgive you your sins.' [26][g]

---

c 17 Isaiah 56:7
d 17 Jer. 7:11
e 19 Some early manuscripts *came, Jesus*
f 22,23 Some early manuscripts *'If you have faith in God,' Jesus answered,* 23 *'truly*
g 26 Some manuscripts include here words similar to Matt. 6:15.

The cursing of the fig tree and the clearing of the Temple are best understood as a single event. Mark has used a 'sandwiching' technique, placing the incident with the tree on either side of the Temple cleansing, and the two passages therefore interpret each other.

We begin with the fig tree. The previous day Jesus had gone into the Temple and 'looked around at everything' (Mark 11:11). Once this inspection had taken place, he then travelled the short distance to Bethany to stay the night. At festival times, it was not uncommon for the visiting pilgrims to camp on the hillsides or stay in villages nearby. At the Passover itself, the pilgrims would seek to sleep within the boundaries of the city (and so Jesus moved on to Gethsemane in Mark 14:32).[8]

The next day, on leaving Bethany to go to Jerusalem, Jesus saw a fig tree in leaf and, being hungry, went over to see if he could find anything on it.[9] The NIV translation is misleading here, as the Greek does not contain the word 'fruit'. In fact, as we will discover, it was not the season for figs (which grow in later summer), so it was unlikely that Jesus would have been searching for them. What he would have expected to be present were the buds (*paggim*) which ripen into figs and are edible. The tree was in leaf but had produced no edible buds. Micah 7:1 comes to mind:

What misery is mine!
I am like one who gathers summer fruit
    at the gleaning of the vineyard;
there is no cluster of grapes to eat,
    none of the early figs that I crave.

A similar sentiment can be found in Isaiah 5:2.

The parallel to Micah is fuller than simply the first verse. The prophet likened Israel itself to the fig tree, and its unfaithfulness to its lack of 'early figs'. As a result:

---

[8] Joachim Jeremias, *Jerusalem in the Time of Jesus: An Investigation into Economic and Social Conditions During the New Testament Period* (Philadelphia: Fortress Press, 1975), 61–2.

[9] Incidentally, we here find Jesus experiencing physical hunger, and this is one of a number of passages that serve to underline the reality of Jesus's humanity: he does not simply *appear* to be human (the error of the Docetists) but *is* human.

The day God visits you has come,
  the day your watchmen sound the alarm.
  Now is the time of your confusion.
(Micah 7:4)

In response to this lack of buds, Jesus pronounced a curse, and we then move on to the Temple where we see a similar pattern play out.[10]

Sometimes the cleansing of the Temple is portrayed as a fit of rage on the part of Jesus, but this does not fit the events themselves. Jesus had been to the Temple the day before and 'looked around at everything'. When he returned the next day, he was not reacting to something newly discovered but rather carrying out a considered act.

The outer Temple courts were open to Gentiles, but over time they had become the location of stalls which sold all the goods needed to operate the Temple. Money had to be changed into suitable coins so that Jewish males aged twenty or over could pay the half-shekel tax,[11] and animals suitable for sacrifice were sold to those who either could not provide their own or had travelled a long distance. Mark specifically mentioned doves being sold, which demonstrates that this trade was being targeted at the poor (see Leviticus 5:7, 12:8).

These stalls had been moved into the Temple from outside, and there is evidence that suggests that this might have been done by Caiaphas just a few years earlier.[12] There was an unfortunate air of corruption around the Temple, particularly in some of the high priestly families, which can be seen in a Jewish tradition which records:

---

[10] The word 'tree' is not present in the Greek, rather we have, 'then he said to it'.
[11] See discussion on Mark 12:13–17 for reasons as to why Roman coinage was not suitable for use.
[12] 'Caiaphas may have been the first High Priest to authorize the sale of sacrificial animals in the temple precincts and may have done so because of a quarrel with the Sanhedrin, which, in turn, may have been related to the Sanhedrin's expulsion from the Chamber of Hewn Stone. Observing this activity and being aware of the factors that had led up to it, Jesus may have reacted the way he did in the temple precincts. Although not implausible, the uncertainty of this chain of reasoning is obvious.' Craig A. Evans, 'Jesus' Action in the Temple: Cleansing or Portent of Destruction?' *The Catholic Biblical Quarterly* 51, no. 2 (1989), 267.

As to Jerusalem's first building, on what account was it destroyed? Because of idolatry and licentiousness and bloodshed which was in it. But as to the latter building we know that they devoted themselves to Torah and were meticulous about tithes. On what account did they go into exile? Because they love money and hate one another.[13]

Jesus began driving out the traders, and Mark used the same verb, *ekballō*, which elsewhere describes the casting out of demons. This act could not fail to attract attention and would make it impossible for the Temple to function. By cutting off the supply of sacrificial animals and the Temple tax, Jesus effectively disrupted the Temple worship.

As was his usual pattern, Jesus then began teaching. His actions were not left uninterpreted, nor was he simply an activist. He cited Isaiah 56:7, which would have been a rebuke to those who had sought to fill the courts of the Gentiles with stalls.[14] The section in Isaiah from which the quote comes (Isaiah 56:1–8) deals with the wideness of God's grace and the gathering of the faithful from all nations in the purposes of God. The immediate context of Jesus's quotation is important.

And foreigners who bind themselves to the LORD
    to minister to him,
to love the name of the LORD,
    and to be his servants,
all who keep the Sabbath without desecrating it
    and who hold fast to my covenant –
these I will bring to my holy mountain
    and give them joy in my house of prayer.
Their burnt offerings and sacrifices
    will be accepted on my altar;
for my house will be called
    a house of prayer for all nations.
    (Isaiah 56:6–7)

---

[13] Cited in Evans, 'Temple', 259. Translation is from Neusner, *Tosefta*. 5.162.
[14] See also Solomon's prayer in 1 Kings 8:43.

Note that the focus was on not on the stalls themselves, but on the fact that they limited access to the worship of God. God brings foreigners to his holy mountain, but the stalls clogged the courts of the Gentiles.

The second quote, from Jeremiah, did criticise the practice of selling goods and implied that the practice was also exploitative. The whole passage from Jeremiah, which would have come into the minds of his Jewish audience, is worth reproducing in whole as it demonstrates that Jesus was acting in a prophetic manner:

> This is the word that came to Jeremiah from the LORD: 'Stand at the gate of the Lord's house and there proclaim this message:
>
> "Hear the word of the LORD, all you people of Judah who come through these gates to worship the LORD. This is what the LORD Almighty, the God of Israel, says: reform your ways and your actions, and I will let you live in this place. Do not trust in deceptive words and say, 'This is the temple of the LORD, the temple of the LORD, the temple of the LORD!' If you really change your ways and your actions and deal with each other justly, if you do not oppress the foreigner, the fatherless or the widow and do not shed innocent blood in this place, and if you do not follow other gods to your own harm, then I will let you live in this place, in the land I gave to your ancestors for ever and ever. But look, you are trusting in deceptive words that are worthless.
>
> "Will you steal and murder, commit adultery and perjury, burn incense to Baal and follow other gods you have not known, and then come and stand before me in this house, which bears my Name, and say, 'We are safe' – safe to do all these detestable things? Has this house, which bears my Name, become a den of robbers to you? But I have been watching! declares the LORD." (Jeremiah 7:1–11)

In response to this, the Temple party sought to kill Jesus, a stark demonstration of the fear they had of him. The reason for this fear was, we should note, his teaching and the amazement it produced in the crowds that heard him.[15] Earlier in the Gospel we saw the Pharisees and Herodians plotting to kill Jesus (Mark 3:6), so we now have a significant number of people from different parts of Jewish life seeking his death. Jesus and the disciples then left the city for the night.

The following day, probably Tuesday, the disciples once more encountered the fig tree, which had now withered from the roots. This was an entire death of the plant, not simply leaves withering in the sun. Peter recalled Jesus's curse of the previous day, but Jesus's response did not explicitly mention the tree. Rather he spoke of faith and prayer, and it might at first sight appear that he was ignoring Peter's comment. However, the 'mountain' Jesus referred to would be the Temple Mount, and so he was making a point as to the relative importance of faith and the Temple. Faith should be placed in God, and not in the Temple. The church should never eclipse the one it serves.

Faith and belief from the heart were to be the key. With that, the Temple Mount itself could be cast into the sea! The Temple paled into insignificance against the importance of faithful prayer. Rather than a pilgrimage to the Temple, it is the heart that is the locus of prayer. Faith, not sacrifice, is the heart of the matter.

It is possible to read Jesus's teaching and to gain the impression that he was endorsing some sort of Prosperity Gospel: 'whatever you ask for in prayer, believe that you have received it, and it will be yours'. That is to go against the grain of the rest of Scripture, and so we should be wary of drawing that conclusion. Jesus himself, when tempted in Mark 1, was given the offer of obtaining riches and influence, yet he spurned this as it was counter to Scripture. The one who truly has faith is the one who does not pray for his or her own prosperity, but for the forgiveness of others, the forgiveness of sins and the glory of God. That is the true faith which leads to prayers that are answered.

---

[15] See, for instance, Mark 1:22.

2. The Temple rejects the Messiah • Mark 11:27–13:2

After Jesus's very public entry, and the no doubt very great controversy stirred up by his cleansing of the Temple, he was now a marked man. All the main parties of Judaism were plotting his death, and there followed several questionings that were all intended to catch him out and to reduce his popularity with the people. Jesus successfully outwitted his opponents, before teaching against them. Finally, and shockingly, he spoke of the destruction of the Temple itself.

All of this activity, coming so close to the great feast of the Passover, represented a great threat to the authorities. It could not be ignored.

The authority of Christ (11:27–33)

The authority of Jesus questioned

27 They arrived again in Jerusalem, and while Jesus was walking in the temple courts, the chief priests, the teachers of the law and the elders came to him. **28** 'By what authority are you doing these things?' they asked. 'And who gave you authority to do this?'

29 Jesus replied, 'I will ask you one question. Answer me, and I will tell you by what authority I am doing these things. **30** John's baptism – was it from heaven, or of human origin? Tell me!'

31 They discussed it among themselves and said, 'If we say, "From heaven," he will ask, "Then why didn't you believe him?" **32** But if we say, "Of human origin" . . .' (They feared the people, for everyone held that John really was a prophet.)

33 So they answered Jesus, 'We don't know.'

Jesus said, 'Neither will I tell you by what authority I am doing these things.'

Jesus returned once more to the Temple courts: a dangerous act, but one from which he did not shy. He was not teaching at this point, simply walking in the courts, but the Temple authorities – the chief priests, teachers of the law and elders who together made up the Sanhedrin – came to him. Their concern was to establish Jesus's authority for 'doing these things', which, presumably, referred both to his clearing out the Temple traders and to his teaching. Here was the establishment seeking from Jesus his credentials. What was his authority?

As he often did, Jesus answered a question with a question, 'so that they might realize their own malice', as Athanasius (c. 296–373) observed.[16] His ministry was closely interlinked with John the Baptist who, after all, proclaimed his coming. John was an Elijah figure and, as we have seen, Malachi looked forward to Elijah's return 'before that great and dreadful day of the LORD comes' (Malachi 4:5). If John's baptism of repentance was indeed heaven sent, then that implied something about Jesus himself since John had pointed to Christ. Moreover, John was held in high esteem by the wider population, and for the authorities to downplay John was to risk the wrath of the people.

It was a politically impossible question to answer, and so they simply shrugged, 'We don't know.' And so Jesus also gave no direct answer but answered with a parable.

Temple squatters (12:1–12)

The parable of the tenants

12 Jesus then began to speak to them in parables: 'A man planted a vineyard. He put a wall round it, dug a pit for the winepress and built a watchtower. Then he rented the vineyard to some farmers and moved to another place. **2** At harvest time he sent a servant to the tenants to collect from them some of the fruit of the vineyard. **3** But they seized him, beat him and sent him away empty-handed. **4** Then he sent another servant to them; they struck this man on the head and treated him shamefully. **5** He sent still another, and that one they killed. He sent many others; some of them they beat, others they killed.

6 'He had one left to send, a son, whom he loved. He sent him last of all, saying, "They will respect my son."

7 'But the tenants said to one another, "This is the heir. Come, let's kill him, and the inheritance will be ours." **8** So they took him and killed him, and threw him out of the vineyard.

9 'What then will the owner of the vineyard do? He will come and kill those tenants and give the vineyard

---

[16] *Letters to Serapion*, 3.2.2. Translation from Athanasius, and Didymus the Blind, *Works on the Spirit: Athanasius's Letters to Serapion on the Holy Spirit, and, Didymus's on the Holy Spirit*, trans. Mark DelCogliano, Andrew Radde-Gallwitz and Lewis Ayres (Yonkers: St Vladimirs Seminary Press, 2011), 129.

to others. **10** Haven't you read this passage of Scripture:

'"The stone the builders
     rejected
   has become the cornerstone;
11 the Lord has done this,
   and it is marvellous in our
      eyes"ᵃ?'

12 Then the chief priests, the teachers of the law and the elders looked for a way to arrest him because they knew he had spoken the parable against them. But they were afraid of the crowd; so they left him and went away.

_____

a 11 Psalm 118:22,23

This parable is closely linked to the preceding passage, and is part of the answer Jesus gave to the ruling party's question, 'By what authority are you doing these things?' (Mark 11:28).

The vineyard was a common Old Testament image for Israel (Psalm 80:8–18; Isaiah 3:14; 5:1–7; 27:2–6; Jeremiah 2:21; 12:10; Ezekiel 19:10–14; Hosea 10:1), and Micah linked an unfruitful fig tree with a vineyard where 'the faithful have been swept from the land' (Micah 7:1–4). Jesus's parable spoke of God – the owner of the vineyard – and his relationship with his tenants. Successive servants were sent to collect some of the fruit, which was the normal payment of rent. It would normally take around four years for new vines to mature, and the tenants had over that period of time come to assume they had ownership of the land. A number of servants were sent, only to be rejected, ill-treated and killed. Such was the lot of the prophets sent by God (see Hebrews 11:35–8). Last of all, he sent his son 'whom he loved' (see Mark 1:11; 9:7), whom they killed. In a final act of derision, they then threw his body from the vineyard, not even giving it a burial.

At this point, Jesus drew his hearers in by asking, 'What then will the owner of the vineyard do?' He was encouraging the Temple authorities to see the justice of what he was about to say, and to see the implications of the words he spoke. Here, before them, was the Son whom God loves (Mark 1:11; 9:7).

The justice of God was then announced: those wicked tenants were killed and the vineyard given to others.

Jesus went on to quote from Psalm 118:22–3,[17] which built upon

_____

[17] The quote is from the Septuagint.

the parable just delivered. The son, who was rejected and killed, would be vindicated by the LORD and become the cornerstone. This text from the Psalms became a key point of witness for the early church, as can be seen in Acts 4:11 and 1 Peter 2:4–7. It is a reminder that we might find more in a text of Scripture than we see at first. Ephrem the Syrian (*c.* 306–373) wondered at this fact:

> Who is capable of comprehending the extent of what is to be discovered in a single utterance of Yours? For we leave behind in it far more than we take from it, like thirsty people drinking from a fountain.[18]

The point was not lost on the Temple authorities, who knew the parable to be directed at them. However, Jesus's popularity with the crowd caused them to keep silence, and they departed. The ruling party bristled at the challenge to their authority, and it would appear that over time they had come to think of the Temple as their own institution rather than a vehicle for the worship of God.

While the parable had the Temple authorities as its target, it applies to all who hold office in the church, or even simply attend. The church is God's and does not belong to any group of people or institution. The church has to remain obedient to the commands of God or risk its own ruin.

Giving dues to God and Caesar (12:13–17)

Paying the poll-tax to Caesar

13 Later they sent some of the Pharisees and Herodians to Jesus to catch him in his words. 14 They came to him and said, 'Teacher, we know that you are a man of integrity. You aren't swayed by others, because you pay no attention to who they are; but you teach the way of God in accordance with the truth. Is it right to pay the poll-tax[b] to Caesar or not? 15 Should we pay or shouldn't we?'

But Jesus knew their hypocrisy. 'Why are you trying to trap me?' he

---

[18] *Diatessaron* 1:18. Translation from Sebastian P. Brock, *Treasure-House of Mysteries: Explorations of the Sacred Text Through Poetry in the Syriac Tradition* (Yonkers: St Vladimir's Seminary Press, 2012), 28.

asked. 'Bring me a denarius and let me look at it.' **16** They brought the coin, and he asked them, 'Whose image is this? And whose inscription?'

'Caesar's,' they replied.

17 Then Jesus said to them, 'Give back to Caesar what is Caesar's and to God what is God's.'

And they were amazed at him.

_____

b 14 A special tax levied on subject peoples, not on Roman citizens

Now that the chief priests, elders and teachers had departed, the Pharisees and Herodians took up the questioning in an attempt to catch Jesus out (we have already seen these two parties plotting together in Mark 3:6). Israel was a nation under foreign occupation, and the very coinage used by the Romans reminded them of the fact. Roman coins bore an image of the emperor and those minted during the rule of the Tiberius (AD 14–37) also carried the inscription, 'Son of the Divine Augustus'. Here was a double offence in the eyes of the Jews: both a graven image and a claim to be the son of a god. In everyday trade the Jews avoided such idolatry by minting their own coins (hence the money changers in the Temple).[19] No less popular was the poll tax which was introduced in AD 6 and triggered a revolt in response.[20]

The question being asked of Jesus, after much flattery, was a trick one: answer 'yes' and he upset Jewish patriots; answer 'no' and he risked the wrath of Rome. He recognised the trap but did not shy away from the question. Rather, he asked for a Roman denarius to be brought to him, an act suggesting that he himself was not carrying such a coin in the Temple. The implied question was, 'What are you Pharisees and Herodians doing carrying such a coin?!'

Jesus went on to answer the question asked of him, and in so doing rejected its either/or basis: it is not God _or_ Caesar, but God _and_ Caesar. The legitimate claims of Caesar are in harmony with the claims of God. This is explored by both Paul (Romans 13:1–7) and Peter (1 Peter 2:13–17), and it is important to note that this does not imply a bare submission to the state. States can – and do – err, and tyranny is an

_____

[19] France, _Mark_, 466.

[20] 'A Galilaean, named Judas incited his countrymen to revolt, upbraiding them as cowards for consenting to pay tribute to the Romans and tolerating mortal masters, after having God for their lord.' Josephus, _Wars_, 2.118. Translation taken from Josephus, _War_, 1.367–9.

ever-present danger. Peter described the role of the governor as 'to punish those who do wrong and to commend those who do right' (1 Peter 2:14). It is not for the governor to set up the moral order or to establish the bounds of right and wrong, but simply to enforce that which is revealed by God. The sovereignty of the state is not absolute, and it has no rights over the kingdom of God. Rather, it is to be an instrument of godly order. The theologian and one-time Prime Minister of the Netherlands, Abraham Kuyper (1837–1920), wrote:

> Thus political authority operates alongside many other author-
> ities that are equally absolute and sacred in the natural and
> spiritual world, in society and family. Every attempt by polit-
> ical authority to try and rule over one of those other areas is
> therefore a violation of God's ordinances, and resistance to it
> is not a crime but a duty.[21]

In the end, the things that bear the image of Caesar may be rendered to Caesar. The challenge in this statement is that it implies that the things that bear the image of God should likewise be rendered to God. We may give some of our coin to the government, but we who are made in the image of God should give all of our very selves to God.[22]

Once more, Jesus caused amazement (see Mark 1:22, 27; 2:12; 5:20; 6:2, 51; 7:37; 10:24, 26; 11:18; 15:5). If we present a Jesus who does not challenge and astonish, we must ask ourselves: are we presenting Christ at all?

The resurrection of the dead (12:18–27)

Marriage at the resurrection

18 Then the Sadducees, who say there is no resurrection, came to him with a question. 19 'Teacher,' they said, 'Moses wrote for us that if a man's brother dies and leaves a wife but no children, the man must marry the widow and raise up offspring for his brother. 20 Now there were seven brothers. The first one married and died without leaving

---

[21] Abraham Kuyper, *Our Program: A Christian Political Manifesto* (Bellingham: Lexham Press, 2015), 22.
[22] Edwards, *Mark*, 364.

any children. 21 The second one married the widow, but he also died, leaving no child. It was the same with the third. 22 In fact, none of the seven left any children. Last of all, the woman died too. 23 At the resurrection^c whose wife will she be, since the seven were married to her?'

24 Jesus replied, 'Are you not in error because you do not know the Scriptures or the power of God? 25 When the dead rise, they will neither marry nor be given in marriage; they will be like the angels in heaven. 26 Now about the dead rising – have you not read in the Book of Moses, in the account of the burning bush, how God said to him, "I am the God of Abraham, the God of Isaac, and the God of Jacob"^d? 27 He is not the God of the dead, but of the living. You are badly mistaken!'

---

c 23 Some manuscripts *resurrection, when people rise from the dead,*
d 26 Exodus 3:6

The Sadducees now came with a controversial question of their own, regarding marriage in heaven. This is the only mention of the Sadducees in Mark's Gospel, and they appear to have been an aristocratic grouping rather than an organised party. They differed from the Pharisees in their beliefs concerning life after death (which they denied) and laid great stress on the free will of the human, most probably to safeguard God from accusations of being complicit in evil. They held that there was no retribution after death and also rejected the many oral traditions of the Pharisees, preferring to hold only to those traditions set out in the books of Moses (the first five books of the Old Testament). They were not particularly popular with the population at large but were well regarded by the wealthy.[23]

The question they posed was deliberately absurd, designed to mock belief in life after death. Although references to the resurrection are present in the Old Testament (e.g., Psalms 16:9–11, 49:15; Job 19:25–6; Isaiah 26:19; Daniel 12:2), these are from the later books and not the books of Moses. A great tradition had grown up around these texts in the period between the Old and New Testaments, and in 2 Maccabees 7:14 we find a tortured young man near to death

---

[23] For a helpful discussion see Gary G. Porton, 'Sadducees', in *The Anchor Bible Dictionary*, ed. David Noel Freedman (New Haven: Yale University Press, 1992). See also Josephus, *Jewish War*, 2.8.14 and also *Jewish Antiquities*, 18.1.4.

proclaiming: 'One cannot but choose to die at the hands of men and to cherish the hope that God gives of being raised again by him. But for you there will be no resurrection to life!' (RSV). It was this thinking that the Sadducees opposed.

The question concerned what was known as levirate marriage, which may be found in Deuteronomy 25:5–6 and which was designed to protect a family's holdings in the case of death. In this imagined scenario, a woman is married successively to seven brothers, all of whom die without children. When she died, the question asked, who would be her husband in heaven?

Jesus was thus invited either to defend something that is set up to be farcical or to deny the resurrection. He did neither, but instead exposed the lack of understanding implied in the question itself. Marriage is an institution that does not persist into the resurrection, presumably as its role in companionship and procreation is no longer necessary. Jesus then took the Sadducees back to the books of Moses to demonstrate that an understanding of life after death is essential to understanding God's speech at the burning bush. When God spoke to Moses at the burning bush, he described himself as the God of the long-dead patriarchs. He has an eternal covenant relationship with them, and they continue to relate to him even though they are dead from a human perspective. To argue against the resurrection is both to ignore the Scriptures that support the view and to ignore the power of God. To say something is 'impossible' is to place arbitrary limits upon God.

The greatest of the commandments (12:28–34)

The greatest commandment

28 One of the teachers of the law came and heard them debating. Noticing that Jesus had given them a good answer, he asked him, 'Of all the commandments, which is the most important?'

29 'The most important one,' answered Jesus, 'is this: "Hear, O Israel: the Lord our God, the Lord is one.e

30 Love the Lord your God with all your heart and with all your soul and with all your mind and with all your strength."f 31 The second is this: "Love your neighbour as yourself."g There is no commandment greater than these.'

32 'Well said, teacher,' the man replied. 'You are right in saying that God is one and there is no other but him. 33 To love him with all your

heart, with all your understanding and with all your strength, and to love your neighbour as yourself is more important than all burnt offerings and sacrifices.'

34 When Jesus saw that he had answered wisely, he said to him, 'You are not far from the kingdom of God.' And from then on no one dared ask him any more questions.

---

e 29 Or *the Lord our God is one Lord*
f 30 Deut. 6:4,5
g 31 Lev. 19:18

The debates Jesus had with the various parties of Judaism drew to a close with a fundamental question from a teacher of the law. It would seem that this was not intended as a trap, but rather came from a genuine interest in what Jesus would have to say. Jesus had won the respect of one teacher of the law, at least.

The question of which is the most important commandment was a familiar one among the teachers of the law, who counted no fewer than 613 commandments in the books of Moses and often sought to rank them.[24] For example, the Babylonian Talmud records a conversation between a Gentile and two rabbis who taught in the decades leading up to the birth of Christ:

> There was another case of a Gentile who came before Shammai. He said to him, 'Convert me on the stipulation that you teach me the entire Torah while I am standing on one foot.' He drove him off with the building cubit that he had in his hand. He came before Hillel: 'Convert me.' He said to him, '"What is hateful to you, to your fellow don't do." That's the entirety of the Torah; everything else is elaboration. So go, study.'[25]

The answer Jesus gave combined Deuteronomy 6:4–6 and Leviticus 19:18, something without precedent in the Jewish writings that survive.[26] Rather than reduce the law to a single principle, Jesus paired the love of God ('the most important one') and of neighbour ('the second'). In fact, the one leads to the other, as Bernard of Clairvaux (1090–1153) taught:

---

[24] France, *Mark*, 477.
[25] Translation from Neusner, *Talmud*, 2:127.
[26] France, *Mark*, 478.

'How can you love your neighbour with purity if you do not love him in God? But he who does not love God cannot love in God. You must first love God, so that in him you can love your neighbour too.'[27]

It is interesting to note that Jesus expanded the quote from Deuteronomy to include 'all your mind'. The word used for mind (*dianoia*) denotes the 'faculty of thinking, comprehending, and reasoning',[28] and by including it Jesus highlighted the importance of using the intellect in loving God. In fact, the debates we have seen Jesus conducting in the preceding passages illustrate precisely that point. Christianity encompasses all our faculties. What is required is no less than a renewal of our minds (Romans 12:2), and that comes by study as well as by prayer. Our faith is reasonable, and we should not shy away from meditating on all that it contains. One should 'Always be prepared to give an answer to everyone who asks you to give the reason for the hope that you have' (1 Peter 3:15).

The reply of the teacher of the law, which began with a parroting back of Jesus's words (except the added 'mind') impressed Jesus. The teacher had employed his 'mind' and understood that our attitude to God and love of him outweighs all the sacrificial system. True faith is not simply an external affair but a love of God which leads us to a love of our neighbour. The Christian life is lived from the inside out.

Son and Lord (12:35–7)

Whose son is the Messiah?

35 While Jesus was teaching in the temple courts, he asked, 'Why do the teachers of the law say that the Messiah is the son of David? 36 David himself, speaking by the Holy Spirit, declared:

' "The Lord said to my Lord:
  'Sit at my right hand
   until I put your enemies
      under your feet.' "[h]

37 David himself calls him "Lord". How then can he be his son?'

The large crowd listened to him with delight.

_____

h 36 Psalm 110:1

_____

27 Bernard of Clairvaux, 'On Loving God', in *Selected Works* (New York: Paulist Press, 1987), 193.

28 BDAG, 234.

After answering a series of questions, Jesus now posed one of his own. He had been hailed as the 'Son of David' by Bartimaeus, and the crowds that welcomed him into the city earlier that week had cried out, 'Blessed is the coming kingdom of our father David!' (Mark 11:10). The notions of Messiahship in ancient Israel were tied up with hopes of a restoration of David's throne by one of his descendants. This 'son of David' would be the Messiah, who would in turn restore Israel to its former glory.

In all of this hope, Psalm 110 (written by David) was important since it spoke of a coming Davidic rule. Given Jesus's line of questioning, it would also appear to have been seen as pointing towards the Messiah. Yet, as Jesus pointed out in his question, it also spoke of one who was greater than David. In this quote, the first 'LORD' (i.e., God – the Hebrew uses the name of God) says to David's lord, 'Sit at my right hand. . .' This second figure is not only called 'lord' by David but is also invited by God to sit at his right hand. Exalted indeed. How can, Jesus asks, such a Messiah be simply described as David's son?

This poses something of a problem. Is Jesus suggesting that the Messiah will in fact *not* be of Davidic descent? This would seem unlikely. Jesus did not rebuke Bartimaeus when he used this title, and Jesus's Davidic lineage was important to early Christianity, as can be seen from the genealogy at the beginning of Matthew's Gospel (see also Luke 1:69; Acts 2:30; Romans 1:3; 2 Timothy 2:8; Revelation 3:7; 5:5; 22:16). It is unlikely that these traditions would have arisen if Jesus opposed them.

The answer is that Jesus was asserting that the Messiah is not *merely* David's son but is also someone greater, someone who might sit at God's right hand: the Son of God. Not a mere general or warrior king, but someone with divine origins. This greater identity of Jesus has been traced throughout the Gospel of Mark (Mark 1:1, 11; 3:11; 5:7; 9:7; 15:39). The large crowd heard all this and was delighted.

In passing, we should note that Jesus described David as 'speaking by the Holy Spirit'. Here is an example of the inspiration of Scripture, acknowledging both David's agency as well as that of the Holy Spirit. A similar description of inspiration is given by Peter: 'For prophecy never had its origin in the human will, but prophets, though human, spoke from God as they were carried along by the Holy

Spirit' (2 Peter 1:21). The Holy Spirit undergirded the writings of the authors of Scripture and guided them as they wrote. The deep currents of the Spirit carry along the authors to his desired end. The one-time principal of Princeton Seminary A. A. Hodge (1823–86) illustrated the principle well:

> 'I have never seen any providence,' sneers Stuart Mill. But this is nothing wonderful. I have never seen the world revolve, though I have lived upon it more than fifty years. The broad current carries the ship with it though you do not mark the track. And the providence of God encircles you, and your vessel, and your ocean too; and while you may take your own little path upon that ocean, the ocean, ship, and passenger are being made subservient to a Higher Will.[29]

True devotion (12:38–44)

Warning against the teachers of the law

38 As he taught, Jesus said, 'Watch out for the teachers of the law. They like to walk around in flowing robes and be greeted with respect in the market-places, **39** and have the most important seats in the synagogues and the places of honour at banquets. **40** They devour widows' houses and for a show make lengthy prayers. These men will be punished most severely.'

The widow's offering

41 Jesus sat down opposite the place where the offerings were put and watched the crowd putting their money into the temple treasury. Many rich people threw in large amounts. **42** But a poor widow came and put in two very small copper coins, worth only a few pence.

43 Calling his disciples to him, Jesus said, 'Truly I tell you, this poor widow has put more into the treasury than all the others. **44** They all gave out of their wealth; but she, out of her poverty, put in everything – all she had to live on.'

---

[29] Charles Adamson Salmond, *Princetoniana. Charles and A. A. Hodge: With Class and Table Talk of Hodge, the Younger, Etc.* (New York: Scribner & Welford, 1888), 181.

As this series of questions came to a close, Jesus warned his hearers to 'watch out for the teachers of the law'. The mix of church and state may bring with it a great respect for church leaders, and with it power. This is a heady mix which may corrupt those in church leadership, or cause others to seek such positions through simply ambition. Even where church and state are not so closely tied, church leadership may still bring honour. Jesus warned his hearers to watch out for prideful teachers. Not all those who seek to teach do so from pure motives but can rather be driven by pride and the desire for money.

In contrast, Jesus pointed to a poor widow who placed two low-value coins into one of the offering vessels placed prominently in the Temple. Although small, her offering was worth much: she gave all she had. It is easy for the rich to make flamboyant donations. Of more value is the donation that is costly to self.

Within many nations, Christianity is held in high regard, and Christian leaders receive honour and a large income. In some places they sit on the legislature; in others they dominate television screens. Jesus counselled us to exercise wisdom when considering to whom to listen, or whose actions we should imitate. Humility is worth far more than pride, and a quiet devotion more than ostentatious show. Jesus's condemnation of those who took money from the poor and paraded around in fine robes was a sobering one: 'These men will be punished most severely.' Their actions belied a love of self rather than the other, or even God. A warning to be heeded.

The destruction of the Temple (13:1–2)

The destruction of the temple and signs of the end times

13 As Jesus was leaving the temple, one of his disciples said to him, 'Look, Teacher! What massive stones! What magnificent buildings!'

2 'Do you see all these great buildings?' replied Jesus. 'Not one stone here will be left on another; every one will be thrown down.'

We now come to a pivotal point in the Gospel. Jesus had entered Jerusalem to great acclaim and entered the Temple. Like the nearby fig tree (Mark 11:13), the Temple had promised fruit, but there was none and so it was cursed. As Jesus went to the Temple to teach, he was confronted by a number of parties who sought to draw him into the controversies of the day and entrap him. This period of controversy in the Temple ended with Jesus warning the crowd about the teachers of the law and – in contrast – commending the actions of a poor widow who donated generously out of her poverty.

It was in this context that Jesus then left the Temple, and one of his disciples drew attention to the magnificence of the building. While these verses sit at the beginning of a new chapter, they fit more naturally with the debates in chapter 12. Rather than forming part of Jesus's teaching of the remainder of chapter 13 they should be viewed as the conclusion of the debates in the Temple, and Jesus's verdict on its leadership.

It may be that the unnamed disciple was overawed by the magnificence of the Temple building, but we would do well to remember that it also symbolised the presence of God within Jerusalem. Psalm 48, for example, sings the praise of the Temple with its tower, ramparts and citadels and proclaims, 'God is in her citadels; he has shown himself to be her fortress' (Psalm 48:3). This disciple had, it appears, not understood the significance of the cursed fig tree and had assumed that the solidity of the Temple assured the permanence of God's presence. Yet the Temple in itself was no guarantee of God's favour. Jesus told the no doubt astonished disciple that all these stones would be cast down. In fact, that is precisely what was to happen in AD 70.[30]

3. The end of the Temple • Mark 13:3–37

The previous section ended with Jesus's prediction of the demise of the Temple, and this would have caused great shock to the disciples. What of God if his Temple is destroyed? Like the Pharisees, the disciples asked about signs, but Jesus cautioned against a reliance upon signs. He instead turned the apostles to the Scriptures, Daniel in particular, and spoke of what was to occur.

---

[30] The Greek reads that there will be no 'stone upon stone', which is an allusion to Haggai 2:15.

When will these things happen? (13:3–4)

3 As Jesus was sitting on the Mount of Olives opposite the temple, Peter, James, John and Andrew asked him privately, **4** 'Tell us, when will these things happen? And what will be the sign that they are all about to be fulfilled?'

Jesus moved on from the Temple and sat a while on the Mount of Olives, which lies to the east of Jerusalem. As he did so, four disciples – the first four he had called – came to him privately. They had heard his prediction of the destruction of the Temple made in the previous passage and wondered when all this would take place. They wished to know what sign they should look for. They seem to have forgotten Jesus's earlier exasperation: 'Why does this generation ask for a sign? Truly I tell you, no sign will be given to it' (Mark 8:12).

Before considering Jesus's answer as a whole, it would be helpful to sketch out its basic structure since this is key to grappling with its contents. It should be remembered that the context of the passage is the destruction of the Temple and the disciples' question, 'Tell us, when will these things happen? And what will be the sign that they are all about to be fulfilled?' (verse 4). There are two questions here: when, and what will be the sign that this is about to occur? Jesus answered both questions, beginning with the issue of signs. His answer took the following form:

What will be the sign?

verses 5–8   Don't be led astray by signs or by false messiahs. Wars do not mean that the end has come, nor do natural disasters.

verses 9–13   Persecution will occur; the disciples should not worry but rather endure. This will be a means of the gospel being spread.

verses 14–19   The true sign of the destruction of the Temple will be the 'abomination that causes desolation'. At that time, flee.

241

| verses 20–23 | 'The days' (i.e., the events of 14–19 surrounding the destruction of the Temple) will be cut short. Beware of false messiahs 'at that time'. |

Encouragement: faith must be maintained as the day of the Lord will come. All is not lost.

| verses 24–7 | 'Following that distress', the longed-for Day of the LORD will occur, and Christ – the Son of Man – will return to 'gather his elect'. |

When will this (the destruction of the Temple) occur?

| verses 28–31 | Soon. In fact, within a generation. |

And when will Christ return?

| verses 32–4 | The precise day or hour is not known, not even by the Son, so be on your guard. |

Conclusion

| verses 35–7 | Keep watch. |

False teachers and misunderstood signs (13:5–13)

5 Jesus said to them: 'Watch out that no one deceives you. 6 Many will come in my name, claiming, "I am he," and will deceive many. 7 When you hear of wars and rumours of wars, do not be alarmed. Such things must happen, but the end is still to come. 8 Nation will rise against nation, and kingdom against kingdom. There will be earthquakes in various places, and famines. These are the beginning of birth-pains.

9 'You must be on your guard. You will be handed over to the local councils and flogged in the synagogues. On account of me you will stand before governors and kings as witnesses to them. 10 And the gospel must first be preached to all nations. 11 Whenever you are arrested and brought to trial, do not worry beforehand about what to say. Just say whatever is given you at the time, for it is not you speaking, but the Holy Spirit.

12 'Brother will betray brother to

death, and a father his child. Children will rebel against their parents and have them put to death. **13** Everyone | will hate you because of me, but the one who stands firm to the end will be saved.

The disciples' desire for a sign prompted Jesus to issue another warning about false teachers. He had earlier warned about those who simply sought worldly honour; now he spoke of those who sought even more. Many, he warned, will come claiming, 'I am' (the Greek is the same as the words of Jesus when he walked on the water). Many will come and many will be deceived. While events will occur which look as if they are the sorts of signs the disciples were seeking – wars, earthquakes and famines – these do not mean that the end has come. They are merely the 'beginning of birth pains', and the wise disciple is not over-concerned with things such as this. The halls of church history are littered with various predictions of the end of things, all tied to events that came and went without the world ending. Better to focus on God and not on signs, which are too easily misinterpreted. We might note that even the destruction of the Temple was not a sign of the apocalypse, but rather a sign of judgment on an institution that had been replaced by the sacrifice of Jesus the Great High Priest (Hebrews 4:14–5:10). That even an event as great as that did not mark the end should give us pause.

Although Jesus sought to calm the anxiety of disciples focused on seeing signs of an apocalypse, he did not suggest that they would be without suffering. Quite the reverse: they were to be on their guard since they would be handed over and flogged, yet even this would be an opportunity to witness to those who hold high office (as we see in Acts 24 when Paul testified before Felix the governor). The gospel must be preached to all nations, and this would be but one means of so doing. Even here the disciple was not to be anxious, since the Holy Spirit would speak through the believer on trial. We might see an example of this in the eloquence with which the martyr Stephen spoke at his trial (Acts 7).

This, Jesus predicted, would also be a time of conflict within families, with many being hated for the sake of Christ. The call in all this is to stand firm to the end, since 'the one who stands firm to the end will be saved'. The Greek word 'martyr' simply means a witness, and our own simple suffering will speak to those around us, often more deeply than our words. To endure is a means of evangelism in itself.

The disciples had asked for a sign of fulfilment (verse 4), and Jesus first warned them not to jump to conclusions. Teachers may be false, and what look like signs of God's disfavour may in fact be the means of evangelisation. He then turned to what would be a cataclysmic event, and one that the disciples must take care to understand: the destruction of the Temple.[31] He now came to answer their question.

The destruction of the Temple (13:14–23)

14 'When you see "the abomination that causes desolation"[a] standing where it[b] does not belong – let the reader understand – then let those who are in Judea flee to the mountains. **15** Let no one on the housetop go down or enter the house to take anything out. **16** Let no one in the field go back to get their cloak. **17** How dreadful it will be in those days for pregnant women and nursing mothers! **18** Pray that this will not take place in winter, **19** because those will be days of distress unequalled from the beginning, when God created the world, until now – and never to be equalled again.

20 'If the Lord had not cut short those days, no one would survive. But for the sake of the elect, whom he has chosen, he has shortened them. **21** At that time if anyone says to you, "Look, here is the Messiah!" or, "Look, there he is!" do not believe it. **22** For false messiahs and false prophets will appear and perform signs and

---

[31] Peter Bolt argues that Mark 13 is focused upon the crucifixion and prepares the disciples for the events of the following chapters. The abomination is the crucifixion, the suffering is that of Jesus upon the cross, the false messiahs are the Temple leaders, the timings mentioned in verse 30 refer to events surrounding Jesus's betrayal and resurrection, the coming of the Son of Man refers to the resurrection and the elect are gathered as the women are told to go to the disciples. There is much to like in this argument, and it is very suggestive, but ultimately it fails to deal with the question asked by the disciples concerning the Temple and the necessity of the gospel being preached to all nations (verse 10). Moreover, the events surrounding the abomination (verse 14–19) do not take place at the crucifixion, and it is odd that he urges the disciples to pray it does not take place in winter when he knows it is to occur very soon. For these and other reasons, Bolt's argument ultimately fails, but is well worth reading. Peter G. Bolt, 'Mark 13: An Apocalyptic Precursor to the Passion Narrative', *Reformed Theological Review* 54, no. 1 (1995).

wonders to deceive, if possible, even the elect. **23** So be on your guard; I have told you everything in advance.

a 14 Daniel 9:27; 11:31; 12:11

b 14 Or *he*

Jesus turned to the question of what the sign would be that the Temple was to be destroyed. He spoke of the 'abomination that causes desolation', a reference to the Book of Daniel (made explicit in Matthew 24:15), with the aside, 'let the reader understand'. This event would be the trigger for the faithful to flee for safety, and the urgency of the flight was underscored by the instruction to not even go back into the house to take anything. Pregnant mothers and those nursing would find this rush exhausting, even more so if it were to take place in winter when the rivers were swollen and the paths full of mud.

Jesus then returned once more to the Book of Daniel, with an allusion to Daniel 12:1, which reads, 'There will be a time of distress such as has not happened from the beginning of nations until then. But at that time your people – everyone whose name is found written in the book – will be delivered.' God is faithful.

Interpretation of this passage turns on the vital question of timing. What is the 'abomination that causes desolation'? Is what is being described the fall of the Temple, which was the question asked by the disciples, or, as some suggest, an antichrist figure prior to the second coming of Christ? If the latter, what do we make of the claim that 'this generation will certainly not pass away until all these things have happened' (verse 30)?

The phrase occurs three times in Daniel. First, in Daniel 9:26–7 we find it used in connection of the death of 'the Anointed One':

After the sixty-two 'sevens', the Anointed One will be put to death and will have nothing. The people of the ruler who will come will destroy the city and the sanctuary. The end will come like a flood: war will continue until the end, and desolations have been decreed. He will confirm a covenant with many for one 'seven'. In the middle of the 'seven' he will put an end to sacrifice and offering. And at the temple he will set up an abomination that causes desolation, until the end that is decreed is poured out on him. (Daniel 9:26–7)

The Hebrew of Daniel 9:26 is obscure and might be rendered 'the Anointed One will be put to death but not for himself' (see NIV footnote), which is significant. There is also a reference in the prophecy to a 'ruler who will come' whose people 'will destroy the city and the sanctuary'. Given all this, and given the question of the disciples in Mark 13:4 about the destruction of the Temple, it is best to understand the 'abomination' as being linked to the destruction of the Temple in AD 70.

This is also a significant grammatical quirk in the Greek of Mark 13:14, noted in the NIV footnote. Whereas we would expect a neuter pronoun when referring to this abomination, we in fact find a male pronoun. This gives the reading, 'When you see "the abomination that causes desolation" standing where *he* does not belong. . .' This suggests that the abomination is not inanimate but is in fact a person. The 'abomination' in Mark would best be understood as a reference to the ruler of Daniel 9:26–7, who might be identified as the emperor Titus, whose people destroyed the Temple in AD 70.

In Daniel 11:31 there is another reference to the abomination, which is also linked to the desecration of the Temple fortress:

His armed forces will rise up to desecrate the temple fortress and will abolish the daily sacrifice. Then they will set up the abomination that causes desolation. With flattery he will corrupt those who have violated the covenant, but the people who know their God will firmly resist him.

Those who are wise will instruct many, though for a time they will fall by the sword or be burned or captured or plundered. When they fall, they will receive a little help, and many who are not sincere will join them. Some of the wise will stumble, so that they may be refined, purified and made spotless until the time of the end, for it will still come at the appointed time. (Daniel 11:31–5)

This passage from Daniel described some being led astray by a false teacher and also described persecutions, themes found in Jesus's teaching in verses 5–13 of Mark 13. In the next chapter of Daniel, we find the final reference to the abomination:

I heard, but I did not understand. So I asked, 'My lord, what will the outcome of all this be?'

He replied, 'Go your way, Daniel, because the words are rolled up and sealed until the time of the end. Many will be purified, made spotless and refined, but the wicked will continue to be wicked. None of the wicked will understand, but those who are wise will understand.

'From the time that the daily sacrifice is abolished and the abomination that causes desolation is set up, there will be 1,290 days. Blessed is the one who waits for and reaches the end of the 1,335 days.' (Daniel 12:8–12)

The passage quoted began with Daniel's complaint of a lack of understanding (Daniel 12:8), to which the reply was given, 'Go your way, Daniel. . .' So it is that Daniel was told that a proper understanding of the prophecy was reserved for a later age ('the time of the end'). The aside, 'let the reader understand', points to the fact that this time had now arrived.

In all these passages, mention is made of the cessation of the daily sacrifice, the heartbeat of the Temple. In the cursing of the fig tree there was a period of time between the curse and the death of the tree. In the cursing of the Temple there was similarly a period of time between its curse and its destruction. A destruction accompanied by a tribulation so severe that all were to flee.

Intriguingly, Eusebius made mention of a flight of Christians from Jerusalem prior to the destruction of the Temple:

But the people of the Church at Jerusalem were commanded by an oracle given out by revelation before the war to esteemed men there to depart from the city and to inhabit a city of Peraea which they called Pella. Those who believed in Christ migrated to this city from Jerusalem, that, when holy men had entirely abandoned the royal capital of the Jews and the entire land of Judaea, the judgment of God might soon overtake them for their many crimes against Christ and His Apostles and utterly destroy that generation of the wicked from among men.[32]

The days of suffering would be cut short, for the sake of the elect, yet the danger would remain. The elect were to be on the lookout for false messiahs and false prophets who may even work signs and wonders. Again, here was a warning to be discerning when it comes to signs. Jesus had forewarned the disciples and assured them that these days would be cut short (verse 20).

This passage, then, does not refer to the return of Christ (which is dealt with in the next portion of Jesus's answer), but rather with the destruction of the Temple.

But what of the argument that all these references in Daniel point to the Greek king Antiochus IV (215 BC–164 BC), who persecuted the Jews and rededicated the Temple to Zeus? Something of the catastrophic anguish of this event is recorded in 2 Maccabees 6:3–6 (NRSVA):

> Harsh and utterly grievous was the onslaught of evil. For the temple was filled with debauchery and revelling by the Gentiles, who dallied with prostitutes and had intercourse with women within the sacred precincts, and besides brought in things for sacrifice that were unfit. The altar was covered with abominable offerings that were forbidden by the laws. People could neither keep the sabbath, nor observe the festivals of their ancestors, nor so much as confess themselves to be Jews.

Surely this would be a better 'target' for Daniel's prophecies? Simply put: it may well be, but that does not mean the prophecies cannot have a double referent. There is an established pattern of what might be termed 'prophetic reapplication'[33] within the Old and

---

[32] Eusebius, *Ecclesiastical History*, 3.5. Translation from Deferrari, *Eccesiastical History*, 145. Pella is beyond the mountains north of Jerusalem in the foothills of the Decapolis to the east of the Jordan.

[33] A happy term of Ah Li Yang of the Lisu Theological Seminary of Myanmar.

New Testaments as can be seen in the reapplication of themes from the Exodus themes in Isaiah. We can also reapply these themes to our own lives, as did those enslaved in America when they sang of Moses and freedom:

When Israel was in Egypt's land,
Let my people go,
Oppress'd so hard they could not stand,
Let my people go.

Refrain:
Go down, Moses.
Way down in Egypt's land.
Tell old Pharaoh:
Let my people go.

As the slaves sang of the oppression of the Israelites, they also sang of their own condition and prayed for release.

The Day of the Lord (13:24–7)

24 'But in those days, following that distress,
' "the sun will be darkened,
and the moon will not give
its light;
25 the stars will fall from the sky,
and the heavenly bodies will
be shaken."**c**

26 'At that time people will see the Son of Man coming in clouds with great power and glory. **27** And he will send his angels and gather his elect from the four winds, from the ends of the earth to the ends of the heavens.

---

c 25 Isaiah 13:10; 34:4

Having dealt with the destruction of the Temple, Jesus turned to his own return in glory. In the parallel passage in Matthew's Gospel (Matthew 24), it is clear that Jesus was addressing *both* the destruction of the Temple *and* his return. In that Gospel, it is recorded that the

---

See Ah Li Yang, 'Paul's Prophetic Reapplication of Isaiah in Romans 9–11', (diss., University of Bristol, 2000).

disciples asked, 'When will this happen, and what will be the sign of your coming and of the end of the age?' (Matthew 24:3). This twofold question is important in gaining a full understanding of this passage, and although we can see this in Mark's Gospel, it is clearer in Matthew's fuller narrative of the event.

Such were the cataclysmic events of the fall of the Temple that it would have been tempting to see them as pointing to the 'Day of the LORD', yet this was not the case. 'Those days' – heralding the return of the Son of Man – would be 'following that distress' (verse 24) and would be of such cosmic significance that the creation itself would bow down. Jesus used language found in Isaiah 13:10; 34:4 and Joel 2:10; 3:16. This will be the time when the people will see 'the Son of Man coming in clouds with great power and glory', an event to which Jesus had referred in Mark 8:38. Angels will be sent out and the elect gathered from across the earth. This is the unmistakable sign of the 'Day of the LORD', and the disciples must be careful not to be misled by other cataclysmic events.

What we have here, then, was both a teaching on the fall of the Temple, in answer to the disciples' question, and an insistence that its destruction would not be accompanied by the return of Christ in glory. That remained for a future time.

The destruction of the Temple is near (13:28–31)

28 'Now learn this lesson from the fig-tree: as soon as its twigs get tender and its leaves come out, you know that summer is near. **29** Even so, when you see these things happening, you know that it^d is near, right at the door. **30** Truly I tell you, this generation will certainly not pass away until all these things have happened. **31** Heaven and earth will pass away, but my words will never pass away.

_____

d 29 Or _he_

Having dealt with the Day of the LORD, Jesus then returned to the issue of the sign of the Temple's demise raised by the disciples in verse 4. The only sign they would receive would be that the events were near, that the process had begun. Jesus used the illustration of a fig tree, which would surely have brought to mind the cursed fig tree of chapter 11. In March/April the leaves come out, and the time is near. The destruction of the Temple was similarly near. In fact, Jesus went on to predict, the current generation would not pass away before this happened. As if to underscore the reliability of his words, Jesus said that his words would endure even longer than the heavens. The Temple may be destroyed, but his words are indestructible.

Be on guard! (13:32–7)

The day and hour unknown

32 'But about that day or hour no one knows, not even the angels in heaven, nor the Son, but only the Father. **33** Be on guard! Be alert[e]! You do not know when that time will come. **34** It's like a man going away: he leaves his house and puts his servants in charge, each with their assigned task, and tells the one at the door to keep watch.

35 'Therefore keep watch because you do not know when the owner of the house will come back – whether in the evening, or at midnight, or when the cock crows, or at dawn. **36** If he comes suddenly, do not let him find you sleeping. **37** What I say to you, I say to everyone: "Watch!" '

_____

e 33 Some manuscripts *alert and pray*

As Jesus brought his answer to an end, he went back once more to the question of his return, which he raised in verses 24–7. The Greek used signifies a change of subject and so suggests that this passage is not to be linked to the destruction of the Temple, which had just been discussed (verses 28–31).[34] In the parallel passage in Matthew's Gospel (Matthew 24), this is much clearer and there is mention of the 'coming of the Son of Man' in Matthew 24:37 and 39, which sets the context.[35]

The answer he gave was that no one knows the precise timing of his return. Not even the Son, but only the Father. So the disciples were urged to be alert and watch, like servants looking out for the

_____

[34] The Greek word *alla* is adversative, 'indicating a difference with or contrast to what precedes, in the case of individual clauses as well as whole sentences'. BDAG, 541–2.
[35] France, *Mark*, 541–2.

return of their master: the return is certain, the hour less so. Jesus illustrated this point by making reference to four periods of the night (the word translated as 'when the cock crows' refers to one of the Roman watches of night, occurring between midnight and 3 a.m.).[36] The disciples were to keep watch at all times.

As we similarly watch and wait for the return of Christ, it is easy for the long years to deaden and dull our attentiveness. It is all too easy to slip into a sort of practical atheism whereby we profess Christ with our words, but our lives are lived as if he is merely a far-distant reality. The watchful Christian lives as if Christ is near and his return imminent. There is no room for putting things off until tomorrow.

NOTE: WHY DOESN'T THE SON KNOW THE HOUR?
Some have found the fact that Jesus is unaware of the timing of 'that day or hour' problematic, suggesting that it denies Jesus's divinity. However, we must beware the error of Apollinarianism, which understood Christ to be a composite of a human body and a divine mind or soul. This was rejected at the Council of Constantinople in 381, which instead insisted that Jesus was fully human *as well as* fully divine. We must therefore allow for times when Jesus exhibited the limits of his human nature, such as when he was tired or thirsty. Or died. Over the years he 'grew in wisdom' (Luke 2:52) and learned obedience (Hebrews 5:8). He developed as any human did and we must not deny Jesus's full humanity.

The logic of the early church was simple: if we are to be saved in entirety, Jesus must be entirely human. If, for example, he did not possess a human mind, our own minds could not be saved. Jesus is as human as we are, except that he does not sin. John of Damascus (*c.* 660–*c.* 750) wrote:

He in His entirety assumed me in my entirety and was wholly united to the whole, so that He might bestow the grace of salvation upon the whole. For that which has not been assumed cannot be healed.[37]

---

[36] BDAG, 41.
[37] St John of Damascus, *An Exact Exposition of the Orthodox Faith*, 3.6, trans. Frederic

Some three centuries earlier, Gregory Nazianzus had stated that Jesus was:

> . . . bounded in body, boundless in spirit, earthly and heavenly, visible and known spiritually, finite and infinite: so that by the same, whole man and God, the whole human being fallen under sin might be fashioned anew.[38]

This logic was present in the Reformation too, with the Belgic Confession (1561) proclaiming:

> For since the soul was lost as well as the body, it was necessary that He should take both upon Him, to save both.[39]

So what are we to make of those times when Jesus displayed a supernatural knowledge such as we find in the healing of the paralysed man, where we read, 'Immediately Jesus knew in his spirit that this was what they were thinking in their hearts' (Mark 2:8)? The answer lies in the verse itself: Jesus knew *in his spirit*. Here we have an example of the work of the Holy Spirit in Jesus's human nature, imparting knowledge.[40] The human and divine natures of Christ work together but are not mixed together.

H. Chase Jr. (Washington: Catholic University of America Press, 1958), 280.

[38] Gregory Nazianzus, *Letters, 101,* 4. Translation from Williams and Wickham, *God and Christ,* 156.

[39] James T. Dennison, *Reformed Confessions of the 16th and 17th Centuries in English Translation: 1523–1552* (Grand Rapids: Reformation Heritage Books, 2014), 2:434.

[40] See Owen, 'Πνευματολογια', 170–71.

6

The Victory of the Messiah

MARK 14:1–16:8

1. Preparation for death • Mark 14:1–11

As Good Friday drew near, the disciples were to be prepared for what was to come. First, a woman anointed Jesus, an act which he said was 'for my burial' (Mark 14:8). His death was near. He then celebrated an early Passover with his disciples and identified himself as the lamb to be sacrificed ('this is my body . . .'). He then foretold denial and abandonment on the part of his followers before going to wrestle in prayer at Gethsemane. The soldiers then came.

The woman and the betrayer (14:1–11)

Jesus anointed at Bethany

14 Now the Passover and the Festival of Unleavened Bread were only two days away, and the chief priests and the teachers of the law were scheming to arrest Jesus secretly and kill him. **2** 'But not during the festival,' they said, 'or the people may riot.'

3 While he was in Bethany, reclining at the table in the home of Simon the Leper, a woman came with an alabaster jar of very expensive perfume, made of pure nard. She broke the jar and poured the perfume on his head.

4 Some of those present were saying indignantly to one another, 'Why this waste of perfume? **5** It could have been sold for more than a year's wages[a] and the money given to the poor.' And they rebuked her harshly.

6 'Leave her alone,' said Jesus. 'Why are you bothering her? She has done a beautiful thing to me. **7** The poor you will always have with you,[b] and you can help them any time you want. But you will not always have me. **8** She did what she could. She poured perfume on my body beforehand to prepare for my burial. **9** Truly I tell you, wherever the gospel is preached throughout the world, what she has done will also be told, in memory of her.'

10 Then Judas Iscariot, one of the Twelve, went to the chief priests to betray Jesus to them. **11** They were delighted to hear this and promised to give him money. So he watched for an opportunity to hand him over.

a 5 Greek *than three hundred denarii*
b 7 See Deut. 15:11.

Mark now places us firmly into the context of the Passover and the Festival of Unleavened Bread which followed it (Numbers 28:16–17), and so provides a lens through which we might view the events of the following chapters. A second context is that of the plotting chief priests and teachers of the law who sought Jesus's death, and so followed the example of the Pharisees and Herodians of Mark 3:6. Jesus's popularity, so amply demonstrated on the previous Sunday, required this group of plotters to act secretly.

The Passover saw the population of Jerusalem swell as pilgrims made their way to the Temple. Josephus estimated that three million were present at the Passover in AD 65 and described the almost industrial slaughter of 256,500 animals a few years later.[1] More recently, Joachim Jeremias, after surveying the various accounts left to us by antiquity, estimated that 180,000 persons would be present in all.[2] Whatever the figure, the thronging crowds crammed

[1] On the Passover in AD 65 see Josephus, *Wars*, 2.280. Regarding the sacrifices a few years later, Josephus wrote, 'So these high priests, upon the coming of their feast which is called the Passover, when they slay their sacrifices, from the ninth hour till the eleventh, but so that a company not less than ten belong to every sacrifice (for it is not lawful for them to feast singly by themselves), and many of us are twenty in a company, found the number of sacrifices was two hundred and fifty-six thousand five hundred; which, upon the allowance of no more than ten that feast together, amounts to two million seven hundred thousand and two hundred persons that were pure and holy; for as to those that have the leprosy, or the gonorrhea, or women that have their monthly courses, or such as are otherwise polluted, it is not lawful for them to be partakers of this sacrifice; nor indeed for any foreigners either, who come hither to worship.' Josephus, *Wars*, 6.423–7. Translation from Whiston, *Works of Josephus*, 749.
[2] Jeremias, *Jerusalem*, 77–84.

into a city to celebrate a feast of liberation would have been a potent mix.

Jesus was staying outside the city walls, in Bethany, which lies on the far slope of the Mount of Olives (see Mark 11:11–12). Also in that village was Simon the Leper, someone who was clearly known to the disciples but is unnamed elsewhere. Given that he was in a position to receive guests, it would appear that his leprosy was not active, and it is possible that he had earlier been healed by Jesus. The woman is unnamed, and since she came during the meal it would appear she had not been invited. She may have been part of Simon's household, or simply a local, but her anonymity is striking given that Jesus foresaw that what she did would be long remembered: 'in memory of her' (verse 9).[3] It is best understood that this was a protective act by Mark.[4] Her anointing of Jesus was a significant political act – the Messiah is the Anointed One – and this would have put the woman at risk.[5]

The oil used, nard, was Indian in origin and costly. The woman broke the jar and poured it over Jesus's head, which would have resulted in the oil running down his face, beard and body (see Psalm 133:2). Some of those present were outraged at the cost of this (more than three hundred denarii, being a year's wages), seemingly oblivious to the significance of the act, or to the oily state of Jesus. He rebuked them, saying that the act was 'beautiful' (the word carries the meaning of being particularly fit for purpose).

Almsgiving for the poor was associated with Passover, but the woman had discerned a greater act. France fittingly comments that 'in the indignant response of the guests, the good has become the enemy of the best'.[6] Caring for the poor is an ever-present task; anointing the Messiah is a higher duty. Her recognition of this fact meant that she was to be remembered always. We should carefully

---

[3] We should be hesitant to quickly equate this woman with the woman in Luke 7:36–50.

[4] 'Their anonymity is for their protection, and the obscuring of their positive relationship to Jesus is a strategy of caution.' Theissen, *Context*, 186–7. Bauckham suggests that this principle also extended to the woman; Bauckham, *Eyewitnesses*, 190.

[5] See 1 Samuel 10:1; 16:1, 13; 1 Kings 1:39; 19:15–16; 2 Kings 9:3, 6; Psalm 89:20.

[6] France, *Mark*, 554.

note that acts of charity flow from our worship of God; they do not come first. The worship of God is paramount: we love God then our neighbour. The one leads to the other.

The fact that Jesus referred to her act as anointing him for his burial need not diminish the messianic imagery in the passage. For Jesus, Messiahship was intertwined with his death.[7]

Judas, presumably still indignant, went to the chief priest to betray Jesus. He may well have described the anointing to the officials, which would explain why his betrayal caused them to act so quickly. A messiah is, literally, an anointed one, and kings were also anointed. A potent mix. Rather than wait until the Passover, where a newly anointed Jesus would be present, they sought to kill him more quickly if the opportunity arose. They promised to pay Judas for his betrayal and in return he watched for an opportunity.

The Passover with the disciples (14:12–26)

The Last Supper

12 On the first day of the Festival of Unleavened Bread, when it was customary to sacrifice the Passover lamb, Jesus' disciples asked him, 'Where do you want us to go and make preparations for you to eat the Passover?'

13 So he sent two of his disciples, telling them, 'Go into the city, and a man carrying a jar of water will meet you. Follow him. 14 Say to the owner of the house he enters, "The Teacher asks: where is my guest room, where I may eat the Passover with my disciples?" 15 He will show you a large room upstairs, furnished and ready. Make preparations for us there.'

16 The disciples left, went into the city and found things just as Jesus had told them. So they prepared the Passover.

17 When evening came, Jesus arrived with the Twelve. 18 While

---

[7] 'What happens in the story is that Jesus recognizes the messianic significance of the anointing but interprets it according to his own understanding of his messianic vocation as entailing suffering and death. Just as readers of Mark know that Jesus' riding into Jerusalem on a colt does not signify messianic triumph of the generally expected kind but constitutes a journey to his death, so the messianic anointing by the woman is redirected by Jesus toward his burial, coherently with the characteristically Markan (though not, of course, only Markan) connection between messiahship and the cross.' Bauckham, *Eyewitnesses*, 192.

they were reclining at the table eating, he said, 'Truly I tell you, one of you will betray me - one who is eating with me.'

19 They were saddened, and one by one they said to him, 'Surely you don't mean me?'

20 'It is one of the Twelve,' he replied, 'one who dips bread into the bowl with me. 21 The Son of Man will go just as it is written about him. But woe to that man who betrays the Son of Man! It would be better for him if he had not been born.'

22 While they were eating, Jesus took bread, and when he had given thanks, he broke it and gave it to his disciples, saying, 'Take it; this is my body.'

23 Then he took a cup, and when he had given thanks, he gave it to them, and they all drank from it.

24 'This is my blood of the[c] covenant, which is poured out for many,' he said to them. 25 'Truly I tell you, I will not drink again from the fruit of the vine until that day when I drink it new in the kingdom of God.'

26 When they had sung a hymn, they went out to the Mount of Olives.

---

c 24 Some manuscripts *the new*

As the Day of Preparation began, as the sun set, the disciples wondered where Jesus might eat the Passover.[8] It was customary on the Day of Preparation to clear the yeast from the room where Passover was to be celebrated, and the disciples may also have anticipated setting up some furniture for the meal, as well as assembling the food needed for the ritual.

In response, Jesus sent two of the disciples into the city (presumably they were staying in Bethany near to Jerusalem), where they were to find a man carrying a water jar. Given that carrying water was normally something done by women, this man would have been noticeable. The water carrier was to be followed to a house, and the two disciples were to approach the owner to ask for a room that, it appears, Jesus had reserved. Furniture was already prepared, and the room was big enough for Jesus and his disciples. The disciples, whom Luke identified as Peter and John (Luke 22:8), found everything just as Jesus had said.

As night fell, Jesus arrived at the room with the twelve apostles and

---

[8] On the chronology of this passage see the introduction.

they reclined to eat the meal, as was the custom for the Passover.[9] As they ate, Jesus gave them the devastating news that one of their number was to be a betrayer. The phrase he used, 'one who is eating with me', underlined the intensity of betrayal. To be in Jesus's inner circle is no guarantee of loyalty to Jesus, and we should beware assigning too much spiritual authority to anyone simply because they hold a position of leadership. As Jesus said elsewhere, 'By their fruit you will recognise them' (Matthew 7:16). Holding office is no guarantee of integrity.

The disciples were distressed by this news ('saddened' is too weak a translation), and one by one they asked him, 'Surely you don't mean me?'[10] Presumably, Judas added his question to those of the other eleven, and it is striking that each of the disciples thought that they may have been the betrayer.

Jesus restated his prediction and further highlighted the intimacy of the betrayer by saying that he dipped his bread into the same bowl as Jesus did himself. This would have brought to mind Psalm 41:9, which reads:

> Even my close friend,
>   someone I trusted,
> one who shared my bread,
>   has turned against me.

Having given them the dread news of his impending betrayal, he passed a woe of judgment upon the one who would betray him.

Jesus then went on to say that all that was to come had already been written, a reference to Old Testament texts such as Isaiah 53 and Psalm 22. There was more in mind, though, than simply a fulfilment of texts, since Jesus's actions would also fulfil much of the Old Testament Law. John Murray, commenting on Hebrews, made the point:

---

[9] Mishnah, *Pesachim* 10 reads, 'On the eve of Passover from just before the afternoon's daily whole offering, a person should not eat, until it gets dark. And even the poorest Israelite should not eat until he reclines at his table. And they should provide him with no fewer than four cups of wine, and even if [the funds] come from public charity.' Translation from Neusner, *Mishnah*, 249.

[10] The Greek phrase invites a negative response.

Christ's own sacrifice is the great exemplar after which the Levitical sacrifices were patterned. We often think of the Levitical sacrifices as providing the pattern for the sacrifice of Christ. This direction of thought is not improper – the Levitical sacrifices do furnish us with the categories in terms of which we are to interpret the sacrifice of Christ, particularly the categories of expiation, propitiation, and reconciliation. But this line of thought is not the characteristic one in Hebrews 9. The thought is specifically that the Levitical sacrifices were patterned after the heavenly exemplar – they were 'patterns of the things in the heavens' (Heb. 9:23). Hence the necessity for the blood offerings of the Levitical economy arose from the fact that the exemplar after which they were fashioned was a blood offering, the transcendent blood offering by which the heavenly things were purified. The necessity of blood-shedding in the Levitical ordinance is simply a necessity arising from the necessity of blood-shedding in the higher realm of the heavenly.[11]

Murray's point –and it is an important one to bear in mind during the Passion – is that Jesus's sacrifice upon the cross is the supreme, the highest and the most real sacrifice. The Old Testament sacrificial system was an anticipation of this later supreme sacrifice and pointed towards it. This understanding, strongly present in Hebrews, was set into poetic form in the next century by Melito of Sardis (*d. c.* AD 190):

For the law is old,
    but the word is new.
The type is provisional,
    but grace is everlasting.
The sheep is perishable,
    but the Lord,
      not broken as a lamb but raised up as God,
    is imperishable.

---

[11] John Murray, *Redemption: Accomplished and Applied* (Grand Rapids: Eerdmans, 1955), 15.

For though led to the slaughter like a sheep
  he was no sheep.
Though speechless as a lamb,
  neither yet was he a lamb.
For there was once a type,
  but now the reality has appeared.
For instead of the lamb there was a son,
  and instead of the sheep a man;
in the man was Christ encompassing all things.
So the slaughter of the sheep,
  and the sacrificial procession of the blood,
  and the writing of the law encompass Christ,
on whose account everything in the previous law took place,
  though better in the new dispensation. [12]

T. H. L. Parker, when referring to Calvin's thought, expressed this process well by describing this as a 'pre-enactment':

The history of the Jews was not only a preparation for the coming of Christ; it was also a deliberate pre-enactment of him and his work. Certain persons and institutions were types or figures or images (he uses the words interchangeably) . . . A type is not for Calvin an accidental resemblance between the two Covenants, but something deliberately set up by God's providence to pre-enact the Incarnate Christ, and thus to stand for Christ and stand for him effectually.[13]

So it is that when Jesus said, 'The Son of Man will go just as it is written about him,' he had more in mind than simply the words of the prophets. He was to fulfil all the Old Testament rituals, which served as his pre-enactment. Jesus, the *real* Passover lamb, was slain at the same time as the Passover lambs that pointed towards him were to be killed. He was the fulfilment and the archetype. With this in

---

[12] Melito of Sardis, *On Pascha*, 4–6. Translation from Stewart, *On Pascha*, 51–2.
[13] Thomas Henry Louis Parker, *Calvin's Old Testament Commentaries* (Edinburgh: T&T Clark, 1986), 74–5.

mind, the Passover becomes a powerful lens through which to view the cross. Through Jesus's sacrifice, we participate in the redemption and liberation of the Exodus. We share in its benefits. To quote the Mishnah, a collection of Jewish oral teaching from the first two centuries AD which themselves represent centuries of tradition:

> In every generation a person is duty-bound to regard himself as if he personally has gone forth from Egypt, since it is said, *And you shall tell your son in that day saying, It is because of that which the Lord did for me when I came forth out of Egypt* (Ex. 13:8). Therefore we are duty-bound to thank, praise, glorify, honour, exalt, extol, and bless him who did for our forefathers and for us all these miracles. He brought us forth from slavery to freedom, anguish to joy, mourning to festival, darkness to great light, subjugation to redemption, so we should say before him, Hallelujah.[14]

Mark's narrative then recounted the Lord's Supper itself, and Jesus performed two symbolic actions as they ate. First, he took bread and, following the normal Jewish practice, gave thanks. The blessing is not recorded, but a common blessing of the time would have been, 'Blessed are you, O LORD, our God, King of the Universe, who brings forth bread from the earth.'[15] He then broke the bread and shared it among his disciples, saying, 'Take it; this is my body.'

Within the Passover liturgy the bread was a symbol of redemption,[16] and as Jesus shared the bread he demonstrated that we are not only redeemed by his body, but also united to him as we eat the bread. Here we might find the roots of Paul's understanding of both the body of Christ and us being 'in Christ'. As he would later write, 'There is now no condemnation for those who are in Christ Jesus' (Romans 8:1).

After the bread, Jesus took a cup (presumably of wine, the 'fruit of the vine', verse 25), blessed it and passed it around. The Mishnah

---

[14] Mishnah, *Pesachim* 10.5.E. Translation from Neusner, *Mishnah*, 250.

[15] See Mishnah, *Berakhot* 6. Translation from Neusner, *Mishnah*, 9.

[16] Mishnah, *Pesachim* 10.5.C.

records the blessing as, 'Blessed are you, O LORD, our God, King of the Universe, Creator of the fruit of the vine,' a phrase echoed by Jesus in verse 25. After they had all drunk from the cup, he identified it as 'my blood of the covenant, which is poured out for many'. In a Passover meal one would expect each person to have an individual cup, and it may well be that Jesus was emphasising the unity of the group by sharing the cup along with the bread.

In this phrase, Jesus brought to mind the confirmation of the Old Testament covenant in Exodus 24:8. This was marked by the sacrifice of fellowship offerings, and the blood was afterwards sprinkled on the altar and the people. Moses then ascended Mount Sinai and received tablets of stone upon which were written the Law and the commandments. Here Christ's death is firmly identified with the sacrificial system summed up in the covenant as a whole. Jesus's death was a pouring out 'for many', the one died in the place of the many. The crucifixion was the perfect sacrifice on which the entire Old Testament sacrificial system was based.

A question arises out of Jesus's words: who are the 'many' for whom Jesus's blood is poured out? Earlier, in Mark 10:45, Jesus had stated that he would give his life as a ransom for 'many', and so we twice see him limiting the effects of his sacrifice to a particular group.[17] There is no room for universalism here, and in the Gospel of John it is clear that Jesus was acting for the benefit of those whom the Father had given him (John 6:37–40; 17). But what of those passages that speak of Jesus coming for the whole world (e.g., John 1:29; 3:16; 4:42) or, more awkwardly, 1 Timothy 2:6 where we finding Paul asserting that Jesus 'gave himself as a ransom for all people'? Is he contradicting Jesus? The answer is, of course, no. The point being made here is that there is but one mediator between God and the human race. Jesus's death is global in its extent, and there is no other saviour. Whatever your nationality or status in life, Jesus is your sole hope. He was sent for the whole world, not simply Israel.

Once the bread and the wine had been distributed, Jesus moved his focus from his crucifixion to the coming kingdom of God when

---

[17] See also Isaiah 53:11–12; Matthew 20:28; 26:28; Romans 5:15, 19; Hebrews 2:10; 9:28.

he would once again drink from the 'fruit of the vine', and 'drink it new'. Since the 'fruit of the vine' is a reference to the Passover blessing, it is natural to look there for the imagery Jesus was using, rather than some hope of the future 'Messianic Banquet'.[18] What makes the wine 'new' is that it has now been fulfilled, since 'Christ, our Passover lamb, has been sacrificed' (1 Corinthians 5:7). Rather than a feast remembering the Passover in Egypt, the newly fulfilled Passover 'proclaims the Lord's death' (1 Corinthians 11:26).

When we celebrate the Lord's Supper, we celebrate all that it achieves, not only our own salvation but also the formation of a new people – the church – drawn from all parts of the globe. That we might be counted among the 'many' whom Christ came to save is to be reminded of the grace of God that extends to those unworthy of his attentions. To receive bread and wine is to remember the torture of crucifixion and the dread cost to himself of Jesus's mission. Is there a more humbling act than to ponder all that Communion represents, and then to partake in eating and drinking the bread and wine? Samuel Stennett (1727–95) captured the awe of it all:

Lord, at Thy table I behold
The wonders of Thy grace;
But most of all admire that I
Should find a welcome place.[19]

As the Last Supper finished, the disciples sang a hymn (possibly one of the Hallel psalms sung after the Passover, Psalms 113–18). They then went to the Mount of Olives, which overlooks the city from the Kidron Valley, but in the Passover regulations is counted as being within Jerusalem.[20]

---

[18] A hoped-for feast marking God making all things new. See Isaiah 25:6–8; Matthew 8:11; Luke 13:29; 14:15; 22:29–30; Revelation 19:9. In other literature of the time, see 1 Enoch 62:14; 2 Baruch 29:5–8; 1QSa 2:11–22.
[19] Samuel Stennett, 'Lord, at Thy table I behold' (1787).
[20] Jeremias, *Jerusalem*, 61–2.

The scattering and Peter's denial foretold (14:27–31)

Jesus predicts Peter's denial

27 'You will all fall away,' Jesus told them, 'for it is written:

' "I will strike the shepherd,
    and the sheep will be
        scattered." d

28 But after I have risen, I will go ahead of you into Galilee.'

29 Peter declared, 'Even if all fall away, I will not.'

30 'Truly I tell you,' Jesus answered, 'today – yes, tonight – before the cock crows twicee you yourself will disown me three times.'

31 But Peter insisted emphatically, 'Even if I have to die with you, I will never disown you.' And all the others said the same.

---

d 27 Zech. 13:7
e 30 Some early manuscripts do not have *twice.*

Having stated that one of the Twelve would betray him, Jesus now predicted that the rest would abandon him. In so doing he quoted from Zechariah 13:7:

'Awake, sword, against my shepherd,
    against the man who is close to me!'
    declares the LORD Almighty.
'Strike the shepherd,
    and the sheep will be scattered,
    and I will turn my hand against the little ones'.

This, then, was no mere fleeing by the disciples in the face of danger but a fulfilment of an earlier prophecy. Significantly, in the chapter following that prophecy, Zechariah went on to describe the fall of Jerusalem, an event Jesus had discussed fully with his disciples just a little time before in chapter 13. This scattering of the disciples was not, however, the end of the matter, since the struck shepherd would rise and 'go ahead of you into Galilee' (see Mark 16:7).

Peter baulked at the suggestion that he would desert Jesus, but Jesus insisted that such a desertion would take place that very night before the cock crowed twice. Peter and the others all continued to assert their loyalty, but the chapters to come would see them scatter. How often it is that loyalty evaporates in the face of danger.

It is a sad fact that in our Christian life we will, at times, betray Christ. As the old *Book of Common Prayer* (1662) confession puts it, 'We have left undone those things which we ought to have done; And we have done those things which we ought not to have done.' A crisis might cause us to question God, or an attack on our faith might cause us to stumble. At this point it is important to remember that to be human is to be fallen and that Christ came precisely to save sinners. We stumble, but we also carry on. Even though Peter was told of his betrayal, he did not drift away but sought to remain close to Jesus. His is the path to follow.

'Yet not what I will . . .' (14:32–42)

Gethsemane

32 They went to a place called Gethsemane, and Jesus said to his disciples, 'Sit here while I pray.' **33** He took Peter, James and John along with him, and he began to be deeply distressed and troubled. **34** 'My soul is overwhelmed with sorrow to the point of death,' he said to them. 'Stay here and keep watch.'

35 Going a little farther, he fell to the ground and prayed that if possible the hour might pass from him. **36** '*Abba*,[f] Father,' he said, 'everything is possible for you. Take this cup from me. Yet not what I will, but what you will.'

37 Then he returned to his disciples and found them sleeping. 'Simon,' he said to Peter, 'are you asleep? Couldn't you keep watch for one hour? **38** Watch and pray so that you will not fall into temptation. The spirit is willing, but the flesh is weak.'

39 Once more he went away and prayed the same thing. **40** When he came back, he again found them sleeping, because their eyes were heavy. They did not know what to say to him.

41 Returning the third time, he said to them, 'Are you still sleeping and resting? Enough! The hour has come. Look, the Son of Man is delivered into the hands of sinners. **42** Rise! Let us go! Here comes my betrayer!'

_____
f 36 Aramaic for *father*

Gethsemane simply means 'olive press', which would suggest that Jesus went to a place in which there was a press to process the olives from a nearby grove. John described the location as a 'garden', which would make sense in that context, and also noted that this was somewhere Jesus often went with his disciples (John 18:1–2). Given its location on the Mount of Olives, there would have been a good view of Jerusalem and, since it was the Day of Preparation, the moon would have been almost full. There would have been enough light for the disciples to keep watch.

When they arrived, Jesus took his inner circle of Peter, James and John with him and told the others to stay where they were. These three had been with Jesus to witness the glory of the transfiguration and now they would see him in great distress. The events that were to occur over the coming days weighed heavily on Jesus, and his distress was such that his soul was 'overwhelmed with sorrow to the point of death' (verse 34). His response to this terror was to pray and, urging the three to keep watch, he went beyond them to meet his Father in deep intercession. Here is a model for us when we face danger: turn to prayer.

The fervour of Jesus's prayer was demonstrated by his falling to the ground. Such was the torment of his soul. He prayed that – if possible – another way might be found and a lesser fate befall him. We would do well to never underestimate the deep, personal cost to Jesus of the cross. This was more than a simple crucifixion, terrible as that would be, but a fate that would cause him to cry out that he was forsaken by God. More than existential angst, this was a spiritual angst that struck at his very relationship with the Father. He was the atoning sacrifice not just for the Jews but for the sins of the whole world (1 John 2:2). He bore our griefs and sorrows (Isaiah 53:4). Terrible as crucifixion was, this was an added torture.

There is deep poignancy in the prayer as the Son of God (Mark 1:1, 11; 3:11; 5:7; 9:7) cried out: 'Abba, Father.' Mark was careful to preserve Jesus's cry in Aramaic. The Son, the one whom God loves (Mark 1:11; 9:7), knew that all things are possible for God, and so begged for the suffering to pass. Yet even here he submitted to the will of God: 'Yet not what I will, but what you will.' This was the only path Christ could take, and the cost was high. Yet it was a path he was prepared to take.

This passage acts as a challenge to us. How often we simply lay our woes before God but stop short of seeking his will. Jesus shows us the path of one who has a deep and unerring trust in the goodness of God, even if that path of goodness at times goes through the valley of the shadow of death (Psalm 23:4). Reflecting on Psalm 4:8 John Favel (*c.* 1627–91) wrote:

> He resolves the sinful fears of events shall not rob him of his inward quiet, nor torture his thoughts with anxious presages: He will commit all his concerns into that faithful, fatherly hand, that had hitherto wrought all things for him, and he means not to lose the comfort of one night's rest, nor bring the evil of to-morrow upon the day, but knowing in whose hand he was, wisely enjoys the sweet felicity of a resigned will.[21]

'The sweet felicity of a resigned will.' This memorable phrase sums up the Christian life.

When he returned from prayer, Jesus found the three asleep. He addressed Peter as 'Simon' – this rock had crumbled into sleep – and rebuked him for not even being able to keep watch for an hour. He urged him to both watch and pray that he would not succumb to the temptation to sleep. Jesus's comment that 'the spirit is willing, but the flesh is weak' neatly summed up the state of all those in Gethsemane. Jesus's spirit was willing to align itself with God, but his flesh recoiled before what was to come. The three disciples' spirits were willing to stay with Jesus to the end (Mark 10:38–9; 14:31), but their flesh desired sleep. How often tiredness hinders our prayers as we only grant God a few minutes of prayer as we wake or before we sleep. Better to give God our best hours.

Jesus returned to his prayer, one hour not being enough, and repeated his desire to the Father. Here we have an example of persistence in prayer, engaging in the struggle until peace is found. He then returned to find the disciples asleep again, and they simply didn't know what to say. The pattern was repeated a third time, and Jesus called a halt. The hour that has been the subject of Jesus's long wrestling in prayer (verse 35) had come. Jesus was to be handed over,

---

[21] From 'Divine Conduct: Or, the Mystery of Providence, Opened in a Treatise Upon Psal. 57:2'. John Flavel, *The Works of the Reverend John Flavel* (London: Baynes and Son, 1820), 4:455.

and the will of the Father was to be fulfilled. He told the disciples to get up: the betrayer had arrived.

NOTE: IS THE SON SUBORDINATE TO THE FATHER?

The submission of Christ's will to the Father's takes us into the heart of the incarnation, the very being of Christ. The councils of the early church were keen to stress that Jesus was both truly God and truly man. These two natures are preserved in the one person of Christ, without any mixture of the two. Jesus's humanity is perfect, as is his divinity. His human nature is the same as our human nature, except that he is sinless. His divinity is begotten from the Father.

In the seventh century there arose a teaching that Jesus had, in fact, only one 'energy' or will. This contradicted the principle that the two natures of Christ were complete and without mixture,[22] but the new teaching took hold until it was finally condemned at the sixth Ecumenical Council, in Constantinople (680–81). Jesus's prayer at Gethsemane was a crucial text in the defence of orthodoxy. Here Jesus's human will was submitted to the divine will and his two wills came together in harmony.[23] In this prayer, Jesus models for us a complete obedience to God's will, a perfect agreement of the human and the divine. Jesus's fear of all that was to come was all too human, and his resolve to live in harmony with the will of the Father was also human. Such humble submission, such willingness to follow God's will is not beyond the reach of human beings. Jesus

---

[22] The Westminster Confession of Faith later defined the natures as being 'without conversion, composition, or confusion' (8.1.2)

[23] One of the great champions of the orthodox position wrote, 'If, however, you understand the subject of the phrase Let not what I will, but what you will prevail to be not the man just like us but the man we consider as Saviour, then you have confessed the ultimate concurrence of his human will with the divine will, which is both his and the Father's; and you have demonstrated that with the duality of his natures there are two wills (θελήσεις) and two operations (ἐνεργείαι) respective to the two natures, and that he admits of no opposition between them, even though he maintains all the while the difference between the two natures from which, in which, and which he is by nature.' Maximus the Confessor (580–662), *Short Theological and Polemical Works*, 6. Translation from Maximus the Confessor, *On the Cosmic Mystery of Jesus Christ: Selected Writings From St. Maximus the Confessor*, trans. P. M. Blowers and R. L. Wilken (Crestwood: St Vladimir's Seminary Press, 2003), 174.

poured out his heart before God but did not simply stop there. He sought to align his will with God's will.

We should be careful here to preserve the full humanity and full divinity of Jesus, and not seek to mingle the two. This passage does not suggest that the divinity of Christ is somehow subordinate to the divinity of the Father. To hold that is to suggest that Jesus only has a divine will and is not fully human. Nor is this an example of what some have termed 'cosmic child abuse', whereby the Father inflicts the wrath of the cross on the Son.[24] That is to simply reduce Jesus to his human nature alone and forget that the eternal second Person of the Trinity is one with the eternal first Person of the Trinity. The three are one and act as one. Father, Son and Holy Spirit *all* decreed that the crucifixion should take place. It was not one Person of the Trinity inflicting something upon the second person of the Trinity against his will. God is one (Deuteronomy 6:4; Mark 12:29).

The Scriptures assert that Jesus is fully God and also fully man. We should be content to let that wondrous and mysterious truth remain and not attempt to 'over-understand' the inner workings of a God greater than anything we can imagine.

Betrayal and arrest (14:43–52)

Jesus arrested

43 Just as he was speaking, Judas, one of the Twelve, appeared. With him was a crowd armed with swords and clubs, sent from the chief priests, the teachers of the law, and the elders.

44 Now the betrayer had arranged a signal with them: 'The one I kiss is the man; arrest him and lead him away under guard.' **45** Going at once to Jesus, Judas said, 'Rabbi!' and kissed him. **46** The men seized Jesus and arrested him. **47** Then one of those standing near drew his sword and struck the servant of the high priest, cutting off his ear.

48 'Am I leading a rebellion,' said Jesus, 'that you have come out with swords and clubs to capture me? **49** Every day I was with you, teaching in the temple courts, and you did

---

[24] Steve Chalke and Alan Mann, *The Lost Message of Jesus* (Grand Rapids: Zondervan, 2003), 182.

not arrest me. But the Scriptures must be fulfilled.' **50** Then everyone deserted him and fled.

51 A young man, wearing nothing but a linen garment, was following Jesus. When they seized him, **52** he fled naked, leaving his garment behind.

As soon as Jesus announced that his betrayer was coming, Judas appeared with an armed mob sent by the chief priests, the teachers of the law and the elders. The fact that Judas was identified as 'one of the Twelve' underlines the extent of the betrayal. This betrayal was further heightened by its manner: Judas kissed Jesus, a common enough greeting at the time and a sign of respect (see Psalm 2:12). A feigned respect for Christ can mask a hatred for him. To simply call Jesus 'Rabbi' is not to own him as such. The true disciple also follows.

At the sign of the traitor's kiss the armed crowd arrested Jesus, and in the fracas one of those with Jesus struck with a sword the high priest's servant, who was presumably leading the crowd.[25] His ear was cut off in the confusion of the night. Chaos.

Jesus challenged the manner of all this, saying that he was no rebel. In fact, Jesus came to achieve something deeper than mere rebellion: he came to restore humanity. The use of arms was not needed, and he had not been hiding away such that an armed party coming at night was warranted. The reason for his arrest was not that he was leading a rebellion, but rather that Scripture must be fulfilled. There are echoes here of Joseph's brothers' betrayal of their younger brother: 'You intended to harm me, but God intended it for good to accomplish what is now being done, the saving of many lives' (Genesis 50:20).

We would do well to recognise that the providences of God are sometimes dark. The path God picks out for us might lead through sorrow, but it is his path nonetheless. Horatius Bonar (1808–89) put it well in one of his hymns:

> The kingdom that I seek
> is thine, so let the way
> that leads to it be thine,
> else I must surely stray.[26]

---

[25] John names the swordsman as Peter, and the servant as Malchus (John 18:10).
[26] Horatius Bonar, 'Thy Way, not Mine, O Lord' (1857).

Jesus asserted that 'the Scriptures must be fulfilled', a phrase that bore witness to his view of the authority of the Scriptures. They carry behind them the weight of God, and so they must be accomplished (see also Matthew 5:18; Luke 16:17; 24:44; John 10:35).

Which Scriptures were being fulfilled? Many! Most immediately we see the disciples deserting him, fulfilling Zechariah 13:7, a verse Jesus had cited a little earlier in Mark 14:27. More broadly, the arrest led to the fulfilment of the Suffering Servant passages in Isaiah (Isaiah 42:1–4; 49:1–6; 50:4–11; 52:13–53:12). Widen out the scope still further and Jesus fulfilled the sacrificial system of the Law. Widen yet further and we find Jesus fulfilling the words uttered to the serpent in Eden:

> And I will put enmity
>> between you and the woman,
>> and between your offspring and hers;
> he will crush your head,
>> and you will strike his heel.
> (Genesis 3:15)

All of this is to say that the rich themes of the Old Testament converge to find their fulfilment in Christ.

As the disciples deserted Jesus, we find a small detail omitted in the other Gospels. Present at the scene was a young man, wearing just a linen cloth, whom the crowd attempted to seize. He too fled, leaving the arresters holding his linen cloth. The young man is often identified with John Mark, the author of the Gospel. We know that John Mark's mother, Mary, had a large house in Jerusalem (Acts 12:12), and it is plausible that the Last Supper was held at that house. Judas would have led the crowd there at first and, finding Jesus not there, went on to Gethsemane. The young John Mark rose from his bed, wrapped his linen sheet around himself, and followed on at a distance. A nice possibility, but no more than that.

2. The four verdicts • Mark 14:53–15:15

This section presents us with four verdicts that were passed on Christ. The council found him guilty of blasphemy, and Peter denied he even knew him. The crowds called for his crucifixion, and Pilate handed him over to that fate.

Jesus before the Council (14:53–65)

Jesus before the Sanhedrin

53 They took Jesus to the high priest, and all the chief priests, the elders and the teachers of the law came together. 54 Peter followed him at a distance, right into the courtyard of the high priest. There he sat with the guards and warmed himself at the fire.

55 The chief priests and the whole Sanhedrin were looking for evidence against Jesus so that they could put him to death, but they did not find any. 56 Many testified falsely against him, but their statements did not agree.

57 Then some stood up and gave this false testimony against him: 58 'We heard him say, "I will destroy this temple made with human hands and in three days will build another, not made with hands."' 59 Yet even then their testimony did not agree.

60 Then the high priest stood up before them and asked Jesus, 'Are you not going to answer? What is this testimony that these men are bringing against you?' 61 But Jesus remained silent and gave no answer.

Again the high priest asked him, 'Are you the Messiah, the Son of the Blessed One?'

62 'I am,' said Jesus. 'And you will see the Son of Man sitting at the right hand of the Mighty One and coming on the clouds of heaven.'

63 The high priest tore his clothes. 'Why do we need any more witnesses?' he asked. 64 'You have heard the blasphemy. What do you think?'

They all condemned him as worthy of death. 65 Then some began to spit at him; they blindfolded him, struck him with their fists, and said, 'Prophesy!' And the guards took him and beat him.

Jesus was taken to the house of the high priest, whom the other gospels name as Caiaphas (Matthew 26:57; Luke 3:2; John 11:49;

Acts 4:6). Here the whole Sanhedrin gathered, comprising the chief priests, elders and teachers of the law.[27] Peter, no doubt conscious of his promise not to fall away from Jesus (Mark 14:29), followed Jesus, but at a distance. He got as close as he was able, even into the courtyard of the house, but would not have been able to gain access to the building. He boldly sat with the guards who had gathered to keep warm around a fire.

With the celebration of Passover near, they were keen to find enough evidence against Jesus to have him put to death quickly. This was more an inquisition than a trial and brought to a conclusion the plotting that had begun during Jesus's early ministry in the north (Mark 3:6). False witnesses were found, but since they could not agree on their allegations, their testimonies could not stand (Exodus 20:16; Deuteronomy 5:20). Eventually the charge was brought that Jesus had said, 'I will destroy this temple made with human hands and in three days will build another, not made with hands' (see John 2:19), but even here the 'witnesses' could not agree as to their testimony. This, though, was enough for the high priest, who stood and asked Jesus to answer the charge.

Jesus remained silent, his silence echoing Isaiah 53:7.

The high priest pressed further, and asked Jesus, 'Are you the Messiah, the Son of the Blessed One?' This line of questioning arose from the charge, since the rebuilding of the Temple was associated with the Messiah (2 Samuel 7:13; Zechariah 6:12), and the Davidic Messiah was understood to be, in some sense, the Son of God (2 Samuel 7:14; Psalms 2:7; 89:26). It also may well be that Judas had related Jesus's anointing at Bethany, as well as Peter's confession at Caesarea Philippi, when he betrayed Jesus to the Sanhedrin.

Whatever the case, it is here that Jesus openly claimed his identity: the Messianic Secret was finally broken. He was both Messiah and Son of God, but also more than both. His divine sonship was no metaphor, and his Messiahship not simply royal. The reply he gave was breathtaking, beginning as it did with the divine name: 'I am'. He then went on to refer to Daniel 7, which reads:

---

[27] The 'all' in verse 53 does not imply every single elder was present, but rather that each party was represented.

In my vision at night I looked, and there before me was one like a son of man, coming with the clouds of heaven. He approached the Ancient of Days and was led into his presence. He was given authority, glory and sovereign power; all nations and peoples of every language worshipped him. His dominion is an everlasting dominion that will not pass away, and his kingdom is one that will never be destroyed. (Daniel 7:13–14).

This describes the inauguration of the kingdom of God. The reign of David was simply a distant echo of the divine rule of Jesus who had been granted sovereign power by God. More than that, he was to be worshipped by peoples of every nation. This worship is a sign of the divinity of the 'one like a son of man' since it is not condemned as idolatry. The fact that God is one (Deuteronomy 6:4) lies at the heart of Judaism and the biblical witness to God. That another is deemed worthy of worship points to the fact that there are Persons within that oneness and leads to our understanding of the Trinity.

This self-disclosure in front of the Sanhedrin was the pivotal moment. There was no more need for witnesses as Jesus had now spoken plainly of his divine Messiahship in their presence. The accused stood self-condemned: he had blasphemed by claiming divine origin. Such was the outrage that the high priest tore his clothes.

Here is the core of Christianity. It is to do with who Jesus *is* and not what he can do for me. We worship Christ because of his divinity and not simply because we hope he might grant us some favour. Everything flows from the fact of Jesus's identity. His words have authority since they are divine words. His teachings are binding since they are divine teachings. Christianity stands apart from Judaism and Islam – the other so-called Abrahamic faiths – as it alone asserts that God is Trinity and Jesus is God. To assert that Christians, Muslims and Jews today all worship the same God is to ignore this fact.

The sentence from all present was that he must die (Leviticus 24:16), but capital punishment was outside their judicial power since they were under Roman occupation (John 18:31), so they contented themselves with abusing Jesus before bringing him to the Roman authorities.[28] To be spat upon is to be humiliated (Numbers 12:14; Deuteronomy 25:9), and they mocked Jesus's claim of divine favour by beating him blindfolded and then asking him to prophecy as to whose fists he had felt. The dark irony here is that Jesus had indeed prophesied that this event would take place (Mark 10:33–4), and their very actions were also prophesied in Isaiah 50:6. Those who are against God nonetheless fulfil his purposes. All are under the providence of God, not simply those who acknowledge him. That, after all, is why we pray.

Once the Sanhedrin was finished with him, the guards took him and continued the beating.

Peter denies Jesus (14:66–72)

Peter disowns Jesus

66 While Peter was below in the courtyard, one of the servant-girls of the high priest came by. **67** When she saw Peter warming himself, she looked closely at him.

'You also were with that Nazarene, Jesus,' she said.

68 But he denied it. 'I don't know or understand what you're talking about,' he said, and went out into the entrance.**g**

69 When the servant-girl saw him there, she said again to those standing round them, 'This fellow is one of them.' **70** Again he denied it.

After a little while, those standing near said to Peter, 'Surely you are one of them, for you are a Galilean.'

71 He began to call down curses, and he swore to them, 'I don't know this man you're talking about.'

72 Immediately the cock crowed the second time.**h** Then Peter remembered the word Jesus had spoken to him: 'Before the cock crows twice**i** you will disown me three times.' And he broke down and wept.

---

g 68 Some early manuscripts *entrance and the cock crowed*

h 72 Some early manuscripts do not have *the second time.*

i 72 Some early manuscripts do not have *twice.*

---

[28] The stoning of Stephen (Acts 7:47–60) was a mob act, not a judicial sentence. Josephus records that the Romans allowed the Jews to kill Gentiles who went into the inner courts of the Temple (Josephus, *Jewish War*, 6.2.4).

While Jesus was being condemned by the Sanhedrin, he was being denied by Peter who was warming himself in the high priest's courtyard. While it is easy to dismiss Peter's actions as cowardly, it is worth remembering that he had taken a great risk even to come into that courtyard. His courage, though, was not without its limits, and his actions bear testimony that even the most ardent of Jesus's followers may stumble. Judas's betrayal was bold and total, but Peter's denial was reluctant and guilt-filled.

A passing servant girl noticed Peter, looked more closely at him and apparently recognised him as a follower of Jesus. The term 'Nazarene' is most probably derogatory since those from Jerusalem looked down on their northern, rural fellow Jews from Galilee. It may be that Peter's accent gave him away (the word used for 'saw' may mean 'noted').

Peter denied the charge, saying that he neither understood nor knew what she was talking about. Here was the first of the three predicted denials. Even though it was passive (he simply claimed ignorance), this was still a disowning of Christ (Mark 14:31). Betrayal may be keeping silent as much as speaking out. He was clearly rattled and moved to the entrance, which would have given him a clearer route of escape. He stepped back and hoped not to be noticed.

The servant girl, noticing that Peter was still within the courtyard, told those standing nearby, 'This fellow is one of them.' Peter made his second denial, but his words were not recorded.

A while later those who were with Peter, and so would have heard the servant girl's accusations, took the matter up for themselves. They knew Peter to be a Galilean (presumably again his accent gave him away) and were certain he was one of Jesus's followers. The word translated 'surely' means 'in truth'. The nagging questions would not cease.

This clear danger brought forth the strongest denial from Peter. He called down curses and swore by an oath that he did not know 'this man'. As Peter made this most categorical of denials, the cock crowed once more. Peter, remembering Jesus's prophecy, broke down and wept. He was a rock no more.

There is a puzzling question as to who Peter cursed. In every other use of the verb in the New Testament, it has an object. The thing to be cursed is named. Here there is no object, which is curious. Why did Peter not relate (or Mark record) what was cursed?

This question has led some to suggest that Peter, in his desire to utterly distance himself from Jesus, cursed him.[29] This might explain Peter's reluctance to use Jesus's name, instead referring to 'this man'. If this was the case, as seems likely, it would have been such a painful and shameful act that Mark awkwardly omitted the object of the verb.

We might also find in this passage another example of how God is pleased to use imperfect people, even in the composing of Scripture itself. Moses murdered, Isaiah was 'a man of unclean lips' (Isaiah 6:5), Paul persecuted the church and Peter denied Christ. It is the carrying along of the author by the Holy Spirit (see 2 Peter 1:21) that produces the Scriptures, not the talent or character of the authors themselves.[30]

Finally, Peter's tears demonstrated the depth of his repentance and stand in stark contrast with the suicide of Judas. He was later restored by the Christ he had denied and stands as a witness to God's gracious forgiveness of those who repent. We should not expect perfection from all Christians, but we should expect repentance.

Jesus delivered to Pilate (15:1–15)

Jesus before Pilate

15 Very early in the morning, the chief priests, with the elders, the teachers of the law and the whole Sanhedrin, made their plans. So they bound Jesus, led him away and handed him over to Pilate.

2 'Are you the king of the Jews?' asked Pilate.

'You have said so,' Jesus replied.

3 The chief priests accused him of many things. 4 So again Pilate asked him, 'Aren't you going to answer? See how many things they are accusing you of.'

5 But Jesus still made no reply, and Pilate was amazed.

6 Now it was the custom at the festival to release a prisoner whom the people requested. 7 A man called Barabbas was in prison with the rebels who had committed murder in the uprising. 8 The crowd came up and asked Pilate to do for them what he usually did.

9 'Do you want me to release to you

---

[29] See the discussion in Helmut Merkel, 'Peter's Curse', in *The Trial of Jesus: Cambridge Studies in Honour of C. F. D. Moule*, ed. Ernst Bammel (London: SCM Press, 1970).
[30] Scott R. Swain, *Trinity, Revelation, and Reading: A Theological Introduction to the Bible and Its Interpretation* (London; New York: T&T Clark, 2011), 62–3.

the king of the Jews?' asked Pilate, 10 knowing it was out of self-interest that the chief priests had handed Jesus over to him. 11 But the chief priests stirred up the crowd to get Pilate to release Barabbas instead.

12 'What shall I do, then, with the one you call the king of the Jews?' Pilate asked them.

13 'Crucify him!' they shouted.

14 'Why? What crime has he committed?' asked Pilate.

But they shouted all the louder, 'Crucify him!'

15 Wanting to satisfy the crowd, Pilate released Barabbas to them. He had Jesus flogged, and handed him over to be crucified.

Having been sentenced by the Sanhedrin and denied by Peter, Jesus was taken to Pilate. The haste of the Sanhedrin was illustrated by the fact that Jesus was taken 'very early in the morning'. They needed him dead by nightfall, which marked the beginning of the Passover.

The Sanhedrin had 'made their plans' (verse 1), but there was a deeper plan at work. After the resurrection, at Pentecost, Peter addressed a crowd in Jerusalem and told them that Jesus 'was handed over to you by God's deliberate plan and foreknowledge; and you, with the help of wicked men, put him to death by nailing him to the cross' (Acts 2:23). Here we find a profound providence indeed: the enemies of Christ were being used to bring about his glory.

This, however, should not be seen as meaning that the actions of the wicked are, in fact, good since they serve God's purposes. God said of Babylon, who conquered Jerusalem and destroyed the Temple:

You are my war club,
    my weapon for battle –
with you I shatter nations,
    with you I destroy kingdoms.
(Jeremiah 51:20)

A little later in the same prophecy we read:

Babylon must fall because of Israel's slain,
    just as the slain in all the earth
    have fallen because of Babylon.
(Jeremiah 51:49)

Babylon was used by God but remained culpable for her actions, which caused the prophet Habakkuk much angst (Habakkuk 1:1–11).

Pilate was prefect (governor) of Judea from AD 26 to 36, and at times of heightened nationalistic sentiment, such as the festivals, he would move from his residence on the coast at Caesarea Maritima to Jerusalem.[31] The Sanhedrin brought Jesus to Pilate since he could pass a sentence of death. He would have had little concern for the sensitivities of Jewish religious law, so the Sanhedrin brought charges of sedition (Luke 23:1–2, i.e., Jesus claimed royal authority opposed to Rome). When Pilate presented the charge, Jesus simply gave a neutral answer: 'You have said so.' These were his last recorded words prior the crucifixion. Before the Sanhedrin he had been 'irritatingly silent',[32] and here he simply did not deny the claim.

The chief priests hurried to bring more accusations which, as we can see from Luke's Gospel, were focused on Roman concerns: 'We have found this man subverting our nation. He opposes payment of taxes to Caesar and claims to be Messiah, a king' (Luke 23:2). They were seeking to force Pilate's hand, and he pressed Jesus for an answer. Jesus, the Suffering Servant, was silent:

> He was oppressed and afflicted,
> yet he did not open his mouth;
> he was led like a lamb to the slaughter,
> and as a sheep before its shearers is silent,
> so he did not open his mouth.
> (Isaiah 53:7)

Throughout the Gospel, people were 'amazed' at Jesus, and Pilate was the last of that long list.[33]

It was not uncommon in the ancient world for prisoners to be released to gain favour with the people, and Pilate appears at some stage to have adopted the practice of releasing a prisoner at Passover (John 18:39). This was now his annual custom, and each year the crowd

---

[31] Strauss, *Mark*, 673.
[32] France, *Mark*, 625.
[33] See Mark 1:22, 27; 2:12; 6:2, 51; 7:37; 10:24, 26; 11:18; 12:17.

came to secure a release (verse 8). Pilate had seen through the charges of the chief priests but, given their seditious nature, he had to be seen to act. This Passover release gave him the opportunity to maintain the strong rule of Rome and still set Jesus free. He went to the crowd.

Pilate was aware of the envy of the chief priests (a closer translation of the Greek than 'self-interest'). Envy is a powerful emotion, which focuses entirely on the self. As one turns inwards towards ambition, one inevitably turns away from God. We might speculate as to precisely what the chief priests were jealous of – popularity, skill in teaching, the working of miracles – but in the end that is left unsaid. What we can conclude, though, is that the working of God in another had brought their envy to the fore.

In the prison was Barabbas, whose name meant 'son of the abba [father]', which was not an uncommon name.[34] Given the fact that Jesus had prayed '*Abba*, Father' in Mark 14:36, there is great irony here. The text refers to an uprising that was clearly well known at the time, but we have no record of the particular event in mind. Barabbas was imprisoned with other rebels from the same uprising, whom we most likely meet at Golgotha (Mark 15:27), and the chief priests stirred the crowd to demand his release. A murderer was to be freed instead of the one who gives life.

Pilate returned to the crowd once more and asked what should be done with 'the one you call the king of the Jews'. For the second time the crowd rejected Jesus, and they called for him to be crucified. The stirring of the crowd by the chief priests only served to undermine their accusation that Jesus was a dangerous rebel, a claim denied during his arrest in Gethsemane (Mark 14:48). Pilate shouted out once more, asking what crime Jesus had committed. That, though, was not the issue. The point was that the Sanhedrin wanted Jesus dead.

Having faced the crowd, Pilate was unwilling to risk civil disobedience by denying their annual request, and so released Barabbas. He wanted to 'satisfy the crowd'. Some see this as a weak action by Pilate, but we know from elsewhere he was ruthless.[35] Better to see this as utter disdain

---

[34] Bauckham, *Eyewitnesses*, 84. It was the twenty-first most popular name among Palestinian Jews (330 BC–AD 200).

[35] Josephus records Pilate sending soldiers to kill protesters (*Jewish Wars*, 2.9.4; *Antiquities*, 18.3.2), and Luke records a massacre of the Galileans (Luke 13:1).

for the Jews and what he saw as their petty infighting. He wanted an easy life and was unwilling to engage with the claims of Christ: a path that usually leads to denying Christ. Pilate handed Jesus over to be flogged, the normal pattern for crucifixion, which was in equal parts torture and execution.[36] His desire was to satisfy the crowd and, as was the case with Herod, this led to the death of a righteous man.

3. The sacrifice of the Lamb • Mark 15:16–47

Here we witness the deepest suffering of the Suffering Servant. His guards performed a mock coronation, and he was crucified under the legend 'The King of the Jews'. Here was his grizzly throne. As he died, a Gentile soldier recognised him as 'the Son of God', and his body was taken for burial. The darkest hour.

The mock coronation of the 'King of the Jews' (15:16–20)

The soldiers mock Jesus

16 The soldiers led Jesus away into the palace (that is, the Praetorium) and called together the whole company of soldiers. 17 They put a purple robe on him, then twisted together a crown of thorns and set it on him. 18 And they began to call out to him, 'Hail, king of the Jews!' 19 Again and again they struck him on the head with a staff and spat on him. Falling on their knees, they paid homage to him. 20 And when they had mocked him, they took off the purple robe and put his own clothes on him. Then they led him out to crucify him.

Jesus was led to the courtyard of Pilate's palace,[37] known as the Praetorium, and the rest of the company joined him. Strictly speaking,

---

[36] Martin Hengel, *Crucifixion in the Ancient World and the Folly of the Message of the Cross*, trans. J Bowden (Philadelphia: Fortress Press, 1977), 28. He quotes Isidore of Seville (AD 560–636) who in a matter-of-fact way commented, 'But hanging is a lesser penalty than the cross. For the gallows kills the victim immediately, whereas the cross tortures for a long time those who are fixed to it..

[37] The Greek word translated 'palace' simply refers to an open place and is also used of Caiaphas's courtyard in Mark 14:54, 66.

a company of soldiers numbered six hundred, but in reality the numbers varied quite widely. Whatever the case here, these soldiers had Jesus to themselves, away from the crowds, and could do with him as they wished.

Jesus had been charged with claiming to be King of the Jews, so the soldiers dressed him up accordingly. A regal purple robe was put around his recently flogged and bloodied body,[38] thorns were twisted into a crown and he was given a mock coronation. They acclaimed him, 'Hail, king of the Jews!' They began to beat him with a staff, reminiscent of the royal sceptre.[39] The language suggests a sustained beating, and this was accompanied by spitting and mock homage. The fulfilment of Jesus's grim prediction on the way to Jerusalem was underway:

> The Son of Man will be delivered over to the chief priests and the teachers of the law. They will condemn him to death and will hand him over to the Gentiles, who will mock him and spit on him, flog him and kill him. Three days later he will rise. (Mark 10:33–4)

All this also fulfils the centuries old prophecy of Isaiah 50:6,:

> I offered my back to those who beat me,
> my cheeks to those who pulled out my beard;
> I did not hide my face
> from mocking and spitting.

Ironic indeed that the King of kings should be crowned in such a manner.

When they had wearied of their task, the soldiers removed the mock regalia and reclothed Jesus. He would have been crucified naked, but it is likely the soldiers did not wish to offend the Jews by parading a nude man through the streets, especially this close to

---

[38] Matthew records a scarlet robe (Matthew 27:28), so the 'purple' robe may have been a military cloak which had faded to a purple colour. The point was the mocking, not the accuracy of the dress.
[39] Probably the mock sceptre Matthew mentions (Matthew 27:29).

Passover when Jewish sensibilities were heightened and the crowds thronged.

As with Jesus, so with those who follow him. How often we are mocked for our beliefs and our obedience to Christ. We should expect no better treatment than the one we follow. The antidote to such taunting is a strong relationship with God and a weak attachment to our sense of self-importance.

The crucifixion (15:21–32)

The crucifixion of Jesus

21 A certain man from Cyrene, Simon, the father of Alexander and Rufus, was passing by on his way in from the country, and they forced him to carry the cross. 22 They brought Jesus to the place called Golgotha (which means 'the place of the skull'). 23 Then they offered him wine mixed with myrrh, but he did not take it. 24 And they crucified him. Dividing up his clothes, they cast lots to see what each would get.

25 It was nine in the morning when they crucified him. 26 The written notice of the charge against him read: THE KING OF THE JEWS.

27 They crucified two rebels with him, one on his right and one on his left. [28] a 29 Those who passed by hurled insults at him, shaking their heads and saying, 'So! You who are going to destroy the temple and build it in three days, 30 come down from the cross and save yourself!' 31 In the same way the chief priests and the teachers of the law mocked him among themselves. 'He saved others,' they said, 'but he can't save himself! 32 Let this Messiah, this king of Israel, come down now from the cross, that we may see and believe.' Those crucified with him also heaped insults on him.

_____

a 28 Some manuscripts include here words similar to Luke 22:37.

As Jesus was being led to Golgotha, Simon from Cyrene in North Africa was coming in from the country, probably arriving to celebrate the Passover which would begin later that evening. That his sons' names are given would suggest that they were known to the early readers of the Gospel. Paul also mentions a Rufus in the greetings at the end of Romans (Romans 16:13).

It was customary for the condemned to carry their own crosses to the place of execution,[40] which in practice meant the crosspiece. Once at the site, this crosspiece would be fixed to an upright which had been set into the ground at the place of execution. Given that Simon was pressed into carrying the cross, it would seem that Jesus had carried it only so far before collapsing from the effects of his beating.

In considering such a well-known passage, it is easy to become accustomed to it. Familiar scenes often lose their shock value. What a sight it would have been to see Jesus, blooded from his flogging and bruised from his beating, dragging his own instrument of execution behind him. What love is this that the Son of God – the one through whom all was created – should take flesh and be willing to have that flesh beaten and slain.

Jesus was led to Golgotha, which means 'the place of the skull'.[41] As with most sites of execution it lay outside the city walls, but the Romans were keen that sites such as these were visible: executions were intended to be a deterrent to other potential offenders and also, where appropriate, a comfort to the relatives of the murdered.[42] There was a grimness to the vengeful justice of the Roman Empire.

Before he was crucified, Jesus was offered myrrh mixed with wine. Some have speculated that this might be a form of anaesthetic, but myrrh does not have such effects, nor was it thought at the time to have them.[43] Myrrh, however, was added to fine wine as a flavouring and, given that it is most likely that the offer was made by the Roman soldiers, it is best seen as a final part of their mock coronation: as the thorn-crowned king was nailed to his throne, he was offered fine wine to drink. Jesus refused.

'And they crucified him.'

In that short phrase so much agony is contained. Crucifixion was

---

[40] Plutarch (AD 46–119), *Morals*, 9.

[41] 'Calvary' comes from the latinised version of this name: *calvariae locus*.

[42] Hengel cites Quintilian (*c.* AD 30–100): 'Whenever we crucify the guilty, the most crowded roads are chosen, where the most people can see and be moved by this fear. For penalties relate not so much to retribution as to their exemplary effect.' Hengel, *Crucifixion*, 51.

[43] Raymond E. Brown, *The Death of the Messiah, Volumes 1 & 2: From Gethsemane to the Grave: A Commentary on the Passion Narratives in the Four Gospels* (New York; London: Yale University Press, 1994), 940f.

an opportunity not only for torture but also for mocking. Some were crucified in comic poses, others had nails put through their genitals and yet others were killed upside down. Here was an opportunity for all the sadism of the executioner to be given free rein. Seneca (4 BC–AD 65) recoiled from the horror of it all:

> Can anyone be found who would prefer wasting away in pain dying limb by limb, or letting out his life drop by drop, rather than expiring once for all? Can any man be found willing to be fastened to the accursed tree, long sickly, already deformed, swelling with ugly weals on shoulders and chest, and drawing the breath of life amid long-drawn-out agony? He would have many excuses for dying even before mounting the cross.[44]

As Jesus was crucified, the soldiers cast lots for his clothing, a disdainful humiliation which was a common practice at the time. As the prisoner died, the captors divided up the spoils (Psalm 22:18).

Mark gave the time of the crucifixion as nine in the morning (lit: 'the third hour'). We should bear in mind that timings in the ancient world were broad, and 'the third hour' simply referred to the morning rather than precisely nine in the morning. This was not a society with a widespread and accurate means of keeping time, which explains why John could refer to the time as 'about noon' [lit: 'the sixth hour'] (John 19:14). If the crucifixion was carried out in the middle of the morning, both would be a reasonable way of describing the time in the ancient world.[45]

The charge was fixed to the cross. Since crucifixion was intended in part as a deterrent, it was important that the bystanders knew the crime. Here indeed was the King of the Jews, but his was an eternal kingdom. Here indeed was a King with the right to judge, but the judge was judged in our place.

Jesus was crucified between two rebels, calling to mind Isaiah 53:12 (which some later manuscripts of Mark cited), and three

---

[44] Cited in Hengel, *Crucifixion*, 30–31. See the full chapter of Hengel's book to gain a sense of the horror.
[45] See the discussion in Johnny V. Miller, 'The Time of the Crucifixion', *The Journal of the Evangelical Theological Society* 26, no. 2 (1983).

different groups mocked him. First of all, those passing by along the thoroughfare insulted him and repeated the false accusation of Mark 14:57–9. Here we find echoes of Psalm 22:7, and also a threefold irony: the verb translated 'hurl insults' (*blaphēmeō*) might also be translated 'blasphemed' – the one who was accused of blasphemy was now being blasphemed; the saviour was being told to save himself; Jesus was indeed going to destroy the Temple by bringing to an end the sacrificial system.

The next group, the chief priests and the teachers of the law, took him to task over his Messiahship. Rather than address Jesus directly, as the passers-by did, they simply talked among themselves. Jesus had kept his Messiahship secret since it would have been misunderstood as a merely political role and not a sacrificial one. The religious party showed they still were looking for a political Messiah, and still sought signs (see Mark 8:11–12).

The final group of mockers were the others who were crucified with him. Here was the lowest blow of all: the despised poured contempt upon him and the humiliated insulted him.[46]

The death of Jesus (15:33–41)

The death of Jesus

33 At noon, darkness came over the whole land until three in the afternoon. 34 And at three in the afternoon Jesus cried out in a loud voice, *'Eloi, Eloi, lema sabachthani?'* (which means 'My God, my God, why have you forsaken me?').[b]

35 When some of those standing near heard this, they said, 'Listen, he's calling Elijah.'

36 Someone ran, filled a sponge with wine vinegar, put it on a staff, and offered it to Jesus to drink. 'Now leave him alone. Let's see if Elijah comes to take him down,' he said.

37 With a loud cry, Jesus breathed his last.

38 The curtain of the temple was torn in two from top to bottom. 39 And when the centurion, who stood there in front of Jesus, saw how he died,[c] he said, 'Surely this man was the Son of God!'

40 Some women were watching from a distance. Among them were

---

[46] Mark chose to omit the penitent thief of Luke 23:39–43 since he was concerned to emphasise the utter abandonment of Christ.

Mary Magdalene, Mary the mother of James the younger and of Joseph,^d and Salome. **41** In Galilee these women had followed him and cared for his needs. Many other women who had come up with him to Jerusalem were also there.

b 34 Psalm 22:1

c 39 Some manuscripts *saw that he died with such a cry*

d 40 Greek *Joses*, a variant of *Joseph*; also in verse 47

As the sun reached its height at noon, darkness fell. Such an event was often linked to God's judgment; accompanying the ninth plague of the Exodus (Exodus 10:21–3) and being seen in the various prophecies of the 'Day of the LORD' (Isaiah 13:9–13; Joel 2:10; 3:14–15; Amos 5:18, 20). This was a darkly portentous sign that underscored the cosmic nature of what was going on. Here was judgment falling upon the shoulders of Christ. Here the ransom was being paid. Here those Jesus came to save were being bought with his blood. Here sin was punished, so that it might be forgiven in those who trust in this sacrifice of Christ.

At three in the afternoon, after hours of suffocating agony, Jesus loudly cried out the first verse of Psalm 22. These are the first words heard from Jesus since the first and only reply he gave to Pilate (Mark 15:2), and they came close to his death (verse 37). They are significant for two reasons.

First, the sense of abandonment contained in the words speaks of the existential cost of the crucifixion. The mere prospect of this caused the deep distress, troubled soul and overwhelming sorrow at Gethsemane (Mark 14:33–4). The agony of pain was one thing, but the cross was more than a mere execution. It was a reconciliation of God to a fallen human race, the most real sacrifice of which the entire Old Testament sacrifice system was a mere shadow. It was a cosmic event where justice was done at an eternal level. Here the new covenant began (Mark 14:24). Christ had 'redeemed us from the curse of the law by becoming a curse for us, for it is written: "Cursed is everyone who is hung on a pole"' (Galatians 3:13, see Deuteronomy 21:23). 'God made him who had no sin to be sin for us' (2 Corinthians 5:21). 'Christ, our Passover lamb, has been sacrificed' (1 Corinthians 5:7). The angel of death had passed over the believer (Exodus 12:23;

Hebrews 11:28). Jesus had given 'his life as a ransom for many' (Mark 10:45). Here was a deep work.

Second, Psalm 22 is significant for the prophecies of the crucifixion contained in its lines, which are particularly striking when read alongside Mark's account:

> But I am a worm and not a man,
>   scorned by everyone, despised by the people.
> All who see me mock me;
>   they hurl insults, shaking their heads.
> 'He trusts in the LORD,' they say,
>   'let the LORD rescue him.
> Let him deliver him,
>   since he delights in him.'
>
> . . . I am poured out like water,
>   and all my bones are out of joint.
> My heart has turned to wax;
>   it has melted within me.
> My mouth is dried up like a potsherd,
>   and my tongue sticks to the roof of my mouth;
>   you lay me in the dust of death.
>
> Dogs surround me,
>   a pack of villains encircles me;
>   they pierce my hands and my feet.
> All my bones are on display;
>   people stare and gloat over me.
> They divide my clothes among them
>   and cast lots for my garment.
>   (Psalm 22:6–8, 14–18)

Some misheard Jesus's cry and assumed he was calling for Elijah. As we have seen earlier in the Gospel, this prophet's return was eagerly anticipated, but we readers of the Gospel know that he returned in the figure of John the Baptist, whom Herod had beheaded.

Someone ran to soak a sponge in wine vinegar and lifted it up to

Jesus on a staff (such was the height of the cross). Soured wine was a common drink among the poorer and was more thirst-quenching than water.[47] The hope was that Jesus, revived, would remain long enough to be disappointed by Elijah's failure to return.

At this point Jesus, with his final effort, gave a great cry and died. How might we capture the paradox of this all? The creator upon the cross. It is best captured by the poets:

'Tis mystery all! Th'Immortal dies!
Who can explore His strange design?
In vain the firstborn seraph tries
To sound the depths of love divine!
'Tis mercy all! let earth adore,
Let angel minds inquire no more.[48]

As well as this paradox, there is the symmetry of the 'tree' of crucifixion (see Galatians 3:13, ESV), undoing the work of the tree of the knowledge of good and evil (Genesis 3:1–6).

In His love there came to us the blessed Tree:
the one wood undid the work of the other,
the one fruit was annulled by the other,
that which brought death by that which is alive.[49]

Will we ever plumb the great profound depths of the work of Christ upon the cross? Is there an end to this reconciling mystery, this eternal sacrifice?

As the great Passover Lamb was sacrificed – 'the Lamb who was slain from the creation of the world' (Revelation 13:8) – the entire Old Testament sacrificial system came to an end. The real, eternal lamb had been slain and there was no more need for the sacrifices that were a mere shadow of the heavenly reality. The Temple veil was ripped in two, from top to bottom, since it was redundant. 'For by

---

[47] BDAG, 715.
[48] Charles Wesley, 'And Can it Be?' (1738).
[49] Ephrem the Syrian, *Hymns on Virginity VIII.1*. Translation from Brock, *Treasure-House*, 61.

one sacrifice he has made perfect for ever those who are being made holy' (Hebrews 10:14). The old Temple, vastly extended by Herod, had been replaced by the temple that is Christ (John 2:19–22). One can only image what the priests, busy with the sacrifice of the Passover lambs in the nearby Temple, made of all this. The Temple was now redundant, as withered as the fig tree of Mark 11:21.

The Roman centurion, a leader of the occupying forces and a Gentile, was the one who finally made the declaration of Jesus's real identity, his words echoing the opening verses of the Gospel. He proclaimed Jesus to be both man and Son of God. Here was a deep irony: the religious leaders with their great knowledge of the Scriptures missed what this soldier, simply observing the manner of Jesus's death, understood. How easy it is to be both well informed and ignorant of the purposes of God.

As the centurion stood at the foot of the cross, many women watched from a distance. The disciples had fled, but the women kept watch. Some had cared for Jesus during his ministry and had come all the way down from Galilee. Others had joined Jesus as he made his journey to Jerusalem. In the number were Mary Magdalene, whom we have not met before in Mark's Gospel, Mary the mother of James the younger and Joseph, and Salome. Mary and Salome were common names in ancient Israel, with more than a quarter of women being called by one of those two names.[50]

These women kept watch over Jesus as he died, a death that was not to extinguish their devotion to him. Throughout his ministry, Jesus had been attended by many women and their service endured beyond his death. Some would follow his body to the tomb, and some would be the first witnesses of the resurrection. Their persistence in following Jesus was richly repaid.

We should also reflect on what this reveals to us of the utter sinfulness of sin. This crucified Christ was the ransom, the Lamb who was slain in our stead. This is what was required to reconcile us to God. This alone should give pause to those who are ready to brush away sin and suppose that God doesn't really mind. The crucifixion stands as an eternal witness that God minds very much.

---

[50] Bauckham, *Eyewitnesses*, 72.

Jesus is buried (15:42–7)

The burial of Jesus

42 It was Preparation Day (that is, the day before the Sabbath). So as evening approached, **43** Joseph of Arimathea, a prominent member of the Council, who was himself waiting for the kingdom of God, went boldly to Pilate and asked for Jesus' body. **44** Pilate was surprised to hear that he was already dead. Summoning the centurion, he asked him if Jesus had already died. **45** When he learned from the centurion that it was so, he gave the body to Joseph. **46** So Joseph bought some linen cloth, took down the body, wrapped it in the linen, and placed it in a tomb cut out of rock. Then he rolled a stone against the entrance of the tomb. **47** Mary Magdalene and Mary the mother of Joseph saw where he was laid.

The Sabbath was close. While the Romans were content to allow victims to remain on their crosses for two or three days, the Jewish regulations required a burial on the same day (Deuteronomy 21:22–3). So it was that a member of the Council (presumably referring to the Sanhedrin) boldly went to Pilate to ask for Jesus's body.

For Joseph of Arimathea to identify himself with Jesus in such a way was a dangerous act yet, we read that he was 'waiting for the kingdom of God', which would suggest that he was a follower of Jesus (John notes he was a secret disciple, John 19:38). Not all the Sanhedrin were hardened to Christ, and in Nicodemus we have an example of another quiet follower. Joseph demonstrated great courage in asking for the body of one so recently executed, and Jesus's death had not deterred his devotion. Here, in contrast to the rich man of Mark 10:17–31, was a wealthy man using his money for the kingdom of God and thereby fulfilling the prophecy of Isaiah 53:9: 'He was assigned a grave with the wicked, and with the rich in his death.'

Given the drawn-out nature of crucifixion and its emphasis on torture, Pilate was surprised that Jesus had died so quickly, and so sent for the centurion to check. The severity of his flogging and beating was such that he was unable to carry his own cross (Mark 15:21), as was the custom, so it may well be that this hastened his death.

On receiving confirmation from the centurion, Pilate duly handed over Jesus's corpse to Joseph (the Greek word designates a dead body).

Custom dictated that a corpse should be prepared for burial, and so Jesus's body was wrapped in linen. One would expect Jesus's body also to be washed, but it would seem that the customary inclusion of spices with the body was omitted in the haste (hence the visit of the women once the Sabbath had passed to finish that gruesome task). That Joseph, a member of the Sanhedrin, carried out the arduous work of taking down the body, wrapping it in linen, carrying it into the tomb and sealing the tomb gives further support to the fact that this was the day *before* the Passover. Such work would be prohibited during that festival.[51]

Joseph was in possession of a tomb hewn from the rock, which speaks to both his wealth and his status. It would be usual for the tomb to contain several separate burial chambers, each carved into the rock. The whole complex would then be sealed by rolling a stone wheel along a channel so that it went across the entrance. As all this took place, the two Marys watched, and it is notable that as the apostles were absent the 'ordinary' Christians stepped up to the task. There is no hierarchy in serving Christ, and they alone followed Jesus along the way to his final destination. Or so they thought.

4. The Resurrection • Mark 16:1–8

The women come to the tomb, but the tomb is empty. Has an absence ever been this significant? All of Jesus's preparation of his disciples had led to this point, and the women were sent to pass on the news Jesus had gone to Galilee 'just as he told you' (Mark 16:7).

The empty tomb (16:1–8)

Jesus has risen

16 When the Sabbath was over, Mary Magdalene, Mary the mother of James, and Salome bought spices so that they might go to anoint Jesus' body. ²Very early on the first day of the week, just after sunrise, they were on their way to the tomb

---

[51] 'The sole difference between the festival and the Sabbath is in the preparation of food alone.' Mishnah, *Besah* 5:2. Translation from Neusner, *Mishnah*, 298.

3 and they asked each other, 'Who will roll the stone away from the entrance of the tomb?'

4 But when they looked up, they saw that the stone, which was very large, had been rolled away. 5 As they entered the tomb, they saw a young man dressed in a white robe sitting on the right side, and they were alarmed.

6 'Don't be alarmed,' he said. 'You are looking for Jesus the Nazarene, who was crucified. He has risen! He is not here. See the place where they laid him. 7 But go, tell his disciples and Peter, "He is going ahead of you into Galilee. There you will see him, just as he told you."'

8 Trembling and bewildered, the women went out and fled from the tomb. They said nothing to anyone, because they were afraid.[a]

---

[a] 8 Some manuscripts have the following ending between verses 8 and 9, and one manuscript has it after verse 8 (omitting verses 9-20): *Then they quickly reported all these instructions to those around Peter. After this, Jesus himself also sent out through them from east to west the sacred and imperishable proclamation of eternal salvation. Amen.*

When the Sabbath had passed and the sun had set, the three women who had watched the crucifixion went to purchase spices so that Jesus's body could be properly anointed for its burial. Early the next morning, which was the first day of the week (Sunday), they went to the tomb.

There is a significance in this being the first day of the week. In Romans 5:14 Paul wrote that Adam 'is a pattern for the one to come' (i.e., Jesus). It was on the sixth day of creation – Friday – that Adam (as well as Eve) was created, and it was on the sixth day of the week that the second Adam brought about the restoration of the fallen nature of the children of Adam. On the seventh day of creation rest was commanded, and Christ lay in the tomb, to rest. The first day of creation saw light being spoken into existence, and on the first day the 'the light of all mankind' (John 1:4) came forth from the tomb into a new creation, a new world. Such was this significance of this event that the church began to meet on a Sunday, the 'Lord's Day' (Revelation 1:10).

The fall of the first Adam was undone. 'For as in Adam all die, so in Christ all will be made alive' (1 Corinthians 15:22). The new Adam had risen, and the new creation had begun. Those who follow that new Adam share in that renewed creation: 'Therefore, if anyone is in Christ, the new creation has come: the old has gone, the new is here!' (2 Corinthians 5:17). As Symeon the New Theologian (949–1022) says:

> O Paradise planted anew by Christ our God! O new mystery and dreadful wonders! There, Adam and Eve lived avowedly among trees which were physical and visible. Both the tree of knowledge and the tree of life were different from each other. But here, the new Adam becomes all things at once for those who believe, both food and a knowledge which does not lead to death nor banish us from the tree of life, but rather which teaches us with what words the serpent ought instead to have been answered: 'Get behind me, Satan!'.[52]

Old Adam's sin has been dealt with.

As these women made the journey, they wondered how they might gain access to the body. The stone would have been large enough to cover the entrance to the tomb, and of a sufficient weight to ensure wild animals did not get in among the bodies. Such was their eagerness to tend to Jesus's body that they set off regardless of this problem, hoping there might be some help nearby.

When they arrived, the stone had been rolled away, which would have been a cause for relief and also some anxiety. The women were not expecting anyone else to carry out their task, and they had set out very early so they would have expected to have been the first on the scene. They went into the tomb, no doubt expecting to have to endure the horror of unwrapping Jesus's mutilated body, but instead encountered a young man dressed in a white robe, nonchalantly sitting on the right side. Unsurprisingly, the women were alarmed.

This young man was more than he seemed, and was clearly waiting for someone to arrive. He did not feel the need to recount how he came to be there, why the tomb was empty, nor describe what had occurred. The strong reaction of the women, even accounting for the gloomy and unsettling interior of the tomb, suggests that

---

[52] Saint Symeon the New Theologian, *On the Mystical Life: The Ethical Discourses* (Crestwood: St Vladimir's Seminary Press, 1995), 108.

there was something remarkable about him. The word Mark used to describe their emotional state (translated 'alarmed') was the same used of Jesus as he entered Gethsemane (Mark 14:33, where the word is translated 'distressed'). The whiteness of the young man's robes also brings to mind the transfiguration and hints at a supernatural origin (see also Acts 1:10; 10:30). Here was more than simply a young man, and Matthew identified him as an angel (Matthew 28:5, see Luke 24:23 and John 20:12).

It is worth considering how the other Gospels record the resurrection since this often causes concerns, or even gives rise to the suggestion that they contradict one another. The problem comes when the reader seeks to impose a modern understanding of history onto documents from another era. It is not the intention of the Gospel writers to give us an exhaustive account of all that Jesus said or did, but rather they seek to present us with only what is needed for their portrayal of Christ (see, for example, John 20:30–31). In recounting the resurrection, their aim was to convince the reader of its truth, not to build a comprehensive record of the events. The differences that trouble some are to do with this selective retelling, rather than contradictions. So, for instance, when Mark referred to a 'young man' he was presenting things from the point of the view of the women, whereas Matthew told us he was an angel. Mark was concerned with the speech of the young man, so only mentioned him, whereas Luke mentioned the second angel. And so on.

As is common with supernatural encounters in the Bible, the first words uttered by this figure were ones of comfort: 'Don't be alarmed' (see Genesis 15:1; Luke 1:13, 30; 2:10; Revelation 1:17). He knew why they had come, which must have given them some comfort, and he was careful to ensure that they understood that he knew *precisely* whom they were seeking: 'Jesus the Nazarene, who was crucified.' They were not to think that he was speaking of another.

Then, with the single Greek word (*ēgerthē*), he entirely subverted their expectations and launched the Christian faith upon the world. Jesus was not to be found in the tomb – the young man pointed the women to the empty chamber – for he had *risen* from the dead. The women were told to go to the disciples, whom Jesus had been training since their calling by the Sea of Galilee, and remind them of Jesus's instructions: 'But after I have risen, I will go ahead of you into Galilee' (Mark 14:28). The resurrection did not signal the end of a process, but rather its beginning: the mission was to continue. The apostles were sent out. The young man mentioned Peter by name, which served to reconcile him after his denial of Christ in the high priest's courtyard.

The women were unsurprisingly left trembling and bewildered by this encounter. They exited the chamber and fled from the tomb, speaking to no one as they went out to the disciples.[53] How often trepidation accompanies discipleship, but we can be confident that Christ goes before us. Fear should be no hindrance to discipleship, but rather is something to be cast out by faith (Mark 4:40; 5:36). What looked like heroic failure was in fact a heroic triumph. This was the message for the disciples, and this is the message for all who follow the crucified Messiah.

So, as we come to the end of his work, how might we summarise Mark's Gospel and his portrayal of the Son of God?

It is the 'good news about Jesus the Messiah, the Son of God' (Mark 1:1) who was long prophesied by the prophets (Mark 1:2) and declared by God to be his beloved Son (Mark 1:11). He, unlike Adam, survived temptation without sin (Mark 1:12–13) and announced that, at last, the kingdom of God was near (Mark 1:15). The call to repentance was issued (Mark 1:15) and 'the way' back to God begun (Mark 1:3). The impure spirits cowered at his presence. Here was the Holy One of God (Mark 1:24) who taught with unique authority (Mark 1:27) and cast out the demons (Mark 1:25). Here was one who forgave sins (Mark 2:5), healed the sick (Mark 1:34, 3:10) – even by mere touch (Mark 5:28) – and raised the dead with a word (Mark 5:41). Like the Father, he fed multitudes in the wilderness (Mark 6:30–44) and he uttered the divine name as he walked on water (Mark 6:45–52). He opened the eyes of the blind (Mark 8:22–6; 10:46–52) and was glorified between Moses and Elijah (Mark 9:2–13). He entered Jerusalem as a returning King (Mark 11:1–11) and passed

---

[53] This would seem to be the best way to understand the sentence, 'They said nothing to anyone, because they were afraid.' The fact that the Gospel exists proves they must have delivered their message to the apostles.

judgment on a much-corrupted Temple (Mark 11:12–25). The true Lamb of God was sacrificed upon a cross, between two criminals, as the now redundant Temple veil was torn (Mark 15:33–8), and the 'way' back to God was secured. Even death could not contain the God of life and he walked out of the tomb (Mark 16:1–8).

Jesus Christ. God and Man. The one who leads his disciples along the way to a new creation and reconciles sinners to God. The key to all this? Faith, even if you have to cry out, 'I do believe; help me overcome my unbelief' (Mark 9:24). Whether you are a fisherman (Mark 1:16–20), a tax collector (Mark 2:13–14), a sinner (Mark 2:15), a young man (Mark 14:51) or a prominent ruler (Mark 15:43).

The abrupt ending to Mark's Gospel leaves the ending open and invites the reader to join Jesus on the way. Jesus calls, 'Follow me.'

Appendix

The longer ending • Mark 16:9–20)

[The earliest manuscripts and some other ancient witnesses do not have verses 9–20.]

9 *When Jesus rose early on the first day of the week, he appeared first to Mary Magdalene, out of whom he had driven seven demons.* **10** *She went and told those who had been with him and who were mourning and weeping.* **11** *When they heard that Jesus was alive and that she had seen him, they did not believe it.*

12 *Afterwards Jesus appeared in a different form to two of them while they were walking in the country.* **13** *These returned and reported it to the rest; but they did not believe them either.*

14 *Later Jesus appeared to the Eleven as they were eating; he rebuked them for their lack of faith and their stubborn refusal to believe those who had seen him after he had risen.*

15 *He said to them, 'Go into all the world and preach the gospel to all creation.* **16** *Whoever believes and is baptised will be saved, but whoever does not believe will be condemned.* **17** *And these signs will accompany those who believe: in my name they will drive out demons; they will speak in new tongues;* **18** *they will pick up snakes with their hands; and when they drink deadly poison, it will not hurt them at all; they will place their hands on people who are ill, and they will get well.'*

19 *After the Lord Jesus had spoken to them, he was taken up into heaven and he sat at the right hand of God.* **20** *Then the disciples went out and preached everywhere, and the Lord worked with them and confirmed his word by the signs that accompanied it.*

The NIV, like most modern translations, places this passage after a comment that it is not present in the earliest manuscripts of Mark.

The issues are discussed in the introduction, but since many will be in churches that consider this longer ending to be original to Mark it seems sensible to offer some comments upon it. In brief, in this ending we find the unbelieving apostles confronted by the risen Christ and sent into 'all the world' in order to 'preach the gospel to all creation' (verse 15).

This passage tells us that Jesus first appeared to Mary Magdalene, and there is a reference to her earlier demon-possession (Luke 8:2). To have been in a spiritually dark place does not preclude someone from encountering the risen Christ, and her darkness had been turned into light. She went to tell the others, but they did not believe her. Their grief blinded them to her witness. Later, Jesus appeared to two travellers – presumably the two on the road to Emmaus (Luke 24:13–35) – but their witness was also dismissed. The phrase 'in a different form' is curious, and would explain why he was not recognised by the two at first.

After this failure to receive the testimony of the first three witnesses – were the disciples once more seeking to police who were Jesus's true disciples? – Jesus appeared to them himself (see Luke 24:36–8). He rebuked their lack of faith and their stubbornness in the face of the testimony of Mary and the travellers. The disciples had no monopoly on Jesus, and he may appear to whom he will.

He then sent them out to preach (see Matthew 28:19). They were to go everywhere and preach to everything: the gospel is cosmic in its reach and is to be preached to all creation (verse 15). Jesus's work leads to a new heaven and a new earth (Revelation 21:1), and as men and women come to Christ the benefits ring out through all the created realm (see also Romans 8:19).[1] Those who believe and are baptised will be saved, but those who do not will stand condemned

---

[1] Thomas Weinandy notes, 'Ultimately the Gospel is about a new creation, a new heaven and a new earth, and not just the rebirth of men and women, but also the re-creation of the whole created order. Nothing of God's good creation will be lost, even if presently the whole of creation is marred by human sin. As humankind is made new in Christ through the transforming power of the Holy Spirit, so the whole of creation will be made new in Christ in that same Spirit, and that apparently includes hyenas, clams, fleas, oak trees, the moon, the sun, and everything else.' Thomas Weinandy, *Jesus Becoming Jesus: A Theological Interpretation of the Synoptic Gospels* (Washington: The Catholic University of America Press, 2018), 443–4.

(see John 3:16–18). This message of salvation rings through the Acts of the Apostles (Acts 2:38; 8:36–8; 16:30–33).

Jesus then went on to speak of various signs, which we also see in the Acts of the Apostles as the gospel went forth. In fact, this passage serves as something of a theological introduction to Acts. We should be careful to note that these signs would not be for their own sake but would confirm the word of the Lord (verse 20; see also Hebrews 2:3–4). They were accompanying signs to confirm the gospel, to point to the teaching of Christ. Once again it was the teaching at the fore, with the miracles serving to give authority to that which was preached.

After speaking with the apostles, Jesus then ascended and sat at the right hand of God. His mission complete, the Son returned to sit with the Father, leaving salvation in his wake.